John Watson Laurie.

NOTABLE BRITISH TRIALS SERIES

General Editor—HARRY HODGE

The Lord Justice-Clerk (Lord Kingsburgh)

Trial of

John Watson Laurie

(The Arran Murder)

EDITED BY

William Roughead

Author of "Bad Companions," "Malice Domestic," &c.

EDINBURGH AND LONDON

WILLIAM HODGE & COMPANY, LIMITED

MADE AND PRINTED IN GREAT BRITAIN
BY
WILLIAM HODGE AND COMPANY, LIMITED
GLASGOW AND EDINBURGH

June, 1932

TO

THE RIGHT HONOURABLE

THE VISCOUNT DUNEDIN, P.C., G.C.V.O.

THIS VOLUME

IS

BY KIND PERMISSION

RESPECTFULLY DEDICATED

BY

THE EDITOR

PREFACE.

In preparing this, the first full account of the Arran murder trial, characterised by the presiding Judge as "certainly one of the most remarkable cases that have ever come before a Court of Justice," I have consulted the original record in the Books of Adjournal of the High Court of Justiciary in Edinburgh. The shorthand writers' notes of evidence, if such were taken in Court, are not now available; but the case was well and accurately reported at the time in the *Scotsman* and *Glasgow Herald* newspapers. Upon a careful collation of these two reports the following text of the evidence adduced at the trial, and of the addresses of Judge and counsel to the jury, is based.

With the exceptions of Lord Dunedin, who, as Mr. Graham Murray, acted as Advocate-Depute in the prosecution, and Dr. Charles Macgillivray, one of the medical experts for the defence, none of those officially concerned in the case survives. Dr. Macgillivray has been so good as to revise the proof sheets of his own evidence. The whole of the medical evidence, both for the Crown and for the defence, has been obligingly read in proof by Professor Sydney Smith, Dean of the Faculty of Medicine in the University of Edinburgh, a favour which the professional reader will as highly appreciate as I do. I have also to thank Mr. Alexander Rae, Depute-Clerk of Justiciary, for facilities afforded to copy and to reproduce certain documents in his custody, connected with the case.

For the illustrations, of which the majority are from my own collection, the four Crown photographs of the *locus* are taken from those produced in Court at the trial. To the courtesy of Lord Kinross I am indebted for the photograph of his distinguished father, when at the Bar. The facsimile of Laurie's letter to the press is from the original MS. preserved in the Justiciary Office.

In my narrative of the events preceding the trial, I have received much assistance from the excellent accounts furnished in the contemporary columns of the *North British Daily Mail*.

The publication of the book has for me a peculiar interest. Forty-three years ago I attended the trial; in 1905 I was commissioned by the publishers to edit a report of it in the present series, but, for reasons with which I had nothing to do, the work was not then proceeded with; and in 1913 I published a brief account of the case, always a favourite of mine, in *Twelve Scots Trials*. That I am now, at the end of the day, enabled to produce it in complete and final form is, at least for myself, a matter of satisfaction. I would fain hope that some readers may share the sentiment.

W. R.

12 BELGRAVE CRESCENT,
    EDINBURGH, *June*, 1932.

CONTENTS.

x

CONTENTS.

APPENDICES.

John Watson Laurie.

Helensburgh, by Greenock, Gourock, Dunoon, Wemyss Bay, and Rothesay, through the Kyles of Bute to the Arran ports: Corrie, Brodick, Lamlash, and Whiting Bay.

On Friday, 12th July, 1889, when the *Ivanhoe* called at Rothesay on her morning run, there boarded her for Arran two young men with whom we shall have much to do. As the steamer passed through the Kyles, the narrow strait between the north end of Bute and the mainland of Argyll, they could hardly fail to notice the house and policies of Ardlamont, which four years later were to be the scene of Cecil Hambrough's tragic shooting expedition with his friend and tutor Mr. Monson.

Of our two passengers—who, as appears, were then unknown to each other, but who made acquaintance on the voyage—one was an Englishman named Edwin Robert Rose. A clerk in the employment of Mr. James Goodman, a builder, of Brixton, London, he was on a fortnight's holiday in Scotland; thirty-two years of age, of slight build, five feet seven in height, of athletic, active habits and agreeable manners; frank and open in disposition, and prone to "take up" with strangers. He was in the best of health and spirits.

The man with whom he forgathered on the trip, though showily dressed, was of the artisan class; a Scotsman, twenty-five years old, half an inch shorter than the other, fresh complexioned, fair haired, notably square shouldered, and wearing a slight moustache and whiskers. Rose, on the other hand, was dark and affected a heavy moustache. Which of them took the first step towards the formation of their fatal friendship we do not know; but from what we do know of their respective ways, it was probably not the Scotsman. He introduced himself to the other as John Annandale.

When the *Ivanhoe* reached Brodick, the two men landed to spend the time during which the steamer continued on her way to Whiting Bay, the farthest port of call, whence she would return in the afternoon to take up her Brodick passengers. How Rose employed himself

2

JOHN WATSON LAUR

INTRODUCTION.

Part I.—The Missing Man.

I.

JULY, 1889, is a red-letter date in the black
crime. On the 18th of that month the diabolic
Jack-the-Ripper perpetrated the seventh and
appalling series of his atrocities, known to his
Whitechapel murders. On the 26th, at
Assizes, the Grand Jury returned a True B
Mrs. Maybrick for the murder of her husband
and on the 31st, before Mr. Justice Stephen,
seven days' trial of that unlucky lady, result
conviction. On the 15th there was committe
land one of the most remarkable murders on r

The Isle of Arran lies in the estuary of t
between Kintyre and the coast of Ayr. It is t
and most picturesque of the Clyde islands; t
Bute and the two Cumbraes, with Ailsa Craig
Rock of the west, are relatively tame and lack i
variety. The savage grandeur of its hills an
one day shrouded in mist, another bathed in s
is only to be matched in Skye; and the outli
island, seen against the western light, whether
Ayrshire shore or from some passing vessel in
way, is of incredible beauty and enchantment.
striking feature is the great, grey cone of Goat
feet above sea level and the highest peak in th
mountains. Glen Sannox, the finest of its ma
is comparable in lonely splendour to Glenc
delectable land may be approached by steam
from Ardrossan or from the higher reaches of t
At the time in question the favourite " sail "
Clyde was the daily run of the steamer *Ivan*

Introduction.

we are not informed; but his companion called at the
house of Mrs. Walker, in the village of Invercloy, and
inquired for lodgings. This was Glasgow Fair week, the
local trades holidays; all the Clyde resorts were crowded,
and Brodick participated to the full in the incursion.
Rooms were not to be had; but Mrs. Walker was able
to provide accommodation in a wooden lean-to structure,
adjoining her house, which enjoyed the advantage of
having a separate entrance of its own, whereby the occupants might come and go at will without disturbance to
the landlady. Mr. Annandale approved the place and
took it for a week. He gave his card, stating that he
came from Tighnabruaich, in the Kyles of Bute; that
he would enter into possession on the following day,
Saturday; and that he would then be accompanied by
a friend, who, however, could stay no longer than the
ensuing Wednesday. Mrs. Walker agreed to the conditions of let, and it was further arranged that Mr. Annandale should take his meals in the lodging, while his
friend should take his " out," to wit, at the adjacent
teashop, locally known as Wooley's. They returned
together to Rothesay in the afternoon. Rose was staying
at the Glenburn Hydropathic, where he had, in his
affable way, become friendly with two other visitors,
Mr. Mickel and Mr. Thom, both hailing from Linlithgow. To these gentlemen he vouchsafed the fact of his
new acquaintance, and when in the evening Mr. Annandale called by appointment, Rose introduced him to his
friends. Mickel and Thom were also going to Brodick
for the week-end; and on Saturday, the 13th, they met
Rose and Annandale on the *Ivanhoe* and travelled thither
in their company. The Linlithgow men were unable to
procure in the village a roof for their heads; they were
fortunate to find a friend's yacht in the bay, aboard
which they obtained shelter. On Sunday, the 14th, the
party did not see much of each other; Mickel and Thom
walked over the hill road to Lamlash, Rose and Annandale
went up Glen Rosa. They all met again in the evening.

3

John Watson Laurie.

On Monday, the 15th, Mickel saw Rose breakfasting alone in Wooley's shop. The impression made by Annandale on him and his companion was distinctly unfavourable; he was silent and uncommunicative, and they failed to find out who he was or where he came from. So when Rose told him that he proposed that day to climb Goatfell with the unknown, Mickel strongly advised him to get rid of him, and, in particular, not to make the ascent in his company. Rose undertook to act upon this advice and promised not to go up Goatfell with Annandale: he said he would " try " to get rid of him—from which it would appear that Rose had his own misgivings as to the wisdom of the association. When Mickel and his friend Thom went back to Rothesay by the *Ivanhoe* that afternoon at half-past three, Rose and Annandale were on the pier to see them off. The effect of Mickel's warning must quickly have worn off under the persuasive power of the stranger, for, though the hour was considerably later than that usually chosen for the purpose, the two men set out forthwith to climb Goatfell.

II.

When Mrs. Walker and her household went to bed that night, they were unaware whether or not the lodgers had returned. She had heard of their intended expedition, and knew they could get into their room when they liked, without reference to her establishment. In the morning there was no sign of them stirring; doubtless they were tired after their excursion and were enjoying what is technically termed " a long lie." But, when eleven o'clock came, she thought it time they should be aroused. She accordingly knocked at their door and, getting no answer, entered the room. It was empty. The one bed seemed to have been occupied overnight by two persons, but her lodgers had vanished, taking with them their respective bags. A straw hat, a pair of slippers, an old waterproof, and a tennis racket had been left behind, sole mementoes of their visitation.

4

LIST OF ILLUSTRATIONS.

JOHN WATSON LAURIE.

INTRODUCTION.

Part I.—The Missing Man.

I.

JULY, 1889, is a red-letter date in the black calendar of crime. On the 18th of that month the diabolical assassin Jack-the-Ripper perpetrated the seventh and last of the appalling series of his atrocities, known to history as the Whitechapel murders. On the 26th, at Liverpool Assizes, the Grand Jury returned a True Bill against Mrs. Maybrick for the murder of her husband by arsenic; and on the 31st, before Mr. Justice Stephen, began the seven days' trial of that unlucky lady, resulting in her conviction. On the 15th there was committed in Scotland one of the most remarkable murders on record.

The Isle of Arran lies in the estuary of the Clyde, between Kintyre and the coast of Ayr. It is the largest and most picturesque of the Clyde islands; the others, Bute and the two Cumbraes, with Ailsa Craig, the Bass Rock of the west, are relatively tame and lack its infinite variety. The savage grandeur of its hills and glens—one day shrouded in mist, another bathed in sunshine—is only to be matched in Skye; and the outline of the island, seen against the western light, whether from the Ayrshire shore or from some passing vessel in the fair-way, is of incredible beauty and enchantment. Its most striking feature is the great, grey cone of Goatfell, 2866 feet above sea level and the highest peak in that isle of mountains. Glen Sannox, the finest of its many glens, is comparable in lonely splendour to Glencoe. This delectable land may be approached by steamer either from Ardrossan or from the higher reaches of the Firth. At the time in question the favourite " sail " down the Clyde was the daily run of the steamer *Ivanhoe* from

John Watson Laurie.

Helensburgh, by Greenock, Gourock, Dunoon, Wemyss Bay, and Rothesay, through the Kyles of Bute to the Arran ports: Corrie, Brodick, Lamlash, and Whiting Bay.

On Friday, 12th July, 1889, when the *Ivanhoe* called at Rothesay on her morning run, there boarded her for Arran two young men with whom we shall have much to do. As the steamer passed through the Kyles, the narrow strait between the north end of Bute and the mainland of Argyll, they could hardly fail to notice the house and policies of Ardlamont, which four years later were to be the scene of Cecil Hambrough's tragic shooting expedition with his friend and tutor Mr. Monson.

Of our two passengers—who, as appears, were then unknown to each other, but who made acquaintance on the voyage—one was an Englishman named Edwin Robert Rose. A clerk in the employment of Mr. James Goodman, a builder, of Brixton, London, he was on a fortnight's holiday in Scotland; thirty-two years of age, of slight build, five feet seven in height, of athletic, active habits and agreeable manners; frank and open in disposition, and prone to "take up" with strangers. He was in the best of health and spirits.

The man with whom he forgathered on the trip, though showily dressed, was of the artisan class; a Scotsman, twenty-five years old, half an inch shorter than the other, fresh complexioned, fair haired, notably square shouldered, and wearing a slight moustache and whiskers. Rose, on the other hand, was dark and affected a heavy moustache. Which of them took the first step towards the formation of their fatal friendship we do not know; but from what we do know of their respective ways, it was probably not the Scotsman. He introduced himself to the other as John Annandale.

When the *Ivanhoe* reached Brodick, the two men landed to spend the time during which the steamer continued on her way to Whiting Bay, the farthest port of call, whence she would return in the afternoon to take up her Brodick passengers. How Rose employed himself

2

Introduction.

we are not informed; but his companion called at the
house of Mrs. Walker, in the village of Invercloy, and
inquired for lodgings. This was Glasgow Fair week, the
local trades holidays; all the Clyde resorts were crowded,
and Brodick participated to the full in the incursion.
Rooms were not to be had; but Mrs. Walker was able
to provide accommodation in a wooden lean-to structure,
adjoining her house, which enjoyed the advantage of
having a separate entrance of its own, whereby the occupants might come and go at will without disturbance to
the landlady. Mr. Annandale approved the place and
took it for a week. He gave his card, stating that he
came from Tighnabruaich, in the Kyles of Bute; that
he would enter into possession on the following day,
Saturday; and that he would then be accompanied by
a friend, who, however, could stay no longer than the
ensuing Wednesday. Mrs. Walker agreed to the conditions of let, and it was further arranged that Mr. Annandale should take his meals in the lodging, while his
friend should take his " out," to wit, at the adjacent
teashop, locally known as Wooley's. They returned
together to Rothesay in the afternoon. Rose was staying
at the Glenburn Hydropathic, where he had, in his
affable way, become friendly with two other visitors,
Mr. Mickel and Mr. Thom, both hailing from Linlithgow. To these gentlemen he vouchsafed the fact of his
new acquaintance, and when in the evening Mr. Annandale called by appointment, Rose introduced him to his
friends. Mickel and Thom were also going to Brodick
for the week-end; and on Saturday, the 13th, they met
Rose and Annandale on the *Ivanhoe* and travelled thither
in their company. The Linlithgow men were unable to
procure in the village a roof for their heads; they were
fortunate to find a friend's yacht in the bay, aboard
which they obtained shelter. On Sunday, the 14th, the
party did not see much of each other; Mickel and Thom
walked over the hill road to Lamlash, Rose and Annandale
went up Glen Rosa. They all met again in the evening.

3

John Watson Laurie.

On Monday, the 15th, Mickel saw Rose breakfasting alone in Wooley's shop. The impression made by Annandale on him and his companion was distinctly unfavourable; he was silent and uncommunicative, and they failed to find out who he was or where he came from. So when Rose told him that he proposed that day to climb Goatfell with the unknown, Mickel strongly advised him to get rid of him, and, in particular, not to make the ascent in his company. Rose undertook to act upon this advice and promised not to go up Goatfell with Annandale: he said he would " try " to get rid of him—from which it would appear that Rose had his own misgivings as to the wisdom of the association. When Mickel and his friend Thom went back to Rothesay by the *Ivanhoe* that afternoon at half-past three, Rose and Annandale were on the pier to see them off. The effect of Mickel's warning must quickly have worn off under the persuasive power of the stranger, for, though the hour was considerably later than that usually chosen for the purpose, the two men set out forthwith to climb Goatfell.

II.

When Mrs. Walker and her household went to bed that night, they were unaware whether or not the lodgers had returned. She had heard of their intended expedition, and knew they could get into their room when they liked, without reference to her establishment. In the morning there was no sign of them stirring; doubtless they were tired after their excursion and were enjoying what is technically termed " a long lie." But, when eleven o'clock came, she thought it time they should be aroused. She accordingly knocked at their door and, getting no answer, entered the room. It was empty. The one bed seemed to have been occupied overnight by two persons, but her lodgers had vanished, taking with them their respective bags. A straw hat, a pair of slippers, an old waterproof, and a tennis racket had been left behind, sole mementoes of their visitation.

4

Introduction.

Annandale had undertaken to pay 17s. for the week, with a further 3s. in respect of Rose's presence. Mrs. Walker perceived that she had been " done "—such incidents were not unprecedented during the Fair week —and decided to bear her loss in silence. She did not report the matter to the police, deeming the loss of her rent the most serious feature of the affair.

On Thursday, 18th July, Edwin Rose was due in London on the termination of his holiday, and his brother went to the station to meet him. His non-arrival alarmed his relatives, who telegraphed to the Rev. Mr. Goodman, a brother of his employer. This gentleman was staying at the Glenburn Hydropathic, a fact which, as they were intimate friends, had induced Rose to visit Rothesay. On Tuesday, the 16th, Mr. Goodman had received from him a letter, dated from " Mrs. Walker's, Brodick," stating that he would be back at Rothesay on the Wednesday for his letters and to say good-bye. On Monday, the 22nd, Mr. Goodman got the telegram from Rose's brother, informing him that Rose had not returned. He went at once to Brodick, learned what Mrs. Walker had to tell, and communicated with the police. On Saturday, the 27th, Mr. Benjamin Rose, of Balham, arrived from London at Brodick to find out what had become of his brother.

The first that the general public heard of the matter was a paragraph in the *Glasgow Evening Citizen* of Monday, 29th July, headed—

AN ARRAN MYSTERY.

SUSPICIOUS DISAPPEARANCE OF AN ENGLISH TOURIST.

AN ACCIDENT OR A CRIME?

After narrating the facts of the case so far as then known, the journal observes : " What has become of the young man Rose is shrouded in mystery. He has not returned to his friends in England, and there is a growing suspicion that he never left the island. Alarmed at his long absence, a brother reached Arran on Saturday, and has been making anxious search." It was learned that before Rose and the stranger left for Goatfell, Annandale was remarked by the villagers to be moody, absent-minded, and meditative. He walked to and fro along the little lane in which their lodging was situated, with bowed head and excited gait, which caused one venerable inhabitant to ejaculate that " she feared the deil was busy with the young man "—a diagnosis only too accurate. It further appeared that the two men were seen together on the summit of the mountain shortly after six o'clock

III.

Mr. Benjamin Rose was not single in his quest. The unusual circumstances of the case aroused in that quiet neighbourhood intense and widespread interest. Every available man, native as well as visitor, was only too willing to assist in the search. On Sunday, the 28th, a large party was organised to scour the hills, but the day proved wet and misty, so that the volunteers had not only a most uncomfortable and even dangerous experience, but all their endeavours were unavailing, as at some points they could not see a couple of yards around them; so they returned to the village disheartened and depressed. It was decided that should the small separate parties of searchers continue during the week unsuccessful, a large party, drafted from Brodick, under the command of Constable Munro; from Lamlash, under Sergeant Munro; from Corrie and Sannox, under Mr. James Douglas and Mr. Alexander Kerr, should, on the following Sunday, comb the mountain in all directions from base to summit, in order, if possible, to solve the mystery.

After a deluge of rain, which continued throughout Saturday till an early hour on Sunday morning, 4th August, the weather cleared rapidly; by eight o'clock

6

Introduction.

the sun broke out, the mist rolled off from the hills, the highest peaks of Arran could be seen distinctly, and the various tracks round Goatfell and over the ridges were boldly and plainly defined. No one unacquainted with the nature of the ground can appreciate the magnitude of the task by which the searchers were confronted. Upon the north and west Goatfell is bounded by a congregation of jagged mountain ridges and fantastic peaks, with deep shadowy glens and grim ravines, the bleak sides of which are furrowed by innumerable gullies and abrupt watercourses—a scene in its awful solitude and grandeur so wild, dreary, and desolate as hardly to be matched in Britain.

Nine o'clock was the hour fixed for the assembling of the company at the Kennels, within the Brodick Castle policies, on the line of the usual route to the summit of the mountain. When the party started it consisted of 150 persons, exclusive of the Corrie contingent of 50, which proceeded by way of Glen Sannox. The gathering at the Kennels was divided into three sections. The first, under command of Mr. John Dewar, the Castle gamekeeper, and Sergeant Munro, Lamlash, went by way of the eastern ridge; the second, under the guidance of Mr. James Crawford and Constable Munro, Brodick, went straight up the face of the mountain; the third, led by Messrs. Robert and Peter Davidson, and Constable M'Coll, Shisken, went westward by Glen Shant and Glen Rosa. The several parties then began their arduous adventure; but, before the second had arrived at the summit, a heavy mist came down, which held them up for nearly two hours. On reaching the top, this party, reinforced by the company from Corrie, again divided, some descending the ridge which unites Goatfell with The Saddle; others going directly down into Glen Rosa.

When about half-way to The Saddle, a shout was heard passing rapidly from group to group, and it was apparent that the object of their quest had been attained.

7

John Watson Laurie.

In a deep, precipitous gully, leading from the ridge of north Goatfell straight down into Glen Sannox, and beneath a great granite boulder, the cavity under which was elaborately built up about the face with no fewer than 42 minor stones, the heaviest weighing over a hundredweight, the crevices between them being artificially filled with pieces of turf and heather, lay the dead and decomposing body of the missing man. Francis Logan, a fisherman from Corrie, being high up on the flank of the mountain, noticed, instead of the clean scents of heather and bog-myrtle, an evil and suggestive odour, which he traced to a large boulder farther up the slope. The place is named Coire-na-fuhren—the gully of fire—which, I am informed, is the correct spelling, though called Corr-na-fourin throughout the subsequent trial.

Nothing was done until Sergeant Munro reached the spot. When the barricade of stones was removed and the cavity behind them laid bare, the body was seen lying at length upon its face, fully clothed, with the skirt of the jacket turned back over the head. It remained untouched and guarded by the police till the arrival about 8 p.m. of Dr. Gilmour. This gentleman, who was sent for as the nearest medical man, was then on holiday at Corrie, from Linlithgow, where he had been long in general practice. With the aid of the police he lifted the body from beneath the boulder; it was at once identified by Mr. Benjamin Rose as that of his brother Edwin, and Dr. Gilmour proceeded to examine its condition. Nothing was found upon the body; all the pockets were empty, and one of them was turned inside out. On removing the jacket, the head and face were seen to be, in Dr. Gilmour's words, " fearfully and terribly smashed." Practically the whole of the face and the left side of the head had been destroyed and were in an advanced stage of decomposition. Otherwise the body was uninjured, but for a fracture of the top of the left shoulder-blade.

8

Introduction.

Meanwhile, others of the company had not been idle. While those who found the body were awaiting the doctor's arrival, a search of the surrounding ground was made. Above the boulder the hillside slopes steeply upward to the ridge at an angle of 45 degrees, on the line of a deep gully and watercourse, often dry in summer, but in which there was then a small stream. The surface of the ground is composed of slabs of granite, patches of heather, sand, and gravel; strewn with boulders big and little, and loose stones. The following articles, later identified as Rose's property, were found higher up the gully at various distances from the boulder:—a walking-stick, lying head downwards, as if dropped; a waterproof, torn into two pieces, "huddled together in a dub, as if they had been trampled upon"; a knife, a pencil, and a button; and a cap, folded in four, with a large and heavy stone on the top of and almost wholly concealing it, lying in the middle of the bed of the burn.

On one side of the gully, above the place where the cap lay, was a clear drop of 19 feet; on the other side, lower down, above where the knife and pencil were found, was a similar fall of 32 feet.

IV.

From Coire-na-fuhren, where the body was found, to Corrie village is some 9 miles of very difficult country. A rude shell had been procured from the hamlet; and when this was brought up to the boulder, the body was laid in it. Eight bearers volunteered to carry it; and about nine o'clock, in the gathering dusk, amid the sinister shadows of the giant peaks, Rose's last journey was begun. Down the precipitous slope of the mountain-side to the bed of the valley beneath, through the track-less upper reaches of the glen and the only less arduous wildness of its widening mouth, past the little burying-ground of Sannox, in which Rose was finally to rest, and so by the coast road to Corrie, the ghastly burden was borne in the deepening darkness, until by one o'clock in the morning it was laid down at last in the coach-house of Corrie Hotel.

There, at one o'clock on Monday, 5th August, by instructions of the Procurator-Fiscal for Bute, tele-graphed from Rothesay, a post-mortem examination of the body was made by Dr. Gilmour, of Linlithgow, and Dr. Fullarton, of Lamlash. This was performed under very unusual conditions; for we read in the *North British Daily Mail* of 6th August: " It was impossible to con-duct the examination with such privacy as was desir-able, so limited was the accommodation; but the group of villagers who gathered round the entrance to the coach-house, although following every movement of the medical men with melancholy interest, refrained from making their presence too obtrusively felt. About an hour elapsed ere the inquiry was completed." It " transpired," as the journalists say, that in the opinion of the medical men the injuries to the head had been inflicted by repeated blows from some heavy instrument, probably a stone. " On the other hand, it is thought that a cowardly push from the murderer sent Rose reel-ing over the precipice, and that death not ensuing imme-diately, Annandale clambered after his helpless victim, and silenced for ever his futile cries for help. Be the method what it may, the whole circumstances point to murder in its blackest aspect, and murder by some one moved by feelings of more than fiendish malignity." This remarkable forecast of the facts reflects much credit on the acumen of the *Mail* reporter.

At four o'clock that afternoon the burial took place. The remains, in a plain black coffin, were taken back along the shore road to Sannox, followed by the deceased's brother and by all the natives and visitors in the district. The funeral service was conducted by the Rev. Mr. M'Dougall, minister of Sannox, and the body was buried in the ancient graveyard at the entrance to

Introduction.

the glen, a beautiful and peaceful spot, rich in old head-
stones, surrounded by a low wall, and sheltered by venerable trees, within sound of the waves that break for ever
on the sands of Sannox Bay.

On 27th September the body was exhumed by warrant
of the Sheriff, to enable Sir Henry (then Dr.) Littlejohn, and Dr. Fullarton to examine it more particularly
as to the condition of the internal organs.

Afterwards, with better intention than taste, a huge
granite boulder, brought from Glen Sannox, was laid
upon the grave, bearing the inscription, "In loving
memory of Edwin R. Rose, who died on Goatfell, 15th
July, 1889." As I first recall it, this stark grey block,
within a massive iron railing, was gruesomely suggestive
of that other sepulchral stone, some 6 miles up the glen.
But time and nature, by embowering it in a wealth
of greenery, have mitigated the harshness of its aspect
and dispersed, so far as possible, that painful association.

Part II.—The Wanted Man.

I.

Meanwhile, the criminal authorities of Bute and
Glasgow had, naturally in the circumstances, not been
idle; but their activities concerned the personality and
present whereabouts of John Annandale.

Researches at Rothesay disclosed that on Saturday,
6th July, a man giving that name and of appearance
similar to that of Rose's companion, engaged a room
from Mrs. Currie, Iona Place, Port Bannatyne, a village
contiguous to the capital of Bute, on the north side of
the famed Rothesay Bay. He lodged there till Tuesday,
the 9th, when he went up to Glasgow, returning next
day with a brown knickerbocker suit and stylish stockings, in place of his previous raiment. On Thursday,
the 11th, he informed his landlady that he was going to
Inveraray. Next day, Friday, 12th July, he told her

11

that he had been invited by a friend to visit Arran, that he meant to " do " Goatfell, and that he would probably not be back till Tuesday. He then left for his week-end trip, taking with him his brown leather bag, and wearing his knickerbocker suit and a straw hat. On the afternoon of Tuesday, the 16th, he reappeared at his Port Bannatyne lodgings, wearing a grey felt hat and carrying a brown-paper parcel containing, as his landlady later learned, a white serge yachting-cap and a chocolate-and-brown striped tennis blazer. In these adornments he arrayed himself during the remainder of his stay. He talked " quite pleasantly " to Mrs. Currie about his visit to Arran, saying he had been up Goatfell, and had enjoyed himself. On Friday evening, the 19th, he asked to have his breakfast at half-past eight next morning, as he intended to see a friend off by the nine o'clock steamer. That day his fortnight's occupation of the room expired; he ordered his dinner for one o'clock and bade the landlady prepare his bill, which amounted to £3 3s. 8d. This she duly did; but the lodger never returned from his morning stroll, and all that Mrs. Currie got in respect of board and lodging was the yachting-cap and a pair of tennis shoes, which were later identified as Rose's property. Annandale had given her his address as No. 6 Cambridge Street, Glasgow, but an application to that quarter produced no response.

The Glasgow *Mail* of 6th August, in a leading article on the facts so far as then ascertained, observes: " The story appears to be that of a man without money, reduced to desperate straits, seeking the acquaintance of a gentleman who seemed to be well off, inducing him to go in his company to a distant and lonely place, and there deliberately and of set purpose murdering him for his money. If there be any other explanation, it is for Annandale to appear and give it." Next day that journal was in a position to announce the identification of the mysterious unknown. The assumer of the

Introduction.

sounding surname was in fact a man named John Watson Laurie, twenty-five years of age, employed as a pattern-maker by Messrs. Sharp, Stewart & Co., at the Atlas Locomotive Engine Works, Springburn, Glasgow. Since 8th June of that year he had been living in lodgings at No. 106 North Frederick Street, until he went to Rothesay on 6th July. The black sheep of a respectable, well-to-do family resident in Coatbridge, he was not unknown to the police, having been, on 23rd March, 1889, at Glasgow Sheriff Court, convicted of theft—in connection with the disappearance from the house of his landlady of jewellery to the value of £18. As his relatives made good the loss, Laurie got off with an admonition.

The "information received," whereby the police were made aware of the wanted man's identity, was obtained from a Glasgow holiday-maker, named James Gillon Aitken, who knew him as Laurie. Aitken also had chanced to go to Rothesay on 6th July and noticed Laurie on the pier. He saw him two or three times in Rothesay during the week; and on Friday, the 12th, happened to be on board the *Ivanhoe* when Rose and Laurie were going to Brodick. Laurie pointed out Rose to him as a gentleman with whom he proposed to stay in Arran. Aitken met him next on the following Friday, the 19th, and observed that he was then wearing a white serge yachting-cap, which strongly reminded him (Aitken) of that worn by Rose on the steamer. Aitken asked him how he and his friend got on in Brodick, to which he replied: "Oh, very well." He gave no details of the visit, but said he was returning to Glasgow, as his holiday was over. On Saturday, the 27th, Aitken met him again at Rothesay; he said he was down for the day. Their next encounter was in Hope Street, Glasgow, on Wednesday, 31st July. By that time Aitken had read in the newspapers of the disappearance of Rose. He hailed Laurie with the pertinent question: "What do you know about the Arran mystery?" The other hesitated—"hummed and hawed." "Dear me," said

13

John Watson Laurie.

Aitken, " have you not been reading the papers? Was not Rose the name of the party with whom you intended going to Brodick? " Laurie still hesitated, and then said it was the same name, but it could not be the same man, " as Rose had returned with him, and proceeded to Leeds." Aitken strongly advised him to communicate what he knew to the authorities, and then asked him " whose cap he was wearing that Friday? " Laurie exclaimed: " Surely you don't think I am a . . . ? " Aitken thought he would have added " thief," but, like Macbeth's " Amen," the word stuck in his throat. Aitken extracted a promise to meet him again that evening and give him further particulars, which, needless to say, Laurie failed to do. The conversation was broken off by Laurie saying he wished to speak to a passing friend; but he went off in the opposite direction. Aitken, his suspicions now thoroughly aroused, forthwith informed the police.

But Laurie, having also read the news from Arran, was already prepared for flight. That morning he had applied to the foreman at the Springburn works for his wages, saying he was leaving to become a traveller in the grain trade. To a fellow-workman he said he was going to Leith on an engineering job; that he had a return-half ticket to London; and that he had been spending his holiday at Brodick with a friend, whom, he euphemistically added, " he had left in Arran," where he was spending some time. The same day he sold his pattern-maker's tools to a broker in the Commercial Road for 25s., and disappeared from Glasgow.

II.

The *North British Daily Mail* of Thursday, 8th August, gives an interesting account of an incident connected with Laurie's visit to Rothesay, not mentioned at the trial—

Yesterday a young man from the Caledonian Railway

Introduction.

Company called at the address in North Frederick Street, where Laurie was lately residing, and asked if Mr. John Annandale resided there. He was surprised to hear that he was not there, and on being asked his business, he said that a gentleman, giving the name of John Annandale and the address of his lodgings in North Frederick Street, was on board the *Caledonia* on Saturday, July 20th, when that steamer ran down a small boat in Rothesay Bay, and that he volunteered to give evidence if required in the case, at the same time giving his card, bearing the name " John Annandale " and his address in North Frederick Street upon it.

This is one more link in the chain of evidence incriminating Laurie, as July 20th was the day he left Rothesay, and he had given his fellow-lodger a detailed account of the *Caledonia* accident, which he said he witnessed.

When his testimony was called for, however, Mr. John Annandale had other things to think about. It is characteristic of the man that he should have thus thrust himself forward at a time when his safety depended on his lying as low as possible. It is of a piece with his wantonly going about Rothesay wearing his victim's yachting-cap and tennis blazer, the very week of the murder.

The excitement caused by the identification of Laurie and his simultaneous vanishing was intense in the district where his name and doings were known. The general opinion was that he had committed suicide. While no one seemed to question his guilt, the greatest sympathy was expressed for his unhappy relatives. The hunt for Laurie, as daily described in the newspapers, brought forth the usual crop of rumours, and irresponsible correspondents were eager in suggesting that he had been seen here, there, and everywhere. On the top of a wall surrounding an old pit shaft at Mossend a workman found materials for a meal, together with a piece of paper, inscribed : " I'm the murderer ! " from which it was inferred that Laurie, abandoning his lunch, had

15

cast himself down the shaft in a fit of remorse. But after a great deal of trouble on the part of the police it was found that the pit, like the story, had nothing in it. Meanwhile, the authorities were informed by Laurie's Glasgow landlady, Mrs. King, that, more fortunate than those hostesses who had enjoyed his patronage at Brodick and Port Bannatyne, she had received from him a remittance for the amount of rent due by him. It was accompanied by a pencil note, posted at Hamilton on 2nd August, and was to the following effect :—

Dear Madam,

I beg to enclose P.O.O. for my rent, as I can't call, for I have to go to Leith. There are some people trying to get me into trouble, and I think you should give them no information at all, and I will prove to them how they are mistaken before very long.

Yours respectfully,

JOHN LAURIE.

The *Mail*, in a leading article on 8th August, took the police sharply to task for their slackness in failing to apprehend the Arran murderer. " We had hoped," says that journal, " that by this time Laurie would have been in their hands. Short of going about the streets shouting ' I am " John Annandale," ' Laurie did pretty nearly all that was possible to put the police upon his track. What strikes one most strongly about his conduct since the night of the tragedy is its sheer stupidity. He acted with the utmost recklessness, apparently on the extraordinary assumption that no inquiry would be made regarding the missing gentleman by his relatives, or at least that the murder would remain unknown and that the body would never be discovered." The writer instances Laurie's going back to his Bute lodgings straight from Brodick, carrying Rose's things with him; his return visit to Rothesay; his wearing of Rose's clothes there; his exhibition of a London return-half ticket, similar to that stolen from Rose; his volun-

16

Invercloy, Brodick, in 1889.

The arrow indicates the hut occupied by Rose and Laurie.

Introduction.

teering to give evidence in the matter of the *Caledonia* accident; and, finally his letter to his Glasgow landlady, which was now public property.

The police, however, had found out more than the *Mail* gave them credit for. They ascertained that Laurie had arrived in Liverpool on Tuesday, 6th August, where he took lodgings at No. 10 Greek Street, paying a week's rent in advance. On Thursday, the 8th, he told his landlady, Mrs. Ennitt, he was leaving that day, as he had obtained a situation at Manchester as a traveller in the cotton trade. He left behind him a box, which on subsequent examination was found to contain certain white shirts, later identified as Rose's, having the name of their new owner, " John W. Laurie," impressed upon them with a rubber stamp, which also was discovered in the box. It does not appear from the evidence led at the trial why Laurie left Liverpool so suddenly; but the *Liverpool Courier* had published that morning the fact of his identity with " Annandale," together with some account of his recent adventures, from which he doubtless inferred that it was time for him to go.

Not content with the considerable degree of notoriety which his singular behaviour had secured for him, and annoyed, perhaps, by the popular attention being now largely transferred to Mrs. Maybrick, then under sentence of death after her seven days' trial at Liverpool, for whose reprieve the " genuine philanthropists " were even more clamorous and insistent than they were to be in due season for his own, Laurie took the astounding step of personally addressing the British public through the medium of the daily press. On Monday, 12th August, the *Mail* published a letter received from him, bearing the Liverpool postmark, to the following effect :—

10th Aug. '89.

Dear Editor,

I feel that I should write a long detailed letter to your paper, but I am in no mood to do so.

I rather smile when I read that my arrest is hourly expected.

John Watson Laurie.

If things go as I have designed them, I will soon have arrived at that country from whose bourne no traveller returns, and since there has been so much said about me, it is only right that the public should know what are the real circumstances which has brought me to this.

Three years ago I became very much attached to Miss ——, teacher, —— School, and residing at ——. My affection for this girl was at first returned . . . until I discovered that she was encouraging the attentions of another man, ——, teacher, ——, who took every opportunity to depreciate me in her estimation.

Since then I have been perfectly careless about what I did, and my one thought was how to punish her enough for the cruel wrong she had done me; and it was to watch her audacious behaviour that I went to Rothesay this and last year. I may say that I became acquainted with another young lady, whose good qualities I sincerely wish that I had learned to appreciate sooner, as if I had I would have been in a very different position to-day.

As regards Mr. Rose, poor fellow, no one who knows me will believe for one moment that I had any complicity in his death.

The morning I left for Arran I was in the company of two friends on Rothesay pier when Mr. Rose came to me and said that he was going to spend a few days with me at Arran.

I was very much surprised at this, as my friends could vouch, for I had not invited him. We went to the top of Goatfell, where I left him in the company of two men who came from Loch Ranza, and were going to Brodick.

I went down to Corrie and met some friends, and we afterwards visited the hotel, where we met several of the gentlemen who were camping out, and I left for Brodick about ten.

I could easily prove that what I say is true, but I decline to bring the names of my friends into this disgraceful affair, so will content myself by wishing them a last adieu.

Yours truly,

JOHN W. LAURIE.

Introduction.

The names mentioned in the third paragraph were deleted by the editor, and the entire paragraph was omitted from the letter as read at the trial. They are those, respectively, of a young lady who had rejected his unwelcome and persistent addresses—he had pursued her even unto Rothesay after the murder—and of another, to whom he believed she had become attached. Laurie afterwards stated, as we shall hear, that his object in writing this letter was to " spite " these two innocent persons. Happily, however, he was hoist with his own petard; for the names were suppressed, and the postmark directed the attention of the police to Liverpool, with the result that they recovered there the box containing Rose's shirts.

The publication of this letter—as to the genuineness of which there was no question—caused a renewal of the public interest in the Arran mystery, and the writer must have been gratified by the consequent rise in his sensational stock. Emboldened by the success attending his first literary effort, the fugitive again addressed the public in a letter, dated 27th August and bearing the Aberdeen postmark, directed this time to the editor of the *Glasgow Herald*. This communication, with the requisite editorial omissions, was duly printed in that journal on 29th August :—

27th August, 1889.

Sir,

I expected that the letter which I so foolishly addressed to the *Mail* would have been my last, but I read so many absurd and mad things in the daily papers, that I feel it my duty to correct some of them, and the first of these is the assertion . . . that I am kept out of the way by friends.

I have not come across a friend since I left Glasgow, nor have I been in communication with any one. I don't deny the fact that I would like to meet some of my friends again, but I am more careful than to allow myself to be lured like the moth to the flame.

Although I am entirely guiltless of the crime I am so much

John Watson Laurie.

wanted for, yet I can recognise that I am a ruined man in any case, so it is far from my intention to give myself up.

I first went to Glasgow in the spring of 1882, but being among strangers, I became homesick, so was glad of the offer held out to me of something to do at Uddingston.

Messrs. John Gray & Co. were at that time making a winding engine, also several steam cranes for the underground railway, and during the months of June, July, and August I assisted Mr. John Swan to make the patterns. I remember Mr. Swan as being a very nice gentleman, but I have no recollection of a man the name of Alexander.

I was not at Hamilton eight weeks ago, and I certainly did not smile to Alexander on the way there. If I had travelled in a train where I was known, don't you think it likely that I would have left at the first stoppage?

The stories about me being seen are all imagination. I have not been seen by any one who knows me, and I have been travelling all the time in England and Ireland; and as I can see that this is no land for me, I will be off again.

It is true that I did take a room for a week at 10 Greek Street, Liverpool, which I paid in advance. I only stayed three days. I did not board with the lady of the house, and after destroying my papers, I left my box, with no intention of ever calling for it again, as it was an encumbrance to me.

The *Mail* takes credit to itself in this case, which does not belong to it at all, for it was a friend of mine who felt it his duty to inform the authorities that Mr. Rose left Rothesay with me; and when I saw from an evening paper that Mr. Rose had not returned to his lodgings, I began at once to arrange for my departure, for I had told so many about him.

Seemingly there was a motive for doing away with poor Rose; it was not to secure his valuables. Mr. Rose was to all appearance worse off than myself; indeed, he assured me that he had spent so much on his tour that he had barely sufficient to last till he got home.

He wore an old Geneva watch with no gold albert attached, and I am sure that no one saw him wear a ring on his tour, and no one saw me wear one, and well —— knew that he was speaking a lie when he said that he saw me wear a ring at

Introduction.

Rothesay. A nice picture this fellow made of me, surely out of ill-will, because I had fooled his precious brother. He says that when he saw me I was wearing a ring, and had one of my hands gloved. This is a preposterous falsehood; indeed, his whole story from beginning to end was a lie.

I met him one morning in Shamrock Street, not Cambridge Street, and I caught hold of his arm, when he asked a boy to call a policeman. There was no striking on either side, but if there had been, I leave those who know us to judge who would come off second best.

—— has changed his opinion about the girl I was more than intimate with from the spring of 1887 to the end of June, 1888. She has now an irreproachable character. It suits him, of course, to say this; but if that were so, this trouble would never have come.

However, these are trivial matters, uninteresting to all but those immediately concerned, and as I am not inclined to say any more, I hope this will be the last the public will hear of me.

Yours truly,

JOHN W. LAURIE.

The references to the lady friend were not read at the trial.

In the same envelope was also enclosed a private letter addressed to the editor, making further scurrilous aspersions upon the character and conduct of this girl, which, of course, was withheld from publication. Both letters were handed to the police, who were satisfied that they, as well as the former letter, were in Laurie's handwriting.

The modest hope expressed in the last paragraph of the *Herald* letter was not destined to be realised. The police believed that the posting of the second letter at Aberdeen was intended to put them off the scent, and that Laurie had in fact returned to his old haunts, as he was reported to have been seen at Uddingston and also at Coatbridge. The net was slowly but surely being tightened. How much money Rose actually had upon him at the time of his death was never proved; but at

John Watson Laurie.

least there must have been enough to enable the murderer
so successfully to elude the vigilance of the police during
the five weeks which elapsed between his absconding and
his apprehension.

III.

On Wednesday, 4th September, 1889, the *North
British Daily Mail* was in a position to give its readers
exceptional value for their money. In bold headlines
it announced: " ARREST OF LAURIE. RECOGNISED AT
LARKHALL. FLIGHT AND PURSUIT. CAPTURED IN A
WOOD. HE ATTEMPTS SUICIDE." So the hunted man
was run to earth at last, and in circumstances appropriately thrilling.

Shortly before the arrival of the Glasgow train, due at
the Ferniegair Station of the Hamilton line, on Tuesday,
3rd September, the stationmaster noticed a man hanging about the entrance. He sent a boy to tell the man,
if he were an intending passenger, " to hurry up, as
the train was due "; but the man said he did not propose
to book, and hastily made off. At that moment Constable Gordon came into the station with a view to joining the train. To him the stationmaster said that a
man who looked like the wanted one had just left.
Gordon went up to the railway bridge over the line,
which commanded a prospect of the immediate neighbourhood, and saw the suspect going along the Carlisle
road. He followed at a rapid walk, and was overtaking
his quarry, when the man looked round, " and seeing
that the officer meant business, bolted through a gate
leading into a grass field." Traversing this at headlong
pace, the fugitive crossed the railway line and reached
the Lanark road. Along the highway he flew, pursued
by Gordon, shouting: " Catch that man; that's
Laurie! " Presently a party of Larkhall miners from
the Bog Colliery nearby, hearing the shouts, joined in
the chase. They threw down their tools and darted down
the road from the pit at breakneck speed. On reaching

22

Introduction.

the Quarry Wood, a mile and a half from Ferniegair Station, they found the panting constable, and asked him where was Laurie. " There; in that wood," he gasped.

It was a small plantation of about two acres, sloping down to the Clyde. The miners were for dashing in at once, but the constable caused them to surround the clump of trees, before any one entered. Meanwhile two boys, who had been in the wood, told how they had seen a man hiding under some bushes in the old quarry from which the plantation is named. Some of the party then went into the wood, and one of the miners soon detected the fugitive, who lay among the undergrowth, with a razor in his hand and a superficial cut on his throat. He was dragged out of his hiding-place and given in charge of the constable. " I am Laurie," said he; " but not Rose's murderer. I wish I had got time to do the job right. I intended to commit suicide to-night." His hand was less capable than at Coire-na-fuhren. Cautioned that anything he now said might be used against him, Laurie rejoined: " I robbed the man, but I did not murder him." He was then taken to the colliery, where his wound was dressed, and was afterwards removed to Hamilton and safely locked up.

The news of Laurie's capture was telegraphed to Rothesay, and the Procurator-Fiscal at once sent two officers by the first steamer—the *Lord of the Isles*—to bring the prisoner back to Bute. Next morning he was conveyed in custody to Rothesay, in order to be formally charged in the Sheriff Court there with the murder of Edwin Rose. One who witnessed Laurie's arrival at the island communicated to the *Sunday Post* of 12th October, 1930, his recollections of that forty-years' old event—

It was the last year of the old white-funnelled boats which for years had overtaken the Wemyss Bay service to the coast, and it was on the *Adela* that he made his passage to Rothesay.

A huge crowd gathered on the pier, but as the *Adela* was circling round the bay a cab was seen speeding in along the east shore. Seated on the dickey was a Rothesay police sergeant, and the crowd at once jumped to the correct conclusion that Laurie had been landed at Craigmore Pier in the hope of avoiding notice.

There was a stampede up to the Court-house, but all that was obtained was a fleeting glimpse of a bowed figure, clad in a brown suit, being hustled in by the big front door.

It was noticed that Laurie's neck was closely wrapped round, and it afterwards transpired that he had tried to cut his throat.

The Court procedure was brief, and early in the afternoon he was conveyed to Greenock Prison, via Gourock.

In his first declaration, being judicially examined before the Sheriff at Rothesay on 4th September, the prisoner admitted his identity, adding, " I have nothing to say to the charge in the meantime." In a second declaration, emitted before the Sheriff at Greenock on 11th September, being shown the cap, waterproof, and other articles belonging to Rose, found near the boulder, he further declared, " I wish to say nothing about any of these articles." At a pleading diet at Greenock on 29th October, the accused formally pleaded Not Guilty, and was remitted to the High Court at Edinburgh for trial.

Part III.—The Trial.

I.

The High Court of Justiciary stands in the Parliament Square, Edinburgh, a backwater of the busy High Street, deserted most days save for King Charles on his leaden charger and Master John Knox in his resting grave. But when a murder trial is afoot the lonely plaza is thronged throughout the proceedings by a curious crowd, each member of which lingers in fond hope to gain admission to the free and popular entertainment within. The exceptional circumstances of the present case attracted a record gathering. " For hours before the time

24

Introduction.

announced for the commencement of the trial," says the *Scotsman* of 9th November, 1889, " the entrance to the Court buildings was besieged by a crowd estimated to consist of about 2000 persons. Anticipating the interest manifested in the trial, the authorities made specially stringent regulations concerning the admission of the public, and the doors were opened as early as nine o'clock."

The sombre walls and lofty windows of the old Court-room have looked down upon many a famous—or rather, infamous—figure, seated in the grim, narrow dock. That very year, on Monday, 18th February, with the same judge upon the Bench and the same counsel for the Crown, I remember witnessing, enthralled, the prosecution and conviction of Jessie King, the notorious baby-farmer and child-murderess, who enjoys the distinction of being the last woman to be hanged in Edinburgh. It was my first murder trial; and I can still hear the dreadful wailing of the condemned woman on the pronouncement of her so well-deserved doom. But the interest attaching to her case pales in comparison with that created by the Laurie trial, of which also it was my privilege to be a spectator.

At a few minutes before ten o'clock, on Friday, 8th November, 1889, the trapdoor in front of the dock was raised and the prisoner, in charge of two constables, came up into Court from the cells below. The appearance of the man was surprising; he looked so unlike one's conception of the supposed murderer. Well dressed and groomed, commonplace, calm, and respectable, could this be the brutal ruffian of Coire-na-fuhren? On the stroke of ten the Lord Justice-Clerk (Lord Kingsburgh) took his seat upon the Bench. The Solicitor-General (Mr.—afterwards Lord—Stormonth Darling, Q.C., M.P.), assisted by Mr. Graham Murray (afterwards Lord President and later Viscount Dunedin) and Mr. Dougald M'Kechnie (afterwards Sheriff of Argyll), advocates-depute, appeared for the Crown. For the defence were the Dean of Faculty (Mr. J. B. Balfour, Q.C., M.P.,

25

John Watson Laurie.

afterwards Lord President and later Baron Kinross) and
Mr. Charles Scott Dickson (afterwards Lord Justice-Clerk).
The Crown Agent was Mr. James Auldjo Jamieson,
W.S.; the agents for the prisoner were Messrs. Webster,
Will & Ritchie, S.S.C.

Monday is the usual day for the opening of an important criminal trial. Why Friday was chosen in this case
I cannot tell; but the fact was attended by the proverbial
ill-luck for all concerned, because the Justice-Clerk having intimated that the case must finish on the Saturday,
the proof on both sides suffered compression, and, even
so, the verdict was not delivered until the discomfort-
able hour of half-past ten at night.

The indictment was as follows:—

JOHN WATSON LAURIE, prisoner in the prison of Greenock,
you are indicted at the instance of the Right Honourable
James Patrick Bannerman Robertson, Her Majesty's Advocate,
and the charge against you is, that on 15th July, 1889, at
Corr-na-fourin, near the head of Glen Sannox, in the Island
of Arran, Buteshire, you did assault Edwin Robert Rose,
Wisset Lodge, Hendham Road, Trinity Road, Upper Tooting,
London, and did throw him down, and did beat him, and did
murder him.

Annexed to the indictment were (1) a list of productions
containing 12 documents and photographs relevant thereto, and 23 articles, the property of Rose; and (2) a list
of 86 witnesses for the Crown. The indictment having
been read by the Clerk of Court, the accused pleaded Not
Guilty; a jury was empanelled, and the prosecutor
adduced his proof.

As the reader is already familiar with the main facts
and the evidence is printed in full in the following
report, it were tedious to take him for the third time over
the same ground. I shall, therefore, merely mention
such points as have not yet been dealt with, and consider,
in particular, the medical evidence for Crown and defence, which, of course, forms the crux of the case.

Introduction.

II.

The fact that Rose was last seen alive in Laurie's company was established by the testimony of several witnesses.

From the sea-level at the beautiful old-time inn of Brodick—now used in connection with the estate—on the north side of the bay, the way to Goatfell lies through the grounds of Brodick Castle, past the Kennels, and thence by the Castle woods to the open moor. Alexander Morrison and Thomas Purdon, respectively brother and brother-in-law to Mrs. Walker, were staying with that lady on the date in question, and knew her lodgers by sight. On the afternoon of Monday, 15th July, these gentlemen, having been up Goatfell, were returning to Brodick, when they met in the Castle grounds, going up, " Annandale " and Rose. Purdon noticed that Rose was then wearing a watch-chain.

The Rev. Robert Hind of Paisley, with his friends Mr. John M'Cabe and the Rev. Joseph Ritson, came from Lamlash that day to climb Goatfell. They started from Brodick at three o'clock, and when they got out upon the open hillside, were overtaken by two young men, one of whom was " exceedingly like " the accused, the other being by his photograph identified as Rose. The fair one (Laurie) kept on ahead and spoke to none of them; the dark one (Rose) chatted awhile with the party, saying that he came from London and had been staying at Rothesay. " He referred to the other young man, and said he [the other] was his guide." Rose was wearing a black waterproof, similar to that produced; but it was then untorn. After continuing in company for half an hour, a shower coming on caused Mr. Hind's party to shelter behind a boulder; the other two carried on. When Mr. Hind's party reached the top about six o'clock, they saw the two young men standing on the farther edge of the summit, looking towards Glen Sannox. The party, having for a quarter of an hour enjoyed the view—one of the most extensive and magni-

ficent in Scotland—descended by the way they came,
reaching Brodick in time for the 8.30 steamer to Lamlash. On the way down they wondered what had become
of the two young men, whom they could see neither in
front of nor behind them, and concluded that they had
gone down by The Saddle.

Two brothers named Francis, from London, also
climbed Goatfell that afternoon. Edward sat down to
rest before tackling the last stiff pull of the ascent;
Frederick went on alone, reaching the summit twenty
minutes before him. When the brother arrived he was
preceded in single file by two young men, one of whom
" closely resembled " the accused. The other was an
Englishman, dark, and wearing a black macintosh, like
that now produced. Witness had some conversation with
the Englishman, who asked him as to the various ways
down. The other did not speak. The last the brothers
saw of them, they were standing on a boulder, with
their backs to Ailsa Craig, and pointing in the opposite
direction. " They were apparently arranging about
going down. They seemed to be on friendly terms and
were talking together." The brothers left the summit
for Brodick at twenty-five minutes past six, and saw
them no more. This is the last that was seen of Rose
alive.

At half-past nine that evening David M'Kenzie, a
shepherd of High Corrie, was " daffing " in the gloam-
ing with two servant girls, employed by summer visitors,
in the leafy lane beside the old burying-ground of
Sannox, when he saw a man emerge from the glen, and
cut across the field beside the graveyard, in the direction
of Corrie. M'Kenzie remarked to his companions that
the wayfarer " was awful tired and worn-out like, and
that he appeared to have had a heavy day's travelling
on the hills." The accused was the man. This is the
first that was seen of Rose's late companion after they
had parted upon the mountain top for ever.

James Wilson, law clerk, Greenock, chanced—it might

Introduction.

have happened to any one—to be in the bar of Corrie Hotel at ten o'clock that night, when he was accosted by a man whom he identified as the accused. The stranger asked Wilson to order for him a bottle of beer, as the hour for supplying non-residents was past. He did so, and left him. Margaret Livingston, the barmaid, corroborated. The stranger subsequently ordered a bottle to be filled with spirits, giving as his reason that he had to walk the 6 miles to Brodick.

Mary Robertson, Kilmarnock, had been on a visit to Brodick. On Tuesday, 16th July, she set forth to catch the early steamer for Ardrossan. Midway between the village and the pier she overtook a man carrying two bags, one black, the other brown. The accused was the man.

Andrew Gilmour, student of medicine, Linlithgow— presumably a relative of Dr. Gilmour—was staying at Corrie. He knew Messrs. Mickel and Thom; and on Saturday, the 13th, was by them introduced to Rose and "Annandale." He, too, left the island on the 16th by the *Scotia* from Brodick at 7 a.m., and the first person he saw on board was "Annandale." That gentleman said he was going to Glasgow. They got into the same compartment of the train at Ardrossan; "Annandale" had either one or two bags, and Gilmour offered to help him with his luggage. He took a black leather bag into the carriage with him, and put it on the rack. Gilmour got out at Greenock. He identified the accused as his fellow-traveller. This is the last that was seen of Rose's bag. How "Annandale" disposed of it is not known.

III.

The accused set his defenders a difficult task by insisting on the line of defence which he had laid down in his letter to the *North British Daily Mail*, namely, that he parted from Rose on the top of Goatfell, and never more set eyes on him, alive or dead.

How, upon that assumption, were the accused's subsequent actings to be accounted for? It was proved that Sergeant Munro, in company with Dr. Fullarton and two constables, going at an ordinary pace, walked from the summit to the boulder in half an hour, and from thence to Corrie Hotel in an hour and forty minutes. Yet Laurie, leaving the top soon after six o'clock, did not reach Corrie Hotel till ten. What was he about during those two superfluous hours? Then, having regained his lodgings and finding that Rose has not returned, he leaves without a word to any one by the first available steamer next morning, taking away with him his friend's luggage—an act only to be explained by his knowledge that Rose could never come back to claim it. This seems to me of itself sufficiently damning, despite the fact that no article proved to have been on Rose's person at the time of his death was definitely traced to Laurie's possession. But it is more than probable that the missing pocket-book, containing his money and return ticket to London, was then in his pocket. It is unlikely that he would leave it unprotected in the open hut at Brodick. However Rose met his death, whether by accident or design, there is no doubt that some one rifled his body and elaborately buried it beneath the boulder. That a casual stranger, coming across the corpse, even if abandoned enough to rob it, would run the gratuitous and fearful risk of burying it, is beyond belief. The defence, therefore, making the best of a bad job, had to concentrate their efforts on persuading the jury that the death was accidental. The charge was murder; if that could be discounted, the robbery, though morally regrettable, was a minor matter.

IV.

The case for the defence was that all the injuries to the body were produced simultaneously, as the result of a single fall over one or other of the steep rocks before

Introduction.

referred to, farther up the gully from the boulder where the body was buried. On the left side, above the place where the cap was found, as already mentioned, was the 19-feet drop, 156 yards beyond the boulder; the 32-feet drop was on the other side, 40 yards lower down, above where the knife, pencil, and button were found. The former fall was that favoured by the defence. There was no indication on the body or clothes of its having been dragged from thence down to the boulder, which, looking to the nature of the ground, would, if done, surely have left unmistakable signs of the process. The only injury to these, apart from the head, was that on the shoulder-blade, with corresponding damage to the flesh, the clothing, and the waterproof. If killed farther up the gully, therefore, the body of Rose must have been carried down to the boulder.

The Crown case, however, was that Laurie, who was familiar with the locality, having induced Rose to descend by way of Coire-na-fuhren, struck him down by a blow with a stone upon the left side of the head, delivered from above and behind, as they clambered down the steep incline. Then, as the wounded man lay helpless on the ground, his face and head were furiously battered so as to prevent recognition, the injury to the top of the shoulder-blade being caused by a blow which missed the head and struck the shoulder. The deed was done beside the boulder, beneath which, having rifled the body, the murderer concealed his victim by erecting the elaborate barricade of stones before described. Why he did not include in this sepulture the several articles scattered about the gully the Crown made no attempt to explain. The defence maintained that these were dropped by Rose as he pitched head-foremost over the rock; but though that might conceivably account for the stick, knife, pencil, and button lying where they were found, how came the waterproof to be torn in two and trampled—" huddled together "—in a pool? And how came the cap, folded in four, to lie in the bed of

31

John Watson Laurie.

the stream, with a stone weighing between seven and eight pounds upon the top of it? The learned Judge suggested that they had been deliberately placed so as to create the presumption of a fall. My own view is that the murderer, having emptied the pockets, threw away the smaller articles as of no importance, and probably overlooked the others until he had completed his sepulchral labours, when even he may well have hesitated to reopen the cavity, preferring rather to hide the cap under a stone in the stream, and let the rest take their chance. I have heard no theory to account for the disjection of the waterproof.

The members of the search party who were at the finding of the body one and all denied that the descent from the ridge to the boulder was either specially dangerous or difficult to a person using ordinary care, and maintained that a man going down on the left side of the gully by what was obviously the natural way, would have no occasion to go near the steep rocks at all. In his cross-examination of the police witnesses, the learned Dean elicited the singular fact that, after the post-mortem in the coach-house on 5th August, the boots removed from the body were taken to the seashore at Corrie and there buried below high-water mark. Sergeant Munro, who gave instructions for their removal, and Constable Coll, who carried out his orders, were severely cross-examined as to their reason for so disposing of them. The boots were the only articles connected with the body which were not preserved as " productions "; and the Dean held that their condition with regard to heels and nails was most vital to the question at issue. The sergeant could give no reason beyond the fact that the boots " were so fully identified " as not to call for preservation. The constable said that Munro " told him to put them out of sight." He thought that if a correct description of them were given, " that is good enough." Pressed again and again as to why the boots were buried, both witnesses took refuge in silence.

32

John Watson Laurie.

Introduction.

Now, I am credibly informed that the carrying out of this curious and irregular interment was due to a Highland superstition, namely, that the dead man's ghost would thereby be prevented from " walking " to the disturbance of the living! If such were indeed the motive, it would seem to imply an imperfect sense of humour on the part of those concerned. Nay, more; there was precedent against it. For did not the ghost of Sergeant Davies " walk," not only bootless but without his clothes, as was solemnly sworn to in the High Court of Justiciary at Edinburgh in 1754? But Sergeant Munro knew not Sergeant Davies.

V.

The real battleground of the case was, of course, the cause of death. The skilled witnesses for the Crown were Drs. Gilmour and Fullarton, who inspected the body at the boulder and performed the subsequent post-mortem examination, and Dr. (afterwards Professor Sir Henry) Littlejohn, who examined the body further on its later exhumation. Into the ghastly details of the injuries to the head and face it is unnecessary now to enter. These will be found by the professional reader fully set forth in the medical reports and in the evidence of the medical witnesses at the trial. It is sufficient here to state that these experts concurred in the opinion that they had been produced by direct violence in the manner alleged by the prosecution. The limbs and extremities were free from fractures and dislocations, and there was no indication of blood upon the body or clothes. The injured parts were horribly decayed; and the fact that the highest cervical vertebra was lying loose when first seen by Dr. Gilmour was attributable to the advanced decomposition of the neck. The entire upper jaw was detached in one piece. These injuries, in Dr. Gilmour's view, must have been caused by repeated impacts, whether due to blows or falls. All the injuries

D

were confined to the left side; and in the case of a sheer, single fall such injuries to the face would not be present. Dr. Fullarton stated that the extent and severity of the fractures were the result of repeated blows with a blunt instrument; he had never seen a head so smashed except by a machinery accident. The injury to the shoulder confirmed this view, for any conscious person falling would have had his hands before him, and the injuries, which in this case were all localised, would have been different. He thought that the first blow was given while the man was standing, and the rest while he lay on the ground. Dr. Littlejohn stated that the condition of the cranium as seen by him was at once suggestive of direct violence by blows. A heavy stone in the hand would be an instrument likely to inflict such injuries. The severity of the bruises would stop hæmorrhage, and the absence of hæmorrhage would account for the speedy decomposition. The detachment of the cervical vertebra was consistent either with decay of the tissues or with dislocation. A fall could not have produced such localised violence without severe injuries to the extremities and to the internal organs, which were intact and uninjured, and remarkably well preserved. He had considerable experience of falls from heights such as the Dean Bridge and the Castle Rock, Edinburgh, but he never saw injuries like these so caused. A fall of such severity *must* have implicated the liver, the condition of which was normal; and there would also be other lesions, not present in this case.

The detached upper jaw, by the way, which figures so prominently in the medical evidence, was preserved by Dr. Littlejohn for professional purposes, and may still be seen by the curious in the laboratory of the Department of Forensic Medicine in the University of Edinburgh.

Three eminent Edinburgh surgeons were called for the defence: Dr. (afterwards Sir Patrick) Heron Watson, Dr. Charles M'Gillivray, and Dr. (afterwards Professor)

34

Introduction.

Alexis Thomson. It is to be observed that none of these gentlemen had seen the body and the actual injuries which it bore; they gave their opinion solely upon reading the three medical reports and hearing the evidence for the Crown. Drs. M'Gillivray and Thomson, however, had visited and inspected the *locus* with reference to the present inquiry. Dr. Heron Watson stated that the injuries which he had heard described were in his view more consistent with a fall than with repeated blows; he considered that they had all been produced simultaneously. The probabilities were in favour of a fall upon the vertex. The vertebræ of the neck were probably broken, so that there would be little bleeding, which in the case of blows would have been copious. The fact that the liver was unruptured did not affect his opinion. As the result of certain grisly experiments, witness described the difficulty of fracturing the human skull by blows, so as to produce the extensive smashing present in this case. His theory was that Rose slipped on the slope, and turning round to the left in attempting to save himself before he reached the edge, fell over the rock headlong and backwards. If the head alighted on a granite surface on which there was a nodule of some size, that would account for the injuries both to the face and shoulder. Dr. M'Gillivray described the nature of the ground, as seen by him at Coire-na-fuhren. The 32-feet drop, which he measured, was hidden from a person coming down. Witness pushed a boulder over, and it was smashed to pieces. Any one falling down the 19-feet drop would land about where the cap was found. If Rose fell over either of these rocks, all the injuries present on the body could have been produced. From the facts so stated, he considered a fall a more probable cause than blows. Dr. Alexis Thomson also gave a description of the gully. The 32-feet drop was above where the knife, pencil, and button were found. A person might find himself on the edge before noticing his danger. The ground at the foot of both drops was shelving granite, with lumps of various forms and ragged surfaces. It was much more probable that the injuries described were produced by a fall from either of these places than by repeated blows.

Skilled medical opinion in a criminal trial is invariably conflicting, greatly to the confusion of the lay mind. But the expert testimony in this case presents a most unusual feature: neither side, on cross-examination, would absolutely negative the possibility of the other's theory. To the lay mind aforesaid it occurs that Rose may have fallen or been pushed over, and then battered with stones—either to death, if not already killed; or with a view to render recognition impossible. "The bearings of this observation," as Mr. Bunsby remarked in another connection, "lays in the application on it."

In addition to their medical men, the defence called only four witnesses: one, an Italian fisherman named Latona, to give expert evidence as a " guide " regarding the dangerous character of the descent by Coire-na-fuhren; another, a girl who had known Laurie at Rothesay, to say that she found him " chatty and agreeable " on his return from the excursion to Arran. It appeared, however, on cross-examination, that the " guide," who had only been three years in the island, was never in Glen Sannox till after the body was found; while the girl admitted that on her asking Laurie how long he took to climb Goatfell, he avoided the question and made no reply. The other two witnesses called were the servant girls who were with Mackenzie at Sannox burying-ground. They did not remember his remark about the man, but admitted that it might have been made.

It was fortunate for the accused's neck that he was tried in 1889 and not in 1898, for then the provisions of the Criminal Evidence Act of that year would have enabled him to give evidence on his own behalf. A man so vain and self-sufficient could not have been kept out of the witness-box; once there, like his blood-brothers, the

Introduction.

competent Mr. Seddon and the plausible Mr. Rouse, he
would infallibly have helped to hang himself.

VI.

The case for the defence being closed, at half-past five
on Saturday, 9th November, the second day of the trial,
the Solicitor-General rose to address the jury on the
part of the Crown. There still, for me, echo across the
forty years the tones of that musical voice; I can still
see the fine and gracious figure of the prosecutor, as he
discharged with perfect fairness his painful duty. Particularly I recall the impressive effect of his opening sum-
mary of the salient facts—

Two young men went up a hill together and only one came
down. The other was found, after an interval of weeks, with
his body horribly mutilated, hidden away among the rocks of
the hillside, and with all his portable property removed. The
one who came down was seen within a few hours of the time
when the death of his friend must have taken place. He
returned from the excursion on which they both started, and
gave no sign or hint that anything had happened to his friend,
or that he had not returned with him. The next morning he
left Arran, and resumed his ordinary occupation until the
hue and cry began. Then, when it did begin, he took to
flight; and finally, when he was about to be arrested, he
attempted to cut his throat.

With regard to the prisoner's conduct, he came to
Rothesay under a false name; he spent the night
of his friend's disappearance in the room which they
had shared; he left by the first steamer next morning
without paying his bill, and leaving the room in such
a state as should suggest that both had occupied it; he
obliterated every trace of Rose except the tennis racket,
which, as it bore its owner's name, would have been an
awkward thing to take with him. He returned to
Rothesay wearing Rose's hat and carrying other property
of Rose's in a parcel; while certain things which also

37

John Watson Laurie.

belonged to Rose were found in the trunk left by him at
Liverpool. The watch and chain and pocket-book, which
Rose was proved to have upon him, were missing; and
though it was not known how much money he had, it
must have been enough to pay his way for the remainder
of his holiday. The question was: Whose hand rifled
the pockets and buried the body beneath the boulder?
He thought the jury would be satisfied that the prisoner
was with Rose till the end; the suggestion of the defence
that these two parted on the mountain top was excluded
by the whole facts of the case. If, then, the prisoner
robbed and buried the body, was his the hand that caused
the death? The suggestion that Rose met his death by
accident, and that the prisoner robbed and buried him,
was so inherently, so wildly improbable that they must
hesitate to accept it. If such were indeed the fact, it
indicated a depravity of mind but little removed from
that which led to murder. Having dealt exhaustively
with the medical theories of each side, the Solicitor-
General said it was for the jury to consider, not so much
what was possible—" because all things are possible
where you are dealing with medical testimony "—but
what probably happened. The prisoner's own behaviour
afforded the readiest solution. He asked them to apply to
it the ordinary standard of human conduct, and to say
whether any man could have so acted who was not the
murderer of Rose. As to motive, the prisoner probably
expected to get more than he got, but having done the
deed, he had to go through with it. Finally, he submitted that the prosecution had established beyond
reasonable doubt that the prisoner was guilty of the
crime charged, and he asked for their verdict
accordingly.

The Dean of Faculty, leader of the Scots Bar, despite
his brilliant gifts and persuasive power of oratory, may
well have had his own doubts as to the success of his
endeavours on behalf of the accused. But notwithstanding the insufficiency of straw wherewith he must effect

Introduction.

his forensic brickmaking, the speech for the defence displays no lack of confidence in the stability of the structure. His hands, of course, were tied from the first by the impossible instructions of his conceited client, who, deeming himself wiser than his legal advisers, insisted that his case be fought on the footing that he left Rose, alive and hearty, upon the mountain. Had he admitted witnessing an accidental fatal fall, and a yielding to the temptation to profit by it, that indeed would have been another story, which might, peradventure, have secured a verdict. The learned Dean said that he agreed with the prosecutor that if the charge were true, this was a murder unprecedented and incredibly atrocious. The onus of proof, therefore, was all the heavier upon the Crown; but he hoped to show that no murder was in fact committed. There were no signs of any struggle or of the dragging of the body; no instrument had been found likely to have inflicted the injuries. All these were upon the left side; no right-handed man would so have attacked Rose, and it was not suggested that the accused was left-handed. He argued that, upon a balance of the medical evidence, all the injuries supported the theory of the defence. Near the spot were two declivities; a fall from either would produce these results. Where, according to the Crown, was this murder committed? If at the boulder, how came the various things to lie where they were found? Their position was quite consistent with Rose's pitching over the rock and the things flying in all directions. The accused's meeting with Rose was casual, the visit to Brodick fortuitous; he could then have had no murderous design. His alleged reticence was due to toothache. There was no evidence that Rose and Laurie were ever together in this world again from the time they were seen on the top of Goatfell.

The Solicitor-General is quite mistaken in stating that the defence admits that the two were together. It must be taken

39

John Watson Laurie.

as a thing not proved that they were together. Whoever removed the body—I hope you will understand that you do not go to deliberate upon your verdict on the supposition that it is the theory or suggestion of the defence that the moving of the body was done by Laurie—nobody knows by whom it was done.

A man of the accused's size and strength could not have carried and buried the body without assistance—one of the stones weighed $1\frac{1}{2}$ cwt.

The Solicitor-General seems to think that we, for the defence, are admitting that Laurie robbed the body of Rose. We admit nothing of the kind. It may be that somebody did it. Very likely, at these Fair holidays, there would be plenty of people on the island who would do that.

This certificate to the character of the local holiday-makers would, no doubt, be gratefully received in Glasgow.

When seen later in the evening, Laurie had no appearance of being a red-handed murderer; but if the Crown case were true, he must have exhibited some traces of the deed. He certainly appropriated improperly some articles belonging to Rose; and if this were a charge of theft, that would be important. But he made no secret of it; he wore the things openly among people who knew them both. Not until Aitken showed that he suspected him did Laurie realise that, having been with Rose in Arran, he might be held responsible for his disappearance. His subsequent conduct was due to that fear; if he had expected this charge he would not have remained in Glasgow till 31st July. When arrested, he said : " I robbed the man, but I did not murder him." That was certainly not a confession that he had rifled the body, but referred to the things which he had taken away from the lodgings. In conclusion, the learned Dean maintained that the Crown had failed to prove, firstly, that there was any murder, and, secondly, if there had been, that Laurie was the murderer. He asked

the jury to return a verdict which would acquit the
accused of this most terrible and appalling charge.

VII.

When the learned Dean sat down, having spoken for
an hour and forty minutes, there was a brief adjourn-
ment, to enable the jury to sustain the judicial charge.
At twenty minutes to nine o'clock the Lord Justice-
Clerk resumed his seat; dead silence fell upon the chatter-
ing benches, and, turning to the jury, his lordship began
his charge. His review of, and comments upon, the
evidence lasted exactly an hour, and the packed audience
hung upon his every word. Perhaps the most composed
of his hearers was the accused, who looked steadfastly at
the Judge, with an occasional glance at the jury, to
see whether they appreciated certain judicial points.
His lordship characterised the case as one of the most
remarkable that had ever come before a Court of Justice.
It was a case of purely circumstantial evidence, and he
proposed first to examine the facts, as to which there
was no doubt. He traced the association of Rose and
Laurie till they were last seen together upon the mountain top. It was proved that the deceased was then
wearing his watch-chain, and they knew that he had in
his pocket-book a return-half ticket to London. These
two did not descend by the ordinary route, but by one
proved not to be dangerous to any one taking reasonable
care. Now, on the way down Rose undoubtedly met
his death by violence, and his body was carefully hidden
by some one. If he died by falling over one or other
of the rocks farther up the gully, it must have been a
work of great difficulty to bring down his body to the
boulder. His lordship then described the rifling of the
body and the disposition of the several articles found in
the vicinity. He then followed the accused on his
emergence from the glen, to the bar of Corrie Hotel, and
so to bed at Brodick, till his departure next morning

John Watson Laurie.

with Rose's belongings; and recalled his wearing of Rose's clothes at Rothesay, his statement that he had a return-half ticket to London, his conversation with Aitken, his flight to Liverpool with a box containing Rose's property, his letters to the press, his apprehension, and his attempted suicide. These were facts about which there could be no doubt; and the Crown said they all pointed to the prisoner's guilt. The defence was that the death of Rose did not take place in Laurie's presence; that, having gone up Goatfell together, they did not descend together—although one met his death on the way by Glen Sannox to Corrie, and the other reached Corrie by way of Glen Sannox. Laurie should have been surprised when he found his friend did not return to their room; but the effect of Rose's non-arrival was that, without a word to any one, he went off with both their bags. The defence maintained that one man could not have carried the body down to the boulder; but the Crown contended that Rose was killed with a stone, which might have happened beside the boulder. The Dean asked, if Rose were killed there, how came the things to be found farther up the gully? But if Rose were in fact killed at the boulder, his murderer might so have disposed of them as to suggest that Rose had fallen over the rocks. The hiding of the cap and the cutting-up of the waterproof must have been done by a human hand after Rose's death. It was very remarkable that the prisoner did not reach Corrie till ten, when those who left the top at the same time reached Brodick before eight-thirty. If the jury could not reconcile these facts with the prisoner's case that he was not " in at the death," there was no escape from the conclusion that his was the hand that hid the cap, tore off the waterproof, and buried the body. After reviewing at large the medical evidence, his lordship observed that those who saw and examined the injuries were in a better position to form an opinion than those who based theirs merely upon the evidence which they had heard. It was not the jury's function

42

Introduction.

to decide between conflicting medical evidence, but to find what, taking the whole facts and circumstances along with that evidence, was the probable cause of death.

The jury then retired to consider their verdict, the Judge left the Bench, and the prisoner was taken to the cells below. For three-quarters of an hour the intense excitement—I know of none more thrilling—always aroused by the jury's absence on their fateful duty, kept the audience in a buzz of expectant whispering, till the ringing of the jury-bell announced that a decision was reached. The Judge came back to the Bench; the accused, as cool as ever, re-entered the dock; the Bar reassembled; the jury filed slowly into their box; the hum of the people was hushed. "The jury, by a majority, find the prisoner guilty." Mr. Graham Murray having moved for sentence, the prisoner unflinchingly stood up to receive his doom. The Lord Justice-Clerk, in pronouncing the sentence of the Court, was visibly affected by the solemnity of the occasion. Not so the prisoner, who heard his fate unmoved, and immediately his lordship had finished, turned round in the dock, surveyed for a moment the crowded Court-room, and said in a loud, firm voice: "Ladies and gentlemen, I am innocent of this charge." The Justice-Clerk at once said that the prisoner could not be allowed to make a speech. Laurie then walked steadily from the dock between the constables and disappeared below; and, the jury having received the customary thanks, the Court rose at twenty minutes to eleven. So the curtain fell upon the last act of the tragedy of the Arran murder.

The *Scotsman* report of the proceedings ends upon a quaint note—

It seems that the jury were very much dissatisfied with the lunch which was provided for them on both days of the Court, and remonstrated with the officials concerning the same.

Surely, if the labourer be worthy of his hire, the lunch should have been worthy of the jury.

43

John Watson Laurie.

I may perhaps be permitted to quote, from the account of the case which I published eighteen years ago in *Twelve Scots Trials*, my recollection of the final picture—

No one who witnessed the closing act of this famous trial can forget the impressive character of the scene. Without, in the black November night, a great crowd silently awaited the issue of life and death. The lofty, dimly-lighted Court-room, the candles glimmering in the shadows of the Bench, the imposing presence of the Justice-Clerk in his robes of scarlet and white, the tiers of tense, expectant faces, and in the dock the cause and object of it all: that calm, commonplace, respectable figure—the callous and brutal murderer whom Justice had tardily unmasked.

Part IV.—The Hidden Years.

I.

The reception of the verdict throughout the country was attended by uncommon circumstances. The lateness of the hour on a Saturday night at which it was delivered, and the unprecedented interest taken by the public in the progress of the trial, were alike remarkable. Glasgow, of course, was especially concerned to hear the result. The verdict was telephoned from Edinburgh to the office of the *Evening Times* as soon as it was given, and fifteen minutes later parcels of a special edition were dispatched to every quarter of the city. The *Glasgow Herald* of 11th November, 1889, gives some interesting details. The printing machines at the head office were kept working till midnight, by which hour 167,000 copies had been sent out and distributed. At Hamilton, we read, copies of the issue sold at fourpence each; there is no record of the price charged for them at Aberdeen. In Paisley, Greenock, and the westward towns the demand was enormous; the police had to regulate the crowds of purchasers, the shops were besieged, and the

44

Introduction.

newsagents had the time of their lives. The conviction came as a surprise, a verdict of Not Proven being generally expected.

Meanwhile the prisoner spent a quiet night in the Calton Jail, and, having had a good breakfast, in order to avoid public attention he was driven in a cab to the Haymarket Station, where, practically unnoticed, he joined the 9.30 train to Greenock via Airdrie, reached Princes Pier Station at midday, and was safely lodged in the local prison.

The news that the execution was appointed to take place in Greenock was received by that respectable burgh with anything but favour. The last person to be hanged there was a man named Boyd, who, on 23rd October, 1834, had suffered appropriately for the murder of his wife. No wonder the citizens failed to appreciate the distinction proposed to be conferred upon them, and were urgent in demanding a reprieve. The narrow majority by which the prisoner's fate was decided, and the recent commutation of the death sentence pronounced on Mrs. Maybrick, were popularly held to justify his getting the benefit of the doubt. Accordingly a movement to that end was forthwith begun in the Coatbridge district, where Laurie's relatives were well known and highly respected. A petition to the Secretary for Scotland (the Marquess of Lothian) was prepared, in which were urged against the carrying out of the sentence the following reasons, namely, that the medical evidence was not conclusive; that the other evidence was purely circumstantial; that the verdict was arrived at by a majority of one; that there was insanity in the prisoner's family; and that he himself from infancy had shown symptoms of mental aberration. The text of the petition is printed in the Appendix. An influential committee was appointed, and arrangements were made for copies to be sent to all the principal towns, where meetings were organised in favour of the petition. In Glasgow, copies were exhibited in the churches, banks, public offices,

John Watson Laurie.

institutions, and shops; in Edinburgh they were laid out on tables in the streets, supplemented by a house-to-house canvass; Carluke even carried on into the night, with a lamplit table beneath the Town Cross. On the 22nd the monster petition, containing 138,140 signatures, was forwarded to Dover House. Glasgow topped the list with 51,000; Coatbridge, 13,000; Edinburgh, 12,000.

It was presently announced that by instructions of Lord Lothian a medical inquiry would be held into the prisoner's mental condition. The alienists appointed for that purpose by the Scottish Office were Sir Arthur Mitchell, K.C.B., Dr. Yellowlees, of Glasgow Royal Asylum, and Professor (afterwards Sir William Tennant) Gairdner, of Glasgow University. These experts, having visited and examined the prisoner, and heard statements by relatives and friends as to his mental history, retired to consider and formulate their report.

Time, however, was getting on; the execution was fixed for the 30th, and the Greenock magistrates had to prepare for the worst. The services of Berry, the eminent specialist, were reluctantly retained to conduct the ceremony; a scaffold, frugally borrowed from Glasgow for the occasion, arrived on a lorry and was erected behind the County Court buildings; and a flagstaff was put up on the roof of the prison. But the Black Flag was not to fly for Laurie. On the 27th it was announced that the Lord Justice-Clerk was in consultation with Lord Lothian at his country seat, Newbattle Abbey, regarding the petition and the report of the alienists, which had then been received; and on the 28th the following official intimation was made by the Secretary for Scotland :—

Newbattle Abbey, Dalkeith.
2 p.m.

In consequence of the Medical Commission having reported that the convict Laurie is of unsound mind, the Secretary for Scotland has felt justified in recommending that he should be respited.

Introduction.

The decision was intimated to the Provost of Greenock by telegram, confirmed by the following letter:—

Office of the Secretary of Scotland,
Whitehall, S.W., Nov. 29/89.

Sir,—I am to signify to you the Queen's command, that the execution of the sentence of death passed on John Watson Laurie, presently in Her Majesty's prison at Greenock, be respited until further signification of Her Majesty's pleasure. —I am, sir, your obedient servant,

LOTHIAN.

You will acknowledge receipt hereof by telegram and return of post.

" The public mind in Greenock," says the *Glasgow Herald*, " is not altogether relieved by the terms of the communication from the Scottish Office." A reprieve had been confidently expected, and there was fear that the execution had only been postponed. This uncertainty was removed on 1st December by the receipt of an official telegram stating that the death sentence had been commuted to penal servitude for life. The text of the Conditional Pardon is printed in the Appendix. The Greenock magistrates tried to recover from the Prison Commissioners the expenses incurred by them in preparing for the execution; but the Commissioners, being, officially, devoid of bowels, left the burgh to pay the bill. On 2nd December the convict was removed to Perth Penitentiary, which had been appointed as the place of his expiation.

II.

On 3rd December the *Glasgow Herald* published an interesting and instructive article entitled, " Laurie in Greenock Prison," which I have thought worth reprinting in the Appendix. " It ought to be stated," says the writer, " that in the opinion of persons who have been coming into close contact with him since his incarceration, his

47

John Watson Laurie.

hand and no other committed the foul deed, and that had the respite been delayed for another day, the world would have been apprised of all the circumstances relating to the crime." His first statement was that he and Rose parted on the summit of Goatfell and that he never saw him again. " After his conviction, and when he had the imminent danger of execution pressing upon his mind, he wrote a letter to Lord Lothian which contained the admission that he had witnessed the fall of Rose from a high cliff, that he had gone to his assistance, that he had taken his bruised and bloody head between his hands, and that when he found Rose dead he robbed him of his valuables and buried the body." But as the day of execution drew near and there was no word from London, he became very uneasy, and just before the arrival of the telegram announcing the respite, he made inquiries as to the proper person to whom to make a confession. " His references to Rose," continues the writer, " were not marked by any exhibition of sympathy for that unfortunate gentleman. On the contrary, he spoke of him as a vain, proud man, always boastful of his money, and desirous of making his hearers believe that he was wealthy. The significance of Laurie's comment upon this point is striking. With singular callousness, he added that *Rose had not very much after all.*" The italics are mine.

Now, this is a very different story from that which Laurie told his legal advisers and upon which they based his case. It is at least a more feasible defence than that advanced for him in Court, and it is probable that, in the skilled hands of the Dean of Faculty, it would, if adopted, have resulted in an acquittal.

The conflicting evidence of the medical experts at the trial was the subject of prolonged correspondence in the press, and Dr. Campbell Black, Assistant Physician to Glasgow Royal Infirmary, and a champion of the " fall " theory, as opposed to the " direct blows " school, published a pamphlet in which he maintained (1) that it

48

Edwin Robert Rose.

was not proved that Rose was murdered at all; (2) that
death was instantaneous, thus accounting for the absence
of much or any hæmorrhage; (3) that Rose fell on the
vertex of the skull, falling backwards, and that all the
fractures thereof occurred then and thereby; and (4) that
the injury to the spinal column was probably the cause
of instant death, and that it could only have been produced in this manner. As the pamphlet has the
imprimatur of Dr. Heron Watson and will interest the
professional reader, it is reprinted in the Appendix.

The *Scottish Leader* of 19th November, 1889, in a
long and able article in favour of the reprieve, observes—

But in addition to the general reasons for asking clemency
for Laurie there are very special reasons more or less apparent
to all who consider the circumstances. In the first place, there
is the uncertainty dwelling in men's mind as to whether an
act literally to be described as murder was actually perpetrated; the dubiety arising from the absence of intelligible
motive. There was no passion in the case; the association
of the two men was accidental and unsought by Laurie; and
all the hope of wealth that was held out cannot be conceived
as tempting any one but an insane creature to an act so
atrocious. If murder were done, then within Laurie's nature
there is enclosed a psychological enigma which the general
human experience is powerless to explain.

Secondly, the journal maintained that the trial was
"unduly hurried." Begun on a Friday, the Judge,
doubtless with the best motives, "announced his determination to finish the case at all hazards within two
days"; and the jury, ill-supplied with food and refreshment, were called upon to give their verdict when worn
out with the strain, excitement, and long confinement
in bad air. "In the third place, there is a powerful
reason for staying the hand of the executioner in the
fact that the verdict was only obtained by a majority of
one vote. . . . It is horrible beyond expression to
think that for this man the difference between absolute

E   49

John Watson Laurie.

freedom and a criminal's death was determined by the vote of a single, fagged-out juryman."

On the other hand, there was a strong body of opinion that the conviction was sound and should not be disturbed. From the mass of newspaper correspondence on the subject I give excerpts from some letters typical of this attitude, addressed to the Glasgow press—

If circumstantial evidence is to go for anything, there could scarcely be a clearer case of guilt than Laurie's. Yet I am surprised to observe certain well-meaning philanthropists are trying to work a reprieve for this man who murdered his victim under the guise of friendship. I cannot believe they will succeed in getting a decent number of signatures to enable them to persevere with any chance of success; but in case they should, and to stifle this mawkish sentimentality in the bud, I propose that petitions be prepared to the effect that the law be allowed to take its course. If Laurie were to escape the death penalty, the hope of conviction by circumstantial evidence might as well be abandoned once and for ever.

JUSTITIA.

New Club, Glasgow, Nov. 18th, 1889.

"A Scotswoman" writes—

In the name of common sense what is coming over us all, that this hysterical howl for a reprieve is raised every time a person is convicted of murder nowadays? If ever circumstantial evidence is to convict, surely it has rightly done so in this case. If ever a foul and brutal murder was brought home to the murderer, step by step, with fatal certainty, by the silent evidence of circumstance after circumstance, this murder of a helpless traveller has been brought home to the man Laurie, so clearly, so convincingly, that unless we are to wait to convict till the murderer selects an audience before whom to do the deed, I fail to see how murder is to be detected. It is high time for persons who are content to abide by the law, and who feel confidence in those who administer it, to raise their voices with no uncertain sound, and try to stem this tide of maudlin sentimentality and secret lawlessness

Introduction.

which is making its way among us. It will be monstrous if we allow this brutal murderer to escape *pour encourager les autres*, and to make our lovely and lonely Highland glens as dangerous to the solitary traveller as the passes of the Apennines or the mountains of Greece.

" Justice " observes—

My firm belief is that Laurie is not insane, and I cannot find any reasons or arguments in " Humanitarian's " letter to make me change that opinion. He says: " Who but a maniac would commit such a deed? " Any person whom the love of finery and money combined with a brutal, vain, and selfish disposition had led away could do it, as this case has proved . . . Many people who are now signing the petition are doing so more for sympathy with them (his parents) than with him. I can only say that I hope the Home Secretary will not accede to public clamour, but will deal out justice without fear or favour.

Another correspondent makes a practical suggestion which undoubtedly would have exercised a chastening influence on the thousands of enthusiastic signatories—

As I feel convinced the present fashion of making heroes of condemned murderers is not for the good of society at large, I humbly suggest that no petitions should be received in future on this subject *unless each signature is signed through a six-penny stamp, payable by the party who signs.*

From a correspondent, whose name, by a curious chance, was Laurie, writing from Greenock, we get an interesting glimpse of the methods pursued in that burgh to promote the success of the petition—

A socialist with a crank placed tables in the streets with sheets, and got all and sundry who could as much as scrawl their names to adhibit their signatures, *many of them going from sheet to sheet and signing it several times in different names.* On Monday, the school children were marched in hundreds " like dumb driven cattle " to sign it. So much for how the petition was manufactured.

51

John Watson Laurie.

And among the reasons heard by this writer as given for signing was: "Only think of the disgrace to our good town to have an execution in it." A strange example, this, of enlightened public opinion!

III.

Considerable dissatisfaction was caused—and expressed —owing to the fact that the report of the medical experts upon Laurie's mental condition was not to be published. The *Saturday Review* of 30th November, 1889, has a leading article, " The Respite of Laurie," which may serve as an indication of the popular feeling—

It was announced last Thursday evening that the Provost of Greenock had received an official communication that morning that Laurie, the man recently convicted of the murder of the English tourist, Mr. Rose, had been respited. The convict, it was further stated " was made very cheerful by the receipt of the news," although when the intelligence was communicated to him he manifested no particular emotion, but confined himself to merely saying " Thank you." Before the public, however, can either share his cheerfulness or re-echo his thanks, it will be necessary to know a little more than we do at present as to the cause of his reprieve. . . .

What was the view taken by the Scottish Office as to Rose's death, and in what precise way did Laurie's alleged insanity operate to bring about his reprieve?

Has it, that is to say, been treated as exculpatory or merely as explanatory? Is it the official theory that he killed Mr. Rose, but that, being of unsound mind, he is not criminally responsible? Or does that theory start with the assumption that Mr. Rose's death was, as Laurie protested in his defence, accidental, and that the latter's insanity only comes in to explain his flight and concealment after the accident took place?

For our part we must admit that we have seen nothing in the case from first to last to raise any presumption of Laurie's insanity; and we trust that the public will be informed, not

Introduction.

only of the grounds on which certain medical experts have
discovered a defence for him which was not so much as
suggested at the trial, but of the complete theory of his connection with the death of Mr. Rose, as that theory has taken
shape in the mind of the Secretary for Scotland.

But to this, as to all other journalistic inquiries, the
Scottish Secretary opposed an official silence. Finally,
a question was asked in Parliament, of which notice was
given for 17th February, 1890—

Mr. Pickersgill—To ask the Lord Advocate, whether he will
communicate to the House the substance of the report of the
three medical experts appointed by the Secretary for Scotland,
to examine the mental condition of J. W. Laurie, who was
convicted of the murder of an English tourist in Arran :

And, whether these experts unanimously reported that in
their judgment Laurie was " not irresponsible "; and, if so,
upon what grounds the Secretary for Scotland advised Her
Majesty to commute the capital sentence.

This question being duly asked, the Lord Advocate
(Mr. J. P. B. Robertson, afterwards Lord President of
the Court of Session and, as Lord Robertson, Lord of
Appeal in Ordinary in the House of Lords) replied as
follows : —

It would be quite contrary to practice for me to communicate to the House the substance of the report received by
the Secretary for Scotland. I may, however, inform the hon.
member that the words quoted in the question were not used
by the medical experts.

The whole question of the criminal responsibility of
the insane bristles with difficulties and has long been a
battleground for experts. As to what constitutes insanity and who, precisely, should be termed insane, that
is another story; but it is not given to every man to
walk solely and always by the light of reason. Indeed,
judged by this high standard and upon a strict account-

John Watson Laurie.

ing, few and fortunate would be those of us found by our alienists to be in all points above suspicion. And it must be borne in mind that at the trial counsel for the defence, with the whole facts and circumstances before them, made no suggestion that the accused was not to be held accountable for his acts. That card was first played by the petitioners and, as we have seen, it won the trick.

But whether or not, and if so, to what extent Laurie, when he committed the crime, was, technically, insane, his behaviour exhibits certain well-marked features which I have noted as common to the many murderers whose conduct I have had occasion closely to study, from Mary Blandy in 1752 to Dr. Pritchard in 1865. None of these practitioners has, so far as I am aware, ever been deemed irresponsible or mentally deficient. All were liars, inveterate and gratuitous—the technical term is, I understand, " pathological " ; but their most striking characteristic is a supreme self-conceit and a total disregard for the claim to consideration of any one except themselves. Your murderer is the perfect egoist. For his especial benefit the sun shines daily, and the pick of the basket is his by right. This pleasant illusion is by the learned termed " megalomania," and, by the vulgar, swollen head. It is not certifiable. A person of such importance cannot, of course, permit anybody else to get between him and the light or stand in the way of his desires. Should somebody do so, why then, so much the worse for somebody : he is liable to become, as our American friends would say, " some " body.

Combined with this intense and overweening selfishness is a callous indifference to the suffering which the application of their ruling principle entails on others. Sometimes, as with Mary Blandy and with Katharine Nairn, it is naked and unashamed; sometimes, as with Dr. Pritchard, it is cloaked by a specious hypocrisy. Thus, while Miss Blandy unfeelingly asked : " Who

54

would grudge to send an old father to hell for £10,000?" and Mrs. Ogilvy imprudently exclaimed, with reference to the purposed poisoning of her spouse: "Divel burst him! I wish I had the dose, I should give it him!" Dr. Pritchard's wife died in his arms, and he had her coffin opened that he might kiss her for the last time. It is merely a matter of taste; the evil spirit manifests itself in different forms. The heroine of Henley and the mistress of Eastmiln would have thought little of Laurie's dreadful remark that "Rose had not very much after all." But it would have shocked profoundly the considerate physician of Sauchiehall Street.

IV.

Had John Watson Laurie known when he entered H.M. General Prison of Perth, that within the walls of that penitentiary and those of the seaside settlement at Peterhead, he should spend the forty-one remaining years of his life, the degree of his insanity would doubtless have been considerably heightened. But at the outset he had no such fear, and was confident that he would regain his liberty in a couple of years.

For four years the granite silence of Peterhead remained unbroken. Then, on Tuesday, 25th July, 1893, the newspapers surprised their readers by the announcement: "Attempted Escape of Laurie, the Arran Murderer." The following paragraph, being of quotable length, is taken from the *Scottish Highlander*:—

On Monday morning, about half-past seven o'clock, a convict, supposed to be Laurie, the Arran Murderer, at present serving a life sentence at Her Majesty's Convict Prison, Peterhead, escaped the vigilance of the warders and civil guard, and set off for freedom. The convict was working at some new warders' houses, which are being erected a little to the

north-east of the prison, the whole being enclosed by a wall
about eight feet high. It is supposed that the convict, taking
advantage of a fog, had managed to cross the intervening
space between the houses and the wall unnoticed by the civil
guard, who paces a platform in front of a sentry-box erected
on the top of the wall, and as there were plenty of ladders
and planks lying about, he had no difficulty in getting over
the wall. He had then crossed the road and made across the
fields to the west, entering a plantation lying to the back of
Bellevue Cottage, occupied by Mr. Macbain. In the meantime
the alarm signal had been given by the prison authorities,
and several warders and civil guards set off in pursuit. Getting a clue of the direction in which the convict had gone,
the civil guards, with loaded carbines, surrounded the plantation, while others proceeded to search the wood. It was not
long before the fugitive was discovered, and having been
shackled he was conveyed to the prison. On the way back to
prison Laurie characterised his captors in language wholly
inconsistent with the ecclesiastical office which he fills—that
of precentor in the convict prison chapel. In less than half
an hour after he threw down the plank and took to flight,
the big gate again closed behind him, and another epoch of
his eventful life was brought to an abrupt termination. It
is understood that the punishment for an attempt to escape
is that the prisoner has a belt of iron rivetted around his
waist, similar bands being put round his ankles, and these
are bound together by heavy chains. He has to wear these
ornaments night and day.

The "unecclesiastical" language may be excused
when we remember that this was the second occasion in
which he had trusted to a wood in vain and been betrayed by a plantation. A fuller and more detailed
report, published in the *Scotsman* on the same date, will
be found in the Appendix.

During 1909 there were divers rumours in the press
that Laurie had been released. These were doubtless
due to the fact that in November the convict would have
completed twenty years penal servitude. From the fact
that Laurie was not liberated, but was transferred, as

Introduction.

we shall find, to Perth, we may assume that his mental condition had so deteriorated as to render him unfit to be at large.

On 27th April, 1910, the *Daily Record and Mail* was able to inform its readers that on the preceding day Laurie, the Arran murderer, had been removed from Peterhead to the Criminal Lunatic Department of Perth Prison. It was understood that "his mental condition has prompted the transfer." Together with a history of the half-forgotten crime, the journal published a photograph: "The Convict Laurie removed to Perth": taken at the railway station and showing Laurie between two warders, leaving the Aberdeen train.

He was removed yesterday in company with five other convicts. The tragic party left Peterhead in charge of three warders at half-past nine in the morning, and travelled in a specially reserved compartment, Aberdeen Joint Station being reached at 11.35. On arrival the convicts, all heavily manacled, were marched hurriedly to one of the waiting-rooms, where they remained for an hour and a half awaiting the 1.10 Caledonian train for Perth. The coach employed for the conveyance of the convicts was attached to this train (having left Glasgow in the morning with half a dozen men for Peterhead). This was coupled to the south-going train, and when all was ready Laurie and his fellow-convicts were put in.

Laurie was easily distinguished. The Arran murderer, however, has aged considerably. His hair, cropped close in accordance with prison rules, is quite grey, and his face wan and haggard. He walks with a stoop, and his whole appearance points to his being in the latest stages of senile decay.

Perth was reached at about four o'clock, and a few minutes later, Laurie and his convict companions were once more within the grim walls of a prison.

Despite the reporter's lugubrious description, Laurie, in the photograph, seems a sturdy figure, his head being bent obviously to defeat the operator. He was officially certified as suffering from progressive dementia.

57

John Watson Laurie.

V.

From his admission to Perth on 26th April, 1910, till his death there twenty years later, nothing more is heard of John Watson Laurie. For all the world knew or cared, he was now as much dead and buried as his victim. But on Monday, 6th October, 1930, there was in the *Scotsman* an echo of the old story—

ARRAN MURDER RECALLED.

The murder of a London tourist, a Mr. Rose, on Goatfell, Arran, in 1889, was brought to mind yesterday through the death of John Watson Laurie in Perth Penitentiary. Laurie, who was sixty-nine years of age and a native of Coatbridge, had been in prison for forty-one years. The first twenty years were spent in Peterhead, and the last twenty-one in Perth Prison. During the major portion of this time he had been confined in the lunacy department.

And the *Glasgow Herald* of that date, in chronicling the event, justly observed that it "recalled one of the most remarkable dramas of crime and retribution in the judicial annals of Scotland." The cause of death was paralysis, of which Laurie had suffered more than one stroke.

VI.

While the Arran of to-day is not the Arran that Rose and Laurie knew; though the quiet villages have broken out in an eruption of bungalows; though the peaceful hill and coast roads are now less delightful to the wayfarer by reason of the ubiquitous motor omnibus; though the majesty of Glen Sannox is affronted by the presence of a light-railway for the working of a barytes mine; yet the mountains and the glens remain, splendid and unrivalled, as of yore. You may still climb Goatfell by the path on which, that fatal July afternoon, the two travellers set forth; behold from the summit the same

Introduction.

incomparable prospect that gladdened poor Rose's sight for the last time; and if you be sufficiently stout and venturesome, you may go down into Glen Sannox by the wild and lonely gully of Coire-na-fuhren, past the boulder—marked now by a cairn—where the body lay concealed; and ponder awhile upon that other boulder by which, in the lovely old graveyard at the foot of the glen beside the sea, is preserved for all time the memory of Edwin Rose's tragedy.

Leading Dates in the Laurie Trial.

1889.

July   6.   Laurie, as "Annandale," takes lodgings in Port Bannatyne.

       12.   "Annandale" and Rose go to Arran from Rothesay for the day; "Annandale" engages a room in Brodick.

       13.   They return to Brodick and occupy the room.

       15.   3.30 p.m. : "Annandale" and Rose set out to climb Goatfell.

             6-6.25 p.m. : Rose last seen alive on the summit of the mountain in Laurie's company.

             9.30 p.m. : Laurie seen at Sannox burying-ground.

             10 p.m. : Laurie seen in Corrie Hotel.

       16.   7 a.m. : Laurie seen going to the pier at Brodick; recognised on the steamer by Andrew Gilmour, who travels with him to Greenock. "Annandale" returns to his Port Bannatyne lodgings that afternoon, wearing Rose's hat.

       18.   Rose fails to return to London from his holiday; his brother telegraphs to Rothesay.

       19.   Aitken meets Laurie in Rothesay.

       20.   "Annandale" decamps from his lodgings at Port Bannatyne; the *Caledonia* incident.

       27.   Aitken meets Laurie again in Rothesay; Rose's brother arrives in Brodick.

       28.   Search party organised in Arran.

       31.   Aitken meets Laurie in Glasgow, and advises him to communicate with the police; Laurie disappears from Glasgow.

August   2.   Laurie writes to his Glasgow landlady.

       4.   Discovery of Rose's body.

       5.   Post-mortem examination at Corrie; Rose buried at Sannox.

       6.   Laurie takes lodgings in Liverpool.

       8.   Laurie leaves Liverpool.

       10.   Laurie writes to the *North British Daily Mail*.

       27.   Laurie writes to the *Glasgow Herald*; exhumation and second post-mortem examination of Rose's body.

September 3.   Laurie recognised and apprehended at Larkhall.

       4.   Laurie examined before the Sheriff at Rothesay.

       11.   Laurie examined before the Sheriff at Greenock.

October 29.   Pleading diet at Greenock; Laurie pleads Not Guilty and is remitted to High Court for trial.

John Watson Laurie.

1889.

November 8. First day of trial: evidence for prosecution.

9. Second day: evidence for prosecution concluded; evidence for defence; addresses of counsel and Judge's charge; verdict and sentence. Execution fixed for 30th November.

25. Medical Commission report Laurie insane.

28. Laurie respited.

29. Laurie reprieved; death sentence commuted to penal servitude for life.

December 2. Laurie removed to Perth Penitentiary.

1890.

February 17. Lord Advocate questioned in House of Commons regarding commutation of sentence; report of Medical Commission called for and refused.

1893.

July 24. Attempted escape of Laurie from Peterhead.

1910.

April 26. Laurie removed from Peterhead to Perth.

1930.

October 4. Death of Laurie in Perth Penitentiary.

THE TRIAL.

FRIDAY, 8TH NOVEMBER, 1889.

Judge Presiding—

THE LORD JUSTICE-CLERK (Lord Kingsburgh).

Counsel for the Crown—

The SOLICITOR-GENERAL (Mr. M. T. Stormonth Darling, Q.C.),

Mr. GRAHAM MURRAY, Advocate-Depute, and

Mr. DUGALD M'KECHNIE, Advocate-Depute.

Agent—

Mr. JAMES AULDJO JAMIESON, W.S.

Counsel for the Pannel—

The DEAN OF FACULTY (Mr. J. B. Balfour, Q.C.) and

Mr. C. SCOTT DICKSON, Advocate.

Agents—

Messrs. WEBSTER, WILL, & RITCHIE, S.S.C.

First Day.

At Edinburgh, the eighth day of November, 1889.

Present—The Right Honourable the Lord Justice-Clerk.

INTRAN.—John Watson Laurie, prisoner in the prison of Greenock, pannel.

INDICTED and ACCUSED at the instance of Her Majesty's Advocate of the crime of murder in manner mentioned in the libel raised thereanent.

The Indictment.

John Watson Laurie, prisoner in the prison of Greenock, you are indicted at the instance of the Right Honourable James Patrick Bannerman Robertson, Her Majesty's Advocate, and the charge against you is, that on 15th July, 1889, at Corr-na-Fourin, near the head of Glen Sannox, in the island of Arran, Buteshire, you did assault Edwin Robert Rose, Wisset Lodge, Hendham Road, Trinity Road, Upper Tooting, London, and did throw him down, and did beat him, and did murder him.   D. M'Kechnie, A.D.

List of Productions.

1-2. Declarations of accused, dated 4th and 11th September, 1889.

3. Medical report by Andrew Gilmour, physician and surgeon, 6th August, 1889.

4. Medical report by Neil Fullarton, M.B., C.M., and said Andrew Gilmour, 5th August, 1889.

5. Medical report by the said Neil Fullarton and Henry D. Littlejohn, M.D., 30th September, 1889.

6. Letter by John Laurie, and envelope addressed to Mrs. Charles King.

7-8. Two letters by John W. Laurie, with their envelopes.

9-12. Four photographs.

Label No. 1. A walking stick.

Label No. 2. Two buttons, stud, and links.

Label No. 3. A cap.

John Watson Laurie.

Label No. 4. A knife.

Label No. 5. A pencil.

Label No. 6. A waterproof coat.

Label No. 7. A small piece of cloth.

Label No. 8. A button.

Label No. 9. A felt hat.

Label No. 10. A cap.

Label No. 11. A pair of shoes.

Label No. 12. A tennis bat.

Label No. 13. Pieces of coat, vest, trousers, collar, necktie, semmit, and drawers.

Label No. 14. A sache or cloth case.

Label No. 15. A brush and comb bag.

Label No. 16. A hair brush.

Label No. 17. A cloth brush.

Label No. 18. A shirt.

Label No. 19. A shirt.

Label No. 20. A shirt collar.

Label No. 21. A box with stamp.

Label No. 22. A trunk.

Label No. 23. A return railway ticket, Glasgow to London.

D. M'Kechnie, A.D.

List of Witnesses.

1-3. (1) Mary Currie, wife, (2) Flora Currie, daughter, and (3) John Currie, son, all of John Currie, Iona Place, Port Bannatyne, Buteshire.

4. Margaret Thomson, wife of Matthew Thomson, Iona Place aforesaid.

5. Francis Ord Mickel, Friarsbrae Villa, Linlithgow.

6. William Thom, commercial traveller, Linlithgow.

7. Andrew Francis Craig Gilmour, student of medicine, High Street, Linlithgow.

8. Rev. Robert Hind, The Manse, St. James Street, Paisley.

9. Rev. Robert Ritson, Avon Street, Motherwell.

10. John M'Cabe, Cramlington Cottage, Leechlea, Hamilton.

11. Alexander Morrison, 14 Carfin Street, Govanhill, Glasgow.

12. Thomas Purdon, 38 Marlow Street, Kinning Park, Glasgow.

13. William Horton Smith, 2 Granby Terrace, Hillhead, Glasgow.

14. Esther Walker, wife of William Walker, Invercloy, Brodick, Arran.

15. Said William Walker.

16. Flora Shaw, widow, Invercloy aforesaid.

17. Isabella Wooley, wife of Alexander Wooley, baker, Brodick, Arran.

18. Benjamin James Rose, 89 Sarsfeld Road, Balham Park Road, London, S.W.

19. William Munro, police sergeant, Lamlash, Arran.

List of Witnesses.

20. William Munro, police constable, Brodick, Arran.

21. Alexander Stewart, police constable, Kilchattan Bay, Bute-shire.

22. Francis Logan, fisherman, Corrie, Arran.

23. David M'Kenzie, shepherd, South High Corrie, Arran.

24. Alexander Kerr, jun., shepherd, Sannox, Arran.

25-26. (25) Evelyn Hay Christian Norrie, and (26) Henry Augustus Christian Norrie, Coltbridge Hall, Edinburgh.

27. Archibald Young, fisherman, Corrie, Arran.

28. Angus Logan, quarryman, South High Corrie aforesaid.

29. Duncan Coll, police constable, Skisken, Arran.

30. John Mackay, chief constable of Buteshire, Rothesay.

31. Ellen King, widow, 106 North Frederick Street, Glasgow.

32. Finlay Kerr, police sergeant, Port Bannatyne, Buteshire.

33. James Gordon, police constable, Rosebank, Dalserf Parish, Lanarkshire.

34. Rev. Gustavus James Goodman, The Manse, Walker-on-Tyne, England.

35. John Borland, missionary, 6 Antigua Street, Greenock.

36. Neil Fullarton, physician and surgeon, Lamlash, Arran.

37. Andrew Gilmour, physician and surgeon, Linlithgow.

38-39. (38) Frederick William Francis and (39) Edward John Francis, 262 Brockley Road, Brockley, London, S.E.

40. James Wilson, 2 Shaw Place, Greenock.

41. John Williamson Macalister, 14 Hamilton Drive, Hillhead, near Glasgow.

42. James Archibald Anderson, 80 Finnart Street, Greenock.

43. Archibald Kerr Bruce, 23 Kelly Street, Greenock.

44. John Barr Cumming Newton, Chesterfield Terrace, Royal Street, Gourock.

45. Margaret Livingston, barmaid, Corrie Hotel, Corrie, Arran.

46. Mary Robertson, 5 Hill Street, Kilmarnock.

47. Jane M'Lellan, residing with Ronald Currie, M.D., Skel-morlie, Ayrshire.

48. Matthew Eaglesome, letter sorter, 106 North Frederick Street, Glasgow.

49. John Eaglesome, 9 Harbour Street, Girvan.

50. James Gillon Aitken, 3 Landsdowne Place, Shawlands, Glasgow.

51-52. (51) Andrew Gilchrist Allan and (52) William Gilchrist Allan, 15 Melton Terrace, Langside, near Glasgow.

53. Margaret Nicolson, laundress, 84 Dundas Street, City, Glasgow.

54. John Alexander Porter Napier, 518 Springburn Road, Glasgow.

55. George M'Master, 294 Springburn Road, Glasgow.

56-57. (56) William Elliott, sub-inspector, and (57) John Neil, criminal officer, Central District, Glasgow Police.

58. Jane Vannan, 3 Commercial Road, South Side, Glasgow.

59. William Johnston, clerk, 26 Sunnyside Road, Coatbridge.

60. Peter M'Lean, grocer, 150 Whifflet Street, Coatbridge.

61. Grace Chalmers, clerk, Caledonian Buildings, Coatbridge.

62. James Reid, station master, Ferniegair Railway Station, Lanarkshire.

John Watson Laurie.

63. Michael Crown, miner, Buchanan's Buildings, Greenfield, Hamilton.

64. Alexander Kirkwood, miner, Merryton Rows, Lanark Road End, near Hamilton.

65. David Paton, Claremont Place, Larkhall, Lanarkshire.

66-68. (66) Mary Rebecca Alice Rose, (67) Louise Rose, and (68) Frederick Louis Rose, Wisset Lodge, aforesaid.

69. Richard M'Elwain Head, 1 Oxford Villas, Wandle Road, Upper Tooting, London.

70. Sydney Alfred Newman, 379 Brixton Road, S.W., London.

71-72. (71) John Silverman and (72) John Frederick Chick, Olive House, High Road, Balham, London, S.W.

73-74. (73) James Baldwin and (74) Reuben George Baldwin, 2 Spring Terrace, Beechcroft Road, Upper Tooting, London, S.W.

75. James Goodman, builder, 1 Mostyn Road, Brixton, London.

76. Alexander M'Killop, joiner, South Sannox, Arran.

77. Alice Barnes, 96 South Lambeth Road, London, S.W.

78. Elizabeth Ennitt, 10 Greek Street, Liverpool.

79. John Pyper, criminal officer, Western District, Glasgow Police.

80. James Ferguson, detective sergeant, City Constabulary, Liverpool.

81. Annie M'Lean, residing with the said Peter M'Lean.

82. Henry Dougall, 78 Grove Street, Cowcaddens, Glasgow.

83. John Boyd, chief constable, Glasgow.

84. William Wharton, station master, St. Pancras Passenger Station, London.

85. Alexander Macdonald, Douglas Hotel, Brodick, Arran.

86. Henry Duncan Littlejohn, M.D., Royal Circus, Edinburgh.

D. M'KECHNIE, A.D.

List of Witnesses for the Pannel, John Watson Laurie.

1. Ann M'Eachern, domestic servant to the Rev. Andrew Brown, Kirkintilloch.

2. Peterina M'Donald, domestic servant, 3 Rillbank Terrace, Edinburgh.

3. Robert Strathern, C.E., Wellington Street, Glasgow.

4. Robert Simpson, C.E., Glasgow.

5. George Garrett, Dambeth House, Coatbridge.

6. Patrick Heron Watson, M.D., Edinburgh.

7. C. W. Macgillivray, M.D., 11 Rutland Street, Edinburgh.

8. H. A. Thomson, M.D., 6a Bruntsfield Place, Edinburgh.

9. Gavin Lawrie, store manager at Gartsherrie.

10. Miss Jeanie Park, residing at Kelburn, Baillieston.

11. Miss Minnie Park, residing at Kelburn, Baillieston.

12. — Latona, guide and residing at Corrie.

13. All the witnesses in the Crown list of witnesses.

14. Duncan Hay, residing at 14 Norfolk Street, Glasgow.

List of Productions.

List of Productions for the Pannel, John Watson Laurie.

1. Ordnance Survey plan of district.
2. Section prepared by Mr. Strathern, C.E.
3. The *Glasgow Mail* of 29th July, 1889.
4. The *Glasgow Mail* of 31st July, 1889.
5. The *Glasgow Mail* of 5th August, 1889.
6. The *Glasgow Mail* of 7th August, 1889.
7. The *Glasgow Mail* of 29th August, 1889.
8. The *Glasgow Mail* of 6th August, 1889.
9. The *Glasgow Mail* of 8th August, 1889.
10. The *Glasgow Mail* of 9th August, 1889.
11. The *Glasgow Mail* of 13th August, 1889.
12. The *Glasgow Mail* of 29th August, 1889.
13. The *Glasgow Mail* of 4th September, 1889.
14. The *Glasgow Mail* of 17th September, 1889.
15. The *Glasgow Evening Citizen* of 29th July, 1889.

The CLERK OF COURT (Mr. Charles Scott, advocate) intimated the plea of Not Guilty, which the prisoner had tendered to the Sheriff at Greenock on the 29th ult.

The LORD JUSTICE-CLERK—Do you adhere to your plea of Not Guilty?

ACCUSED—Yes, my Lord.

The pannel, having pleaded Not Guilty, was remitted to the knowledge of an Assize, and the following jury was balloted :—

1. Archibald Jamieson, fishmonger, 56 Castle Street, Edinburgh.
2. James White, saddler, 12 Athole Place, Edinburgh.
3. John Cran, engineer, Clareview, Restalrig Road, Leith.
4. John Sanderson Dunn, farmer, Gilston, Herriot.
5. John Brown, clothier, Olive Bank, St. Albans Road, Edinburgh.
6. William Oliphant, grocer, 10 East Adam Street, Edinburgh.
7. Robert Bruce Watson, grocer, Gibraltar Villa, St. Leonard's Lane, Edinburgh.
8. John Henderson, joiner, Muir Park Place, Dalkeith.
9. John M'Connochie, missionary, 31 Bernard Street, Leith.
10. Edwin Park, commercial traveller, 78 Brunswick Street, Leith Walk, Edinburgh.
11. George Stenhouse, brewer, Lothian Vale, Horse Wynd, Abbeyhill, Edinburgh.
12. Ebenezer Miller, 21 Upper Gilmore Place, Edinburgh.
13. Richard Ross, farmer, Beild, Biggar.
14. James Robertson Gavin, slater, 7 Rosevale Place, Leith.
15. James Lochhead, coal merchant, 125 Morrison Street, Edinburgh.

John Watson Laurie.

The CLERK OF COURT having read over to the jury the charge against the pannel, they were all lawfully sworn to try the libel.

The trial then proceeded.

Evidence for the Prosecution.

ALEXANDER MACDONALD, examined by Mr. M'KECHNIE—I live at the Douglas Hotel, Brodick, Arran. I was asked by the police in the county of Arran to take several photographs of certain parts of Glen Sannox, as well as one showing the summit of Goatfell. [Shown Productions Nos. 9-12.] I identify the markings on these photographs, which were made from information given by the police.

Cross-examined by the DEAN OF FACULTY—Photograph No. 10 was taken from the lower part of the gully, looking upwards?—Yes.

How far down the gully from the spot where the body of the deceased was found?—From about 200 yards farther down.

Do you say that this photograph, taken from a point 200 yards farther down the gully from the spot where the body of the deceased was found, gives an accurate idea of the declivity above that spot?—No, it cannot give an accurate idea of the declivity. It is necessarily foreshortened.

BENJAMIN JAMES ROSE, examined by the SOLICITOR-GENERAL—I live at 89 Sarsfield Road, Balham Park Road, London. I am a brother of the deceased, who was a clerk in the employment of James Goodman, builder, London. He was thirty-two years of age, about 5 feet 7 inches in height, and was of slight build. He enjoyed fairly good health, was of active habits, and brisk in his walk, brisk on his feet. He was not by any means what you would call a lazy man. He was not an athlete, but he was a lawn tennis player, engaging in the game about twice a week for two or three years before his death. In the season also he was a cricketer, belonging to a cricket club. He was on good terms with his family, and was of an agreeable and cheerful disposition. He was in the habit of taking holidays out

70

Evidence for Prosecution.

Benjamin J. Rose

of London every year. I am not quite sure about the last time I saw him in life, but I believe it was on leaving church, in the district of London where we resided, on the last Sunday in June last—the Sunday preceding his departure for Scotland. He lived with my father at Wissit Lodge, along with four sisters and one brother. When I saw him on that occasion, he intended to leave upon holidays shortly, but he had not then decided where he was going. He was then, apparently, in his usual health and spirits.

On the 20th of July I heard through my father and my sister that he had gone to Scotland, and that he had not returned on Thursday evening, 18th July, as he had promised. The family had consequently taken alarm. They tried to telegraph that same Saturday evening, but found it too late to do so. The first thing on Monday morning, the 22nd, however, they telegraphed to the Post Office at Brodick and to the Rev. Mr. Goodman, a son of my brother's employer, who was staying at the Glenburn Hydropathic, Rothesay. The replies were not satisfactory; and at last, on 26th July, I went down myself, arriving at Brodick on the following day—a Saturday. I had communicated with the chief constable of Buteshire, Mr. Mackay, and on the next day—Sunday—a search was organised and was kept up almost continuously until the following Sunday, the 4th of August. I was in Arran all that time with the exception of one night—a Wednesday—when I went to Rothesay to see the chief constable. On Sunday, 4th August, my brother's body was found. I was in the search party on the hill, although I was not in that particular section of the party that found the body, being, in point of fact, about a mile or so distant. When I was brought to the spot where the discovery was made, I saw the body lying under a boulder —the boulder I see marked in the photograph I have now before me. [Shown Production No. 12.] The stones had been removed from the top of the body, and the body was lying on its face. I had no doubt about it being my brother's body, although it was not from the face but from the general contour of the body that I recognised it.

By the COURT—The face was not recognisable.

Examination continued—Why?—It was decayed. The

71

John Watson Laurie.

bones of the head had been broken, and the head had been smashed in. The body was not removed until Dr. Gilmour had examined it. It was removed, and taken down to Corrie after nine o'clock the same night; and on the following day it was buried in the Sannox burying-ground at the foot of the glen. Dr. Gilmour made his examination of the body on the spot, the body being buried after the post-mortem examination. [Shown Label No. 1.] I recognise the walking stick made of West India wood now before me as my brother's. It was found close to the boulder under which the body was found [shown Label No. 3], and the tweed cap now shown me was also found. I believe this tweed cap was my brother's. It was made of the same material as the suit my brother wore, and was found a little above the boulder. I identify the two buttons, the stud, and the sleeve links now shown me as having been worn by my brother, the buttons bearing the name of the makers of his suit—Silverman & Birch. [Shown Label No. 2.] I think the hat now shown me was my brother's, although I am not able to swear to this. [Shown Label No. 9.] It bears the name of a hatter in Brixton Road, whose predecessor my brother was in the habit of dealing with, and the shop was near his place of business. [Shown Label No. 10.] I could not say that the white yachting cap now shown to me was my brother's, but it is similar to the one my brother wore. [Shown Label No. 12.] I readily identify as my brother's the tennis racket before me. I am confident of that.

Cross-examined by the DEAN OF FACULTY—You told us that your brother was expected back on Thursday, 18th July. Was that because his holiday had run out?—Yes, he was due on Friday, the 19th July.

Rev. GUSTAVUS GOODMAN, examined by the SOLICITOR-GENERAL—I am a minister of the Presbyterian Church at Walker-on-Tyne, and I am a son of Mr. Goodman, builder, Brixton, London. Walker-on-Tyne is about 3 miles down the Tyne from Newcastle. I knew the late Edwin Robert Rose. I remember his going to Rothesay last summer on a holiday. It was very largely the fact of my being there

72

Evidence for Prosecution.

Rev. Gustavus Goodman

that induced him to go there. He resided at the Glenburn Hydropathic while he was there, and I saw a good deal of him. I saw him on board the steamer *Ivanhoe* going to Arran on Friday, 12th July, with about twenty from the Glenburn Hydropathic, who went the round that day. I saw him on the evening of that day, and walked up and down the corridor with him, and we had a short conversation. That was the last opportunity I had of speaking to him. On the following morning I was out rowing a boat, and I met him going down the slope from the Hydropathic, on the way to the *Ivanhoe*, I believe. He was unusually cheerful and was enjoying his holiday. He had mentioned that he would like to go to Arran for a day or two, and that he would call at the Hydropathic on the following Wednesday for any letters that might be forwarded. So I did not say good-bye to him on that occasion. He was due in London on Thursday. I received a letter from him on the following Tuesday—that would be the 16th—dated 15th July, from Mrs. Wooley's, confectioner, Brodick. I have got it with me.

The DEAN OF FACULTY—I do not object to this being produced, if you like.

The SOLICITOR-GENERAL—No; I do not know what is in it.

Examination continued—What was the next you heard of him?—A telegram from one of the members of his own family, on Monday, 22nd, saying that he had not arrived. I immediately went over to Brodick myself and made inquiries at Mrs. Wooley's and also at Mrs. Walker's, and when I found that he had not reappeared I communicated with the police. [Shown Label No. 9.] I recognise the soft grey hat shown to me as that which Constable Kerr brought to the Hydropathic on the Sunday morning, and which I conclude belonged to Rose. I saw him wearing a similar hat while he was at Rothesay. [Shown Label No. 10.] As regards the white yachting cap shown to me, I saw him wearing a hat like that at Glenburn. It specially took my attention, because it seemed a little more rakish in appearance than is general in yachting caps. When Constable Kerr put it before me, it seemed to coincide in appearance with that which Mr. Rose wore. I would not

John Watson Laurie.

swear with absolute certainty, but my impression is that that is the same cap.

WILLIAM MUNRO, examined by the SOLICITOR-GENERAL—I reside at Lamlash, Arran, and I am a sergeant of police for Buteshire. I received a telegram on 25th July to meet the chief constable at Brodick. Thereupon a search was organised. It began on Sunday, the 28th, and went on till the following Sunday. On 4th August the portion of the ground searched was Glen Sannox, on the east side of Goatfell. The search party consisted of about 150 persons collected from Brodick and other 50 from Corrie—in all about 200. I was with the party that went up Glen Sannox. When the body was found a cry was raised. I was distant about a quarter of a mile at the time; I went straight up to the spot. There were a good many collected there by that time. The body was lying under a boulder, and there was an erection of stones below the boulder. In the cavity below the boulder the body was discovered, and there were about 20 inches of stones of various sizes built up in front of it. I have no doubt that these stones were put there by a human hand. There was some turf placed along the top, for the purpose of concealing the body. When I got up, nothing had been done. We removed the stones, and there we found the body of a man lying on its face, with the skirt of the jacket turned over the head. I took command of the party when I came up, and did not allow the body to be moved until a doctor was sent for. Dr. Gilmour, who was living in the island, arrived first, and after him came Dr. Fullarton. Meanwhile I went to order a box to convey the body, leaving three constables in charge of the body, with orders from me that nothing should be touched until the doctors came. I did not see the face, but about the head there appeared a living mass of maggots. [Shown Labels Nos. 1 and 6.] I identify the walking stick and waterproof produced as having been handed to me by Alexander Kerr, jun. I did not see the articles found, but I was afterwards present at the examination of the body of Edwin Rose, and I identified it as the same body as that found on Goatfell. The name of the place where the body was found is Corr-na-Fourin,

Evidence for Prosecution.

William Munro

at the head of Glen Sannox. I afterwards traversed the route from the top of Goatfell, down the ridge to Corr-na-Fourin, and from the boulder to Corrie Hotel. I went from the top of the hill to the boulder in half an hour and from the boulder to the hotel in an hour and forty-four minutes. Constables Munro and Coll and Dr. Fullarton were with me. We went at an ordinary pace, and it could be done in less time, walking more smartly than we did. As a matter of fact, I have done it in less time, for I have gone from the boulder to the hotel in an hour and twenty-four minutes.

By the COURT—Do you mean walking or running?—Walking.

Examination continued—Do you know that part of the island well?—Yes.

If you wish to go from the top of Goatfell into Glen Sannox, does the boulder lie on the usual line?—Not if you go down The Saddle and Corrie Glen. If you go from the top of Goatfell into Glen Sannox, you go down The Saddle and then straight down Glen Sannox, The Saddle is at the top of Glen Sannox.

Is that road by the boulder one that is commonly taken by the people?—No, it is an out-of-the-way road.

What sort of road is it? Is there any sort of track?—No, there is no track. It is a very difficult road, with long heather and large boulders.

What sort of ground is it between the ridge and the boulder?—It is not very difficult at the top, but near the foot it is difficult. It is pretty steep, with flat rocks.

Is it a road that with care an ordinary man should have no difficulty in traversing?—Oh, yes. I have gone down five times that way. There is a gully or watercourse in the centre of the hill. It is very often dry in summer, but there was a little water in it at the time. [Shown photograph No. 10.] The watercourse takes the line of the letters upon this photograph.

By the COURT—Where was the cap found?—The place where it was found was pointed out to me by Angus Logan, one of the witnesses. I measured the distance, and from the boulder to the cap it was 156 yards 2 feet.

John Watson Laurie.

William Munro

Examination continued—From the boulder to where the knife and pencil were found was 132 yards 2 feet, and from the boulder to where the waterproof was found was 110 yards 2 feet. That place was pointed out to me by Alexander Kerr, a witness. The place where the stick was found was 24 yards from the boulder. That place was also pointed out to me by Alexander Kerr.

Tell us, as near as you can, a little more about the nature of the ground between the place where the cap was found and the boulder—the channel of the watercourse you have mentioned. Is it dry rock?—Yes, except a small quantity of water. There is no vegetation on it.

Do you consider it a slippery part? Is there any slope on it? Is it a sheer fall or a slope?—It is a slope. Along part of the way on each side there is a line of rock several feet high, highest when looking down the watercourse on the right side, the highest part being where the waterproof was found.

On which side is there vegetation, grass, or heather?—On the left side of the ravine. There is not much on the right side. On that side there is the projecting rock I have mentioned, so that anybody in the watercourse would be concealed from one side of the hill. On each side of the gully there is a rock—about 9 feet or 10 feet high on the one side and 28 feet on the other. I believe that anybody in the watercourse would be concealed from it on both sides —for 58 feet on the left and 10 feet on the right.

Then you say that the top of the rock is 8 feet or 10 feet high?—That on the left side is higher—between 30 feet and 40 feet.

By the COURT—Supposing you are looking down the watercourse, which is the high side?—The right.

The DEAN OF FACULTY—That is just the opposite.

Examination continued—The high side of the ravine is the side on which the waterproof was found. On the other side, the left side going down, the rock is only 8 or 10 feet high.

There is a certain amount of vegetation?—There is no vegetation on the top of the rock.

The dull colour on the east side of the rock [in the

76

Evidence for Prosecution.

photograph] is heather or grass?—Grass or heather interspersed among the rock.

Now, any one going down there into Glen Sannox, who wished to take the usual route, would naturally come down —on which side of the watercourse?—He might take either side.

By the COURT—I would take either side.

Examination continued—With safety?—With safety.

You were present at the exhumation of the body on 23rd September?—Yes, and I identified it then as the body of Rose.

Cross-examined by the DEAN OF FACULTY—How long have you lived in Arran?—Thirty-one years.

Are you quite accustomed to the hills there?—Yes.

You know all the routes?—I was not very well acquainted with Goatfell till this occasion. I am well accustomed to the hills.

Much more than a man from the town?—Some men from the town know the hills very well.

Yes, but some do not. Did you observe the condition of the body?—Yes.

Particularly?—Yes.

Did you observe the condition of the neck?—No.

Did you on that occasion or at Corrie notice anything about the neck?—No.

You did not observe whether the neck was broken?—I cannot say.

Whether it separated at the top of the bone or not?—I cannot say.

Was the clothing ever stripped off at any time while you were present?—Not altogether.

Were there boots on it?—Yes, boots with iron heels and sprigs.

Where are the boots now?—I cannot say. I do not know.

Do you know if they were preserved or not?—They were not preserved.

Why?—Because the body was fully identified by the brother.

Were not the clothes buried with the body, except a few samples kept for production?—Yes.

77

John Watson Laurie.

William Munro

I want to know what was done with the boots with the iron heels?—I believe they were buried on the beach at Corrie.

Below high-water mark?—Above high-water mark.

By whose orders was that done?—I do not know.

Well then, who did it?—I believe it was the witness Duncan Coll. He is one of the police.

By whose instructions did he bury the boots?—The chief constable was present.

Have you any objection to telling me by whose instructions Constable Coll buried these boots?—I believe I told him to take them out of the shed. I did not tell him what to do with them.

Now, why did you put these boots away? Why did you order these boots to be put away?—Because they were not preserved.

I know they were not preserved. I want to know why?—Because the body was so fully identified by Rose's brother.

We will see about that. Why were the man's boots the only things that were put out of sight—the only things separated from the rest of the body and buried on the beach?—There was none of the clothing preserved; it was buried with him and we know where to find it.

Did you ever know such a thing to be done in an inquiry relative to murder?—The body was so fully identified.

I ask you—did you ever know such a thing being done in the investigation of any crime before?—[No answer.]

Well, Sergeant, I ask you further, did you not think it might have been material to the ends of justice to see these boots, and particularly the iron heels?—I did not consider so at the time.

Have you thought of it since?—No.

You have described the place where the different things were found as consisting of smooth slopes and hard stones. Is not that so?—Parts of it.

Some of it very steep?—Middling steep.

Well, middling steep. Did you not think, if there was any question whether the man fell or whether he came to hurt in any other way, it might have been material to have seen the boots with the iron heels? To see not only

78

Evidence for Prosecution.

William Munro

whether they were iron heels, but as regards their condition whether they were worn or not?—They were worn.

You say so. Have you anything more to explain about these boots?—Everybody in the habit of traversing hills wears boots with iron heels. I wear them myself and I went down five times.

If the question arose whether a man fell or came to hurt otherwise—don't you see, Sergeant?—[No answer.]

Very well, you have no answer to give to that. There were also iron sprigs?—Yes.

Might it not be important for the jury or others investigating this case to see the condition of these sprigs?—They were just iron sprigs.

There are such things as sprigs worn and sprigs not worn. Sometimes they may catch and sometimes they may slip. Now, have you any explanation to give as to why one of your policemen was asked to take these boots and bury them on the beach? Don't you see it is very unfortunate? Have you any answer to give?—[No answer.]

> [Witness was then shown a plan, No. 2 of productions for the pannel, on which he pointed out The Saddle, which he had described as the ordinary way down from the ridge. The plan and the place marked was afterwards shown to the judge and jury.]

The ordinary route to Glen Sannox, as you have said, is there shown by The Saddle?—Yes.

The other is quite the reverse of the ordinary one, where Rose was found, of course; but you can go that way with safety?—Some people go, yes.

But it is not the ordinary route?—No.

[Shown Production No. 10.] Does this photograph give a fair idea of the character of the place and of the declivity? —Yes.

The declivity is very steep?—Yes.

Is it not on the average half a right angle?—[No answer.]

Perhaps you do not undertsand that. You have told us about the character of the ground and have said it was a

79

John Watson Laurie.

very difficult road?—Only a part of it. It can be traversed with safety.

Besides being a difficult road, do you think it would not be correct to say that to people unfamiliar with it and unfamiliar with mountain roads, it might be a dangerous one?—I do not think so.

There are long flat slabs of smooth stone?—Yes, but a person is not obliged to walk on them.

There is no path on either side?—Yes, there is for half-way down.

I thought you said there was no track?—You can walk down on the east side.

But pray distinguish; I asked you whether there is a track—a marked track?—You can go down with safety.

That is not an answer to my question. Is there any marked track on either side, at or near the place the body was found? . . .

By the COURT—The question is, is there any pathway a person can see?—Yes.

Cross-examination continued—Is that on the right side or the left side?—On both sides.

Is there a great deal of traffic there?—There has been a great deal of traffic since this happened.

Do you mean that there is a path now?—Yes, and before.

Is that what you mean?—I mean that it can be traversed with safety. Shepherds go down there.

Yes, perhaps by shepherds and sergeants of police.

By the COURT—Is there any marked pathway you can see? —Yes, on the east side.

You said on both sides?—Particularly on the east side.

How is that marked : by a wearing of the stone or what?— Yes, and by treading on the ground.

But there is not much of a track?—Not much.

Shepherds coming down at haphazard have a line they take which leaves a slight track?—Yes.

Cross-examination continued—Were you ever there at all yourself until you went recently with the search party?— No, never.

Although you have been thirty-one years on the island! Now let us be a little more sure in regard to the description

80

GLEN SANNOX

X WHERE BENVENT IS SUPPOSED TO HAVE TAKEN PLACE INTO GLEN SANNOX

CORRIE GLEN

TO SADDLE

GLEN ROSA

SUMMIT OF GOATFELL

The Summit of Goatfell.

From the photograph produced in Court.

Evidence for Prosecution.

William Munro

of it. You told us of the bare rock and of the rock screen. You said something which I did not quite understand—that a person might be concealed in the ravine. You mean that a person walking down the gully might not be visible to persons on the sides?—Yes.

The LORD JUSTICE-CLERK—He said: "for 58 feet on the left and 10 feet on the right."

Cross-examination continued—These are the distances for which a person would be concealed?—Yes.

How would you describe the ravine or gully with relation to where the cap or other things were found?—His cap was found 44 feet from the head of the ravine.

Did you observe whether on the left side of the stream going down, very nearly opposite to where the cap was found, there is a clear drop of 19 feet?—No, it is only 8 feet. I measured it.

Perhaps there are more drops than one there?—10 feet is the highest.

Is there not at or near the place where the cap was found, on the right side going down, a drop of 32 feet clear?—It is 46 yards from where the cap was found—lower down near the boulder.

Did you measure the drop?—No, I did not, because it would not be safe to go near it. It is projecting over the gulley.

By the COURT—The height of this drop is about 30 feet.

Cross-examination continued—You told us about the waterproof coat. [Shown Label No. 6.] Would you look at the two pieces of it? The sleeve on one side would seem as if it had been worn with the white side out and the other sleeve with the black side out?—No, sir.

Is not this the white side and this the black?—That might have been turned in taking it off the body.

Exactly what I was going to ask you. Is it a reversible coat? You can wear it inside out?—Yes.

Is there not a hole in it above the sleeve?—That is what would be the top of the shoulder.

You say quite correctly it might be reversed in taking it off. Suppose that that sleeve had been turned like the

John Watson Laurie.

William Munro

other one, would not that have been about the top of the left shoulder?—The right shoulder.

Right, as it is now; but if the sleeve were turned it would be the left. Did you observe any injuries on the body at or about the top of the left shoulder?—No, sir; I did not examine the body.

I thought you were present at the post-mortem examination?—So I was.

But it is enough if you say that you did not observe?— The injury might be done by dragging the body along the road, or dragging it among the rocks.

It is facts I want from you, not opinions. As you speak of dragging, were there any signs of dragging on the body? —No, none that I saw.

What did you mean by putting in that suggestion about dragging?—I suspected it might be dragged down among the rocks.

I suppose that at that time of the year there are a great number of people in Arran?—A good many.

You had no difficulty at all events in gathering 200 people on the island?—No, but most of them were natives.

But there were a good many visitors besides?—Yes.

Re-examined by the SOLICITOR-GENERAL—In regard to these boots, you gave no orders about their disposal?—None. The boots had a rim of iron round the heel—ordinary iron heels —and sprigs on the sole, and were of the same description as those worn by shepherds and other people who traverse Goatfell. Any other kind of boots would not do for walking on such a hill as Goatfell; these boots are much safer. There was nothing else noticeable about them. They were of the ordinary lacing kind. [Shown Production No. 9.] That is a photograph of the top of Goatfell, and to go down by the boulder the only route would be that shown by the arrow on the photograph. The other ridge, The Saddle, is marked to the left. The road by the boulder, although not so common as the other road, is the one which is taken by people going down the hill. It is the shorter of the two, and I have known it to be taken by ladies.

The overhanging rock, which you told the Dean of Faculty

Evidence for Prosecution.

about and which is on the right-hand side of the gulley, is shown on photograph No. 10 as projecting. Supposing anybody fell over that rock, would it be possible for the person's cap to get into the position in which the cap of Mr. Rose was found?—Every bone in his body would be broken.

But confine yourself to the question of the cap in the meantime. It would be impossible for the cap to reach that position?—Yes, it would be impossible.

Further cross-examined by the DEAN OF FACULTY—I did not see the cap found. The place was pointed out to me.

By the COURT—Is there any high rock of any kind near that place?—No, except the one just referred to.

How far from this boulder is the nearest rock from which a person might hurt himself?—About 398 yards.

Any person falling from there and found at the boulder must have dragged himself there or been dragged there?—Yes.

What is the depth of the gully?—About 9 feet. It is just an ordinary mountain gully.

Now, about these boots; who was present when the boots were buried?—I was not present. I cannot say who was.

You said something about the chief constable being present? —He was in charge; he was the responsible officer.

You said you told a constable to take the boots out of the shed?—Yes. That was while the post-mortem was going on and after the body was put into the coffin.

Did you tell the constable what to do with the boots?—No.

You do not know what was done with them? You only heard that they were buried? But his duty would be to go to the chief constable, I suppose. If you told him simply to take them away, his duty would be not to dispose of them in any way without orders?—I might have told him to take them down to the shore.

You mean that they were to be put away?—Yes.

ALEXANDER STEWART, examined by Mr. GRAHAM MURRAY— I am a police constable, and I live at Kilchattan Bay. In the month of July last I was stationed at Loch Ranza. I

83

John Watson Laurie.

Alexander Stewart

took part in the search which was instituted for the body of the missing man Rose. I was with the party which was in Glen Sannox on the Sunday on which the body was found. I was the first police officer to arrive at the spot at which the body was discovered. The body was actually found by another person, not a policeman, and I heard him cry that the body had been found. When I got up to the place, I found Logan at the boulder. He had touched nothing, and I told him not to touch anything until the sergeant came. When the sergeant came we looked at the condition of the boulder. It lay in such a way as to leave a big cavity underneath it. The boulder just overhung the cavity. When we looked into the cavity we saw a lot of stones gathered underneath, and the body beyond them. The stones were arranged in such a way as to suggest that they had been put there to cover the body. They had evidently been put there by the hand of man for the purpose of concealing the body. There were also clumps of heather there. The result of the total construction was such that we could not see what was behind—I could only see one small piece of clothing. When we took this construction down, we found the body of a man lying on its face.

By the COURT—On the front?—Yes.

Examination continued—What position was the clothing in?—The jacket was turned up over the head. The body was not moved at that time and a doctor was sent for. Dr. Gilmour eventually arrived, and after that the body was moved. Until he came it had not been touched at all. When it was moved, the pockets were searched. I saw that done. There was nothing found in the pockets.

Did you see anything else as to the position of the pockets? —Yes; there was one of the pockets turned inside out, before any of our people touched it—it was lying inside out. There was no watch on the body. [Shown shirt stud and half-set of sleeve links, Label No. 2.] These articles were handed to me by Dr. Gilmour at the time they were taken off the body. The button which is produced [Label No. 8] was handed to me by Alexander Young who had found it. The body was taken down to Corrie the same night, and handed over to the care of the chief constable.

84

Evidence for Prosecution.

William Munro

WILLIAM MUNRO, examined by Mr. GRAHAM MURRAY—I am a police constable of Brodick, Arran. On Tuesday evening, 16th July, I heard something about lodgers having left Brodick without paying. After that I heard that a certain Mr. Rose had disappeared, and I took part in the several searches which were instituted in order to recover the body.

Were you there on 4th August when the body was discovered?—No, not at the time it was discovered. I was close by.

I ask you, were you with the search party?—Yes. I was not, however, with that portion of the search party that actually discovered the body. Soon after its discovery our search party was informed, and we accordingly went to the place where the body had been found. I found on arriving at the boulder that the stones, which had been in front of it, had been removed, so that the body was visible when I got there. It was not touched until the arrival of Dr. Gilmour, and then it was lifted out of the place in which it had lain.

What condition was it in?—From the mouth upwards the head was all smashed in, and round the top of the head.

Will you describe in your own words what the face was like?—It was all broken up from the mouth to the back of the head. Broken bones remained in the boulder cavity on the spot where the head had lain.

Was the face so smashed as to be unrecognisable?—The face could not be recognised, there was no face there—just a mass of battered features. [Shown links and buttons, Label No. 2.] I saw these taken from the body by the doctor at the time. [Shown cap and knife, Labels Nos. 3 and 4.] That cap was handed to me by Angus Logan and I then labelled it. The knife was handed to me by Mr. Young. I was present when the body was taken down to Corrie on 4th August. On Saturday, 14th September, I joined Dr. Fullarton, Sergeant Munro, and Constable Coll at the point of the ridge immediately above the boulder, and from the ridge I went down to the boulder. I then started from the boulder and walked down Glen Sannox to Corrie Hotel. Going at a fairly smart walk, but not walking

John Watson Laurie.

William Munro

" against time," the time occupied was an hour and thirty-nine minutes. On 12th August I had walked from the top of Goatfell to the top of the ridge; and though I was carrying some photographic apparatus, I did the distance in twenty-five minutes. I timed myself from the ridge to where the cap was found, and found it to be six minutes. I had been there only once before this case happened, and cannot consequently say what are the paths ordinarily taken by tourists. I should imagine that down by the boulder is the way that is travelled by people who, being on the top of Goatfell, want to get down by Glen Sannox. The road by the boulder is fairly easy. There is nothing to deter a young man in good health and of fair agility from going down that road. There is nothing in the character of the ground, which, in my view, would make it specially dangerous. I was present at the exhumation of the body and identified it as that which had been buried.

Cross-examined by the DEAN OF FACULTY—You told us that the face was not recognisable. Was it manifest that there had been a good deal of decay and decomposition of the face and other parts of the body?—In the face.

Was not the skull full of maggots?—Yes. I was present at the post-mortem examination, but I did not take any particular notice as to whether any other injury was discovered on the body.

When you arrived, was the body still in the place where it had been found?—Yes. I observed when the body was removed that some parts of the skull were on the ground. They were lifted and put into the skull by Dr. Gilmour.

By the COURT—I saw the pieces of skull picked up and handed to Dr. Gilmour.

Cross-examination continued—You said that there was nothing to make the place specially dangerous. Is there not a considerable amount of hazard connected with travelling at the place you have spoken of—does not the whole of that slope, from the top of the ridge down to the boulder, consist of very smooth granite blocks?—No.

You said it was not specially dangerous?

Evidence for Prosecution.

The LORD JUSTICE-CLERK—Mr. Graham Murray went specially into that question.

The DEAN OF FACULTY—No doubt, for good reasons. [To witness]—You assented to the view that there was nothing specially dangerous?—Yes.

Yet there are considerable slopes of smooth granite rocks as you go down by the west or left side?—There are short pieces of 3 feet or 4 feet on the west side which do not afford a good foothold, and there might be plenty of room for a man to slip and fall; but, of course, it would depend upon where the smooth piece was.

Were you told where the cap was found?—Yes. I made a particular examination of the rock. There was a considerable drop on the rock about 40 yards down the gully. On the east side (the right side going down) there is a clear drop of about 20 feet. On the right hand side of the gully, going down from where the cap was found, there is a drop of about 10 feet.

Do you mean to say that the biggest drop you noticed going down that place was 10 feet?—Yes.

Did you measure this?—I did.

You observed near where the cap was found a drop on the right side of 32 feet?—I did not.

Did not you observe on the left side of the gully near where the cap was found a drop of 19 feet?—No.

Re-examined by Mr. GRAHAM MURRAY—This drop of 20 feet is farther down the gully. If a man had tumbled down that drop, could his cap, in falling off, have got to the place where this cap was found?—I should say not.

Apart from decay, was the smashing of the face such as to render the features unrecognisable?—I should say so.

Was Dr. Gilmour the first person to touch the body?—Yes. The bones before mentioned were not handed to Dr. Gilmour until he had seen and so far examined the body.

By the COURT—The detached portions of the skull were found exactly at the place where the part of the head was found, attached to the body.

DUNCAN COLL, examined by the SOLICITOR-GENERAL—I am a police constable and I live at Shisken, Arran. I took

John Watson Laurie.

Duncan Coll

part in the search for the body of Mr. Rose, and on 4th August, in answer to a shout, I went to the exact spot where the body was found. After the arrival of Dr. Gilmour I assisted in removing the clothing and personally searched it. I found nothing at all in any of the pockets, but the lining of one of them, on the left side of the jacket, was turned inside out. Pieces of the skull bones were lying on the ground where the head lay.

It seems that you afterwards buried a pair of boots which were on the body?—Yes, on the seashore at Corrie.

Was that your own idea or were you told to do so?—I was told by Constable Munro to put them out of sight and I did so. I went down to the seashore and put stones on the top of them.

Why did you do that?—I thought that when I was told to put them out of sight he meant me to bury them; and I did so. What he told me was to take them out of the shed.

What were they like?—They were common lacing boots with iron heels and small sprigs in the soles. The iron heels were such as are worn by people in climbing the hills.

And they are safer for climbing than plain ones?—Yes, I should think they are safer for climbing than plain ones.

Cross-examined by the DEAN OF FACULTY—I suppose that would depend very much upon whether the metal was worn? —It would.

If the metal was much worn, might not the iron both of the heels and of the sprigs become a source of danger instead of safety to the person going over smooth granite?—Well, they might be slippery.

That is exactly what I mean. Did you merely bury these boots because you were ordered to do so?—Yes.

Was no reason given to you?—There was no reason I could form.

Did it seem to you a very strange thing that your sergeant told you to put them out of sight? Is Munro your superior? —It was not the sergeant, it was Constable Munro, who is in charge of the district and of all these productions.

The way he took charge of these productions was to tell you to put the boots out of sight. Did you put any other production out of sight?—No.

Evidence for Prosecution.

Why did you preserve the rest of the productions, and put the boots out of sight?—[No answer.]

Do you think now that it was an important matter that these boots should have been produced here?—If a description of them was perfectly given, that is good enough.

Do you think your description is as good as seeing them? —Others saw them too.

Would it not have been better for the jury to have had an opportunity of seeing them for themselves?—No doubt it would.

You buried them below high-water mark?—Between low-water and high-water mark.

Well, that is below high-water mark?—Yes.

So that you made sure they would be well out of sight?— Well, I simply put a lot of stones on top of them.

And you never went back to look for them again?—They were never asked for.

Did it not occur to you that when this became a matter of charge, it would have been proper to get these boots and let them be judged of like the other productions?—I do not know.

Have you no opinion about it?—No.

Did you hand the pieces of the skull to the doctor or put them in a box?—I handed them to the doctor. The doctor lifted some of them and looked at them.

Did you observe if there was anything wrong with the left shoulder?—It was dislocated and the bone was sticking out.

Was there any appearance of injury on the soft tissues of the left shoulder?—I could not say. The bone was sticking out of the joint.

The body was not stripped of the clothing at all?—No, the clothes were merely cut up front and back, and were thrown out from both sides. Of course, there would be parts where the clothes were still gripping.

At any time when you were present, was there any examination made to see the external surfaces of the left shoulder?—The doctors examined the shoulders.

You know the place where the body and the different things were found. Is it not a very rough place there?—It is very

89

John Watson Laurie.

rough at the place where the different productions were found; but some of the stones are smooth and polished.

Is it not a place where a person going down might slip? —They generally pick their way.

But if they did not pick their way, and if a man made a mistake, might he not very readily slip?—He might.

And are there not parts there where, if a man were to slip, he would be very apt to pitch down heavily on his head?— Yes, there are some precipices.

Is it not the case that if a man slipped, just about the place where the cap was found, he might go head-foremost over a drop of 30 feet?—He would go a good length.

Would it not be quite enough to be damaging to the head? —Yes.

Have you any doubt that if a man fell over there he would be killed?—I do not know.

Have you not a very shrewd opinion you would not like to fall there head-foremost?—I would not like to give an opinion.

Re-examined by the SOLICITOR-GENERAL—When you talk of precipices, where do you mean they are?—All over the hill.

Near the place where the waterproof and cap and things were found, are there any rocks with a sheer fall of more than 30 feet?—No, it is just a gradual slope down.

But at the side there are, here and there, rocks with a sheer drop, the biggest of which is how much?—Well, about 20 feet or 30 feet, I believe, in some places.

And these places are about 40 yards below where the cap was found? . . .

The DEAN OF FACULTY—He has not said that. That is not what he said to me.

Re-examination continued—Are these places about 40 yards below where the cap was found?—It is about that distance, I believe.

At the place where the cap was found or immediately above it, is there any sheer drop of any height at all?—Well, there is just one slope that I know of; it is not a perpendicular drop.

Any man slipping there would not fall sheer down?—He would slip down.

90

Evidence for Prosecution.

Duncan Coll

By the COURT—Is there one slope so steep that a man could not recover himself if he fell? He could not get a hold again if he once got away?—No, my Lord, he could not get a hold.

Where is that place?—On the south side of the place where one can get down, below where the body was found.

FRANCIS LOGAN, examined by the SOLICITOR-GENERAL—I am a fisherman of Corrie, Arran. I was in the search party on 4th August, and I was the person who actually found the body of the deceased. I was some distance below the boulder when a smell attracted my notice to it. When I went up, I found there was a dyke built in front of the boulder so as to close up the opening. Behind this dyke the whole body, with the exception of an arm was hidden. The body was pretty well concealed except for the arm. There were pieces of turf among the stones. I saw that the body was lying on its face. The policeman and others came up after I had given the alarm. I did not remove anything. Sergeant Munro removed the stones, but the body was not touched till Dr. Gilmour arrived. When I first went up to the boulder I saw two or three footmarks. They were faint, as if they were washed out by the rain; but when the other searchers came forward they were altogether obliterated. These footmarks were just in front of the boulder.

Cross-examined by the DEAN OF FACULTY—Were there many stones in the dyke?—I counted them and found them to number forty-two.

Were they heavy?—The heaviest of them would weigh about 1 cwt. and a half; but there were not many nearly so heavy as that.

That is a very heavy stone, is it not?—It is not very heavy.

Would it not be better to have two men to carry such a stone? You say that was the heaviest. Were a number of the others, though not heavy, still good big lumps?—No, they were not very big.

It is a very rough place up the glen above where this body was found, is it not?—Yes, it is very rough.

91

John Watson Laurie.

Francis Logan

About the roughest part on the hills?—Yes, on that side.

You said you saw two or three footmarks. Was that just when you came up?—Yes.

Did you make any particular observation of them, or did the people come up immediately?—No, I did not think about it.

On Monday last you showed Dr. Macgillivray and Dr. Thomson over the place, and pointed out to them the various spots where the body and the different productions were found?—Yes.

Near where the cap was found, were there points where the granite was smooth and slippery?—Yes.

By the side of the stream right above where the cap was found, there is a sheer drop. Did you see it measured?—Yes, it was 19 feet; while on the other side of the stream, lower down, there is a clear drop of about 32 feet, which I also saw measured.

Re-examined by the SOLICITOR-GENERAL—Were all the stones which lay upon the body such as one man might lift?—Yes.

Were there plenty of stones about?—Yes.

Would the rough boulder rock at the side of the stream give a foothold to any one with iron heels on his boots?—Yes, any one with tackets in his boots.

That drop of 19 feet above where the cap was found is not in a regular line down?—It is at the side.

So that any one going down from the ridge to the boulder could not get down perfectly well past that drop of 19 feet?—Yes.

People coming down from Goatfell to Glen Sannox usually come down by The Saddle?—Yes, but since this happened many people go by the boulder.

The spot where the cap was found was pointed out to you. Was that a place where the cap would naturally lie if a man had fallen over that 19-feet rock?—No, it would have to be put there. Some one would have to put it there.

Further cross-examined by the DEAN OF FACULTY—The Solicitor-General put a question, in which he said that a

Evidence for Prosecution.

Francis Logan

person coming down the recognised way would not get near this drop at all. There was no recognised way, so far as you know, till this tragedy occurred?—No.

Then you do not mean by that to suggest that a man going there might deviate from the path?—No.

You say that a man would have been the better of iron heels going down. Do you mean hobnails such as people use in the country?—Yes, I mean the big kind of hobnails.

A good deal would depend on whether they were new or old—whether they were worn smooth or not. If they were a good deal worn and polished smooth, a man would be more apt to slip than if he had no metal at all in his shoes? —Yes.

You never saw the cap actually lying?—No, the place where it was found was pointed out to me in the bed of the stream.

Was the drop of 19 feet into the bed of the stream?—Yes.

If the drop was into the stream, and if the cap was in the stream, why is it not possible that the cap might have come off when the person was falling down? Might not that have happened?—It could not lie yonder.

Do you mean it would have been washed away with the stream?—There was a stone on the top.

That is another matter; but, apart from that, if the drop was into the middle of the stream, and the cap was in the stream, what was to prevent the cap having fallen off as the person fell down over the rock?—That might be.

By the COURT—You said there was a stone upon the cap. Never mind about that stone. Suppose that the man fell over that 19 feet with the cap on, and that when he was falling his cap came off, do you think it could have lain where it was found?—No.

Why not?—The water would have carried it off.

Was it in the stream?—Yes, it was sitting in the water with this stone over it.

Could it have fallen into that place in the water if a man had fallen from the top? Would it have lain where it was supposing it had fallen, or would it have been carried down?—It would have been carried down.

93

John Watson Laurie.

Alexander Kerr, jun.

ALEXANDER KERR, jun., examined by Mr. GRAHAM MURRAY—I am a shepherd in Sannox. I am well acquainted with the place. I was one of the search party who, on Sunday, 4th August, found the body of Mr. Rose, and I was quite near to Logan—perhaps about 20 yards away—when he discovered the body. I heard Logan shout: " I have got him." I then went down and saw the boulder, and was on the spot when the doctor came. Until then I did not see any one touch the body. When I got down I looked round about to see if I could find anything else. [Shown Labels Nos. 1 and 6.] I found the walking stick produced and handed it to Constable Munro. I also found the water-proof shown to me. The stick was lying as if it had been dropped, and the waterproof was split in two bits, the parts lying together in a little pool of water and huddled up as if they had been tramped upon. The waterproof might just have been dropped there. The letter S in the photo-graph produced [Production No. 10] marks the place where the walking stick was found, and the letter W the place where I found the waterproof. When tourists go to the top of Goatfell, the ordinary way to descend is by going down to Glen Sannox over The Saddle. The way down by Corr-na-Fourin is shorter, but steeper. There is nothing to prevent any one who is ordinarily athletic from coming down by Corr-na-Fourin. I do not know whether this road is taken by both old and young, but there is nothing to prevent a fairly good walker from descending that way. I do not consider it at all dangerous. [Shown Production No. 11.] The cross on the skyline of that photograph indi-cates clearly the way in which a person wanting to descend by this short road from the top of Goatfell would proceed. There is no track to guide any one on the way.

Would a person coming down have to keep to the right of the gully?—Yes.

But it would be possible to travel by the left?—Yes, but a person would naturally take the right side.

Cross-examined by the DEAN OF FACULTY—Is there any marked track on either side of the gully?—No.

94

Evidence for Prosecution.

Alexander Kerr, jun.

As a shepherd you are very much accustomed to the hills; you spend your life among them?—Yes.

You are probably more surefooted than one less accustomed to such work?—I do not know.

Till this thing happened, was the route by The Saddle down to Glen Sannox from Goatfell not the way that nearly everybody went?—Yes, but a few had always come down by Corr-na-Fourin.

When you found the stick and waterproof, were you walking by the stream?—Yes, looking for things, and I first came upon the stick and then upon the waterproof. I was about to go still farther, but the ground was getting very steep about that place, and the people cried to me to come back.

And did you do so?—Yes.

Were you on the right-hand side of the stream going up? —Yes.

Just at the place where you had reached, did not the ground begin to get very steep, close by the gully?—Not very steep, but there were slippery granite rocks.

Was it not a place where a person might readily slip?— You could go up.

Re-examined by Mr. GRAHAM MURRAY—Do you remember whether there was any water in the watercourse in the middle of July?—No.

If a man was right down in the bed of the watercourse, would he be concealed from persons on other parts of the hill?—Yes.

Would people up on Goatfell or on The Saddle see him?— They might not.

At the place where you found the waterproof is one concealed from view from the right and left but not from below? —Yes.

Further cross-examined by the DEAN OF FACULTY—Unless in places where a person had got out of sight into the actual bed of the stream, would he be seen from The Saddle going down that way?—Yes.

The ordinary line of the gully is visible from The Saddle? —Yes.

John Watson Laurie.

Archibald Young

ARCHIBALD YOUNG, examined by Mr. GRAHAM MURRAY—I am a fisherman and reside at Corrie. I was one of the division of the search party in Glen Sannox on Sunday, 4th August. After the body had been found I looked round to see if I could discover anything. [Shown Labels Nos. 4 and 8.] I found the knife now produced and also this button, which I handed over to Constable Munro. The knife and button were both lying together straight up above the boulder.

ANGUS LOGAN, examined by the SOLICITOR-GENERAL—I am a quarryman and I live at South Corrie, Arran. I was one of the search party in Glen Sannox when the body of Rose was found. I went up when I heard Francis Logan shout out that he had found the body. After that I looked about to see if I could discover anything, and I found the pencil [Label No. 5] now produced. I afterwards went searching farther up and I found the tweed cap now shown. [Label No. 3.] It was folded in four, with a stone about 6 inches square and 3 inches thick, and 7 lb. or 8 lb. in weight, lying on the top of it. The cap was in the water, there being a small stream of about 3 inches. As the cap lay in the water I could only see a little bit of the snout [peak]; the rest of it was hidden by the stone. The watercourse at that point was about half a yard broad.

What was the character of the ground at the edge of the stream; was it heather or grass?—Going up the stream on the left-hand side, it was rock. There was a projecting piece of rock on the right-hand side. There was a little sand or gravel under the projecting rock.

Did you see any marks on the ground?—I saw nothing.

Anywhere within a few yards of it?—Nothing—only the gravel was a little trampled.

Are you sure there was trampling?—The sand was not lying as the water had left it; it was trampled up.

Were the marks as if the gravel had been disturbed by some foot?—I thought so, but I might be wrong.

Did it look like a human foot or the foot of a beast?—I could not say what kind of foot it was, but I found it was turned up.

96

The descent by Coire-na-Fuhren.

The marks indicate the ridge and the boulder.

From the photograph produced in Court.

Evidence for Prosecution.

Angus Logan

Was it a place a beast was likely to be in?—I could not say whether a beast could have got into the place or not.

How far was the gravel turned up; how far did it extend? —The gravel would only be about 2½ yards long and a yard wide.

Was the turned-up mark over the whole extent?—Only part of it, so far as I observed.

What was the impression made on your mind at the time by the state of the gravel?—I did not form any opinion about it. I simply lifted the cap, and said to some one or other that I had found it.

Was it possible that the turning up of the gravel had been done by any of the people helping in the search, or were you there before anybody else got there?—I was there first. I am not aware that any of the search party was there before me.

Do you think the cap could have got as you found it by accident, or that it had been put there by design?—I do not think it could have been so covered up by accident.

You know the hill well?—Yes. I was an ordinary shepherd at one time.

Do you know how tourists used to get down from the top of Goatfell who wanted to see Glen Sannox? Did they generally take The Saddle way?—I know The Saddle is accounted the right way.

Have you seen people going otherwise?—I cannot say.

> [At this stage the witness was shown a marked photograph [Production No. 11] and said that the mark on the photograph represented the way a person might take in coming from the summit of the ridge down to the boulder.]

Is there anything in the character of the ground to prevent them coming down that way?—They could come.

Cross-examined by the DEAN OF FACULTY—After the waterproof and pencil had been found, it was suggested that by further search something more might be found?—Yes.

Did Archibald Young go ahead of you?—Yes.

Where were you?—I was pretty much towards the bed of

H

John Watson Laurie.

Angus Logan

the stream and he was on the right above me. I tried to go up the bed of the stream and found I could not do so. Young then hooked the crook of his stick into mine and pulled me up, otherwise I question if I could have come up. The rocks were very slippery.

Do you think you could have come down?—Yes.

Perhaps rather quicker than you would have liked! If you had not had the help of Alexander Young's stick, could you have managed it at all?—Owing to the slipperiness of the rocks, I question very much if I could have got up.

The slipperiness would be a source of danger to any one coming down?—I think I could risk it coming down.

Ah, to come down; but the rocks are very slippery there? —Yes.

A great part of the rocks up that gully are smooth granite? —Well, they are smooth where the water flows on them, but in other places they are pretty rough.

Or where water has flowed on them?—Yes.

Did you get on a shelf of rock above Young?—Yes.

Was it on the shelf you saw a cap?—No; just as I was about to get into the crevice where the cap was, I saw it.

Yes, but we are following the course up. Don't you recollect, after you got on the shelf of rock, Young warning you not to go there?—Young did not warn me; Kerr did.

Did you say you would try it?—Yes.

Then did he say he would stand below and "kep" you if you fell? That must have been rather a ticklish place?— At first sight it appeared to be.

Was that just before you saw the cap?—I did not see the cap until all that had passed.

How far down the stream was it this happened, before you saw the cap?—It was about 4 or 5 yards.

When the body was found under the boulder, did you notice whether there was a small hole in the clothing behind the left shoulder?—Yes. I cannot describe it in any other way than by saying it was a small hole about 2 or 3 inches in size.

Did you think the shoulder was dislocated?—I paid no attention to it.

To be sure about the place, was it just after you had been

98

Evidence for Prosecution.

Angus Logan

pulled up that the knife and button were found?—I think Young had the knife before he drew me up. The button, I think, he got afterwards.

That was at the place where he pulled you up?—Yes.

Re-examined by Mr. GRAHAM MURRAY—About this slippery place where you were pulled up, was that in the bed of the stream?—Yes.

Was that at a place where a person coming from the top of the hill would have come down naturally or not?—I would not think he would.

If he did not come by this particular place, there were several places where he could have got along well enough?—Yes.

About this place where you climbed up and somebody stood to "kep" you if you fell—supposing you had fallen there and your cap had fallen, would the cap have been found where you found this one?—No, because the cap I found was above this place.

What was the character of the bed of the stream immediately above where the cap was found?—I think it was loose stones and gravel.

Above, was there any place where a man would require to be pulled up by sticks?—If he happened to get in there, I do not know how he would get out.

Could a man have gone straight up from the cap?—I do not think so.

But you could have got out on either side?—Yes, I got easily out the way I went in.

Dr. ANDREW GILMOUR, examined by the SOLICITOR-GENERAL —I have been in general practice as a physician and surgeon in Linlithgow for thirty-eight years. I am a licentiate both of the Royal College of Physicians in Edinburgh and of the Faculty of Physicians and Surgeons in Glasgow. I am also a surgeon-major in the auxiliary forces and have medical charge of the detachment of soldiers stationed at Blackness. In the month of July last I was staying as a summer visitor in Arran and heard of the disappearance of a young Englishman named Rose. On the 4th of August I was called to the place known as Corr-na-Fourin to view his body, and

John Watson Laurie.

Dr Andrew Gilmour

when I got up I found that the body had been retained in its original position. The body was lying under a large boulder, and all that had been done was that stones had been removed from the front. It was lying face downwards. With the assistance of one of the constables I lifted the body and put it down outside the boulder. I partly examined the body while it was lying under the boulder and after it was removed I made a most careful and exhaustive examination on the spot, to a certain extent before the body was touched. The results of my examination on the spot have been embodied by me in the first report [Production No. 3], dated 6th August, 1889. That is a true report.

I want you to read that report to a point at which I shall stop you. The reason is that other medical gentlemen are in Court, and we are only going to take matters of fact. You will stop when you come to opinion ?—" I, Andrew Gilmour, physician and surgeon in general practice, Linlithgow, do hereby certify, on soul and conscience, that on the evening of Sunday, the 4th August, 1889, Alexander M'Millan and another man belonging to Corrie informed me that the body of the supposed Edwin Robert Rose had been found at the foot of a steep cliff high up on the mountain side of Glen Sannox. They informed me that the constables who were in charge of the body would not remove the body from its resting place until examined by a medical man. I at once volunteered to go up and inspect the body before removal. Beneath a large boulder or flat stone, 12 or 14 feet long, there was a pretty large open space, quite sufficient to conceal a man, looking towards the north or bottom of the glen. In this sort of recess the body was lying at full length, head north-west, feet south-east, face and belly downwards, boots and stockings on and entire. Trousers, coat, vest, suspenders, and shirt entire and free from rents, showing no indications of rough usage, bottom of trousers rolled up. Skirt of coat drawn carefully up over the head, probably to conceal or hide from view the ghastly appearance of the head, while covering the body with stones. With the assistance of one of the constables we turned the body over and drew it out from beneath the boulder, and then made a careful examination of the clothes and body. All

100

Evidence for Prosecution.

Dr Andrew Gilmour

the clothes were free from tears and rents or rough usage.
We also rifled the pockets in all the clothing; they were all
empty, not a scrap or vestige of anything. Arms, legs,
and body, including fingers, were free from injury or
fractures. The body in some parts was a little decayed,
but very little decay in either the arms or legs. The left
shoulder-blade near the top, where it forms the upper and
outer boundary of shoulder joint, was broken off
probably . . .''

Just pass over the remainder of that sentence which contains your opinion?—'' On examining the head and face,
both were fearfully and terribly smashed. Lower jaw dislocated on left side; upper jaw detached from its connections with the other bones of the face; nasal bones lying
loose and separated from the frontal bone. The bones of
the left side and top of the head were all fractured, and
portions of them lying inside the skull or brain cavity,
which was empty of brain matter. All it contained was
a heap of maggots and pieces of fractured skull bones, which
appeared to have been crushed in on the brain. The frontal,
parietal of left side, temporal of left side, and back or
occipital bones were fractured. Parietal, temporal, and
frontal bones were broken into many pieces, and portions
of them lying inside the brain. The occipital—a very
strong bone—was fractured across its whole length near its
upper boundary.''

That will do, thank you; I do not want you to read the
last paragraph of your report. Look at this photograph.
[Shown Production No. 12.] Does that represent accurately
the boulder under which you found the body?—Yes, it
represents it pretty accurately.

Tell us a little more particularly about these bits of bone
which were in the cavity of the skull. I suppose you did
not discover them until the body was laid on its back
outside the boulder?—Before we turned the body round and
when we were drawing it out I could see in, and could see
distinctly a portion of the head. The portion I saw presented a large ragged surface and a large hole on the left
side leading into the centre of the brain. When I first saw
the body the jacket or coat was thrown over the head. Until

John Watson Laurie.

Dr Andrew Gilmour

the jacket was drawn back I did not see the head at all. When that was done the side of the head presented to my eye was the right side. The head was turned slightly over so that I saw part of the hole on the left side.

Did you notice pieces of bone in the cavity of the skull?— I felt them. From the position I could not well see. Then we drew the body out as carefully as possible and turned it on its back, so that I might make a more careful examination.

Tell the jury in popular language what condition you found the face in?—On turning the body round on its back, with the face and front upwards, it presented a very ghastly spectacle. The face was almost denuded of flesh. The greater part of the left side of the head was completely denuded of the integuments, muscles, and flesh. Towards the right region of the matrix of the skull there was a ragged edge of the scalp, with dark hair adhering to it. The lower jaw was dislocated, and the upper jaw was detached from the cheek-bone and lying quite loose. By dislocated, I mean detached from the suture. The cheek-bone on the left side was lying loose. I could put my finger on it and lift it. The nasal bones on both sides were detached from their attachments and were lying loose.

And the eyes were gone?—Completely gone. The body was a skeleton. Upon the left side it was completely denuded to the central medial line over the frontal, and extended backwards to the occipital bone. There was a large irregular cavity with pieces of bone, showing a series of fractures radiating in every direction. I counted no fewer than nine pieces. Most of these pieces were found lying within the skull. The whole of the brain matter had been destroyed by maggots, and the bones were mixed up with the maggots and lay in the lower part of the skull. There is no doubt that many portions of these bones were knocked in at the time the injuries were inflicted, and, as the brain matter decayed, they fell into the cavity. I made a full superficial examination of the body on the spot. I found the clothing entire and free from rough usage. I could not see whether there was any blood on the clothing. There may have been,

102

Evidence for Prosecution.

Dr Andrew Gilmour

but from the colour of the tweed it would have been difficult to distinguish it.

Was there any injury on the body, so far as you then observed, as distinct from the head, except the fractured shoulder-blade?—None.

Did you form any opinion as to how the fracture on the shoulder had been caused?—It was a slanting fracture from above downwards. I examined the spine. I examined the legs, and a hole appeared to have been eaten through the trousers and into the flesh, this, I suppose, had been done by rats. After being examined, the body was put in a box and taken down to Corrie, and on the following day Dr. Fullarton, of Lamlash, and I made a joint examination of the body.

Did it strike you at the time that decomposition had attacked chiefly the upper part of the body?—Decomposition had attacked those portions which had been broken at the time of death. Those parts of the body which had been protected by the skin from the atmosphere were in a better state of preservation.

Did you make another examination of the body along with Dr. Fullarton, of Lamlash, in the coach-house at the Corrie Hotel?—I did, on the following day.

[Shown Production No. 4]—Is that the report?—Yes.

Is it a true report?—Yes.

Mr. GRAHAM MURRAY then read the joint report of Drs. Fullarton and Gilmour, which was as follows :—" We, Neil Fullarton, physician and surgeon, Lamlash, Arran, and Andrew Gilmour, physician and surgeon, practising at Linlithgow, but presently residing at Corrie, Arran, do hereby certify, on soul and conscience, that we have this day, Monday, 5th August, 1889, at one o'clock p.m., in the coach-house of the Corrie Hotel, made a post-mortem examination on the body of a man which had been discovered, on the afternoon of the day previous, in South Glen Sannox, Arran. The body was contained in a rough deal box in which it had been carried from the place where found, and was in charge of constables. Upon the box being opened by the police, the body of the man was found lying upon his back with his legs extended and the arms by the sides. There

John Watson Laurie.

Dr Andrew Gilmour

was a portion of a black glazed waterproof coat covering the upper part of the trunk and head, and in the box was a small tweed cap and a stained white linen pocket-handkerchief. The body was dressed in a tweed suit similar to the cloth of cap, and had on a pair of strong lacing boots, brown merino socks and drawers, a white linen shirt, and a white knitted semmit; the suspenders of trousers were intact and fixed, and the clothing was whole, with the exception of a hole over the left hip and one at left shoulder; these holes extended through all the clothing covering these parts. Round the calf of each leg under the trousers was strapped a leather padding about 6 inches deep. The body was in an advanced state of decomposition, and was covered with maggots, which swarmed all over it and the box in which it lay. Upon removing the waterproof from the upper part of the body we found that the whole of the soft tissues of the neck were gone, exposing the cervical vertebrae, the uppermost one of which was detached and lying separate in the box. The head lay upon its right side, and still attached to it by the ligaments of its right articulation was the lower jaw-bone; this bone was quite denuded of soft parts, and was disarticulated on the left side. The greater part of the skull on the right side of the head, as well as portions of the back and left side, still remained intact, although a fracture was plainly visible extending down through right parietal bone into the temporal of same side. This intact portion of bones of head had the hairy scalp still adherent to it, and what was left of this showed the hair to be black and about 2 inches long. The whole of facial part of skull (with the exception of a piece of right frontal portion), as well as greater part of left side, corresponding to a line of fracture which will presently be described, was awanting, and the parts awanting were found packed in the interior of what was left of the skull. The line of fracture through skull began on the left side immediately in front of and above the glenoid fossa of the left temporal bone, and extended backwards and slightly upwards three-fourths of an inch above the external auditory meatus, through the squamous portion of the temporal as far as the ridge running back from the zygoma, where it turned downwards and back-

Evidence for Prosecution.

Dr Andrew Gilmour

wards through the mastoid portion of the temporal. Crossing the occipito-mastoid suture it entered the occipital bone,
and curving upwards and towards the right it passed an inch
to the left of the external occipital protuberance, then through
the occipito-parietal suture into the left parietal bone,
through which it extended upwards, forwards, and to the
right, crossing the sagittal suture into right parietal, extending into same to the depth of half an inch, when it curved
again towards left, and crossed the same suture into parietal
of left side, from whence, passing forwards, it crossed the
coronal suture slightly to left of central line of forehead,
and was prolonged downward, outward, and to right through
frontal bone on right side into right orbit, from which it
passed exactly through the line of attachment of the right
malar or cheek-bone to the upper jaw-bone on the right side.
All the bones inside the line of fracture thus described were
completely denuded of soft tissues, and the temporal, occipital,
left parietal, and frontal were broken into several pieces,
the occipital into two large pieces by a fracture extending
upward and forward, the others into much smaller fragments, the portion of the right parietal broken off being
still attached to a larger fragment of its neighbour bone of
left side by the suture. The whole of the part of face comprising the upper jaws was detached in one piece, the malar-
bone of the left side being broken off from the left upper jaw-
bone, and detached separately by a fracture through left
zygoma at a point exactly corresponding to a line drawn
in front of condyle of left lower jaw-bone. On the base of
skull inside the line of fracture extended from the squamous
part of left temporal bone obliquely and irregularly towards
the right front, where it joined the external line of fracture
on that side through the orbital plate of frontal bone. The
opening or cavity into skull produced by these fractures
measured from before backwards in its greatest length 9
inches, and transversely it measured at its widest part behind
4½ inches, and same in front 6 inches. We then proceeded
to strip body, and upon taking off boots and socks, although
skin of feet was shedding off, there was plainly discernible
a well-marked red line extending from the heel to roots of
toes on each foot. Next we ripped up the clothing in front

John Watson Laurie.

Dr Andrew Gilmour

of body and limbs, and found that there were no broken bones in limbs or in any part of the trunk, with the exception of a fracture which extended right across left scapula immediately below the origin of the coracoid and acromion processes of said bone, and which were thus together detached. The ' umerus or upper-arm bone of this side was not dislocated, although the parts all about joint were stripped of flesh. The first and second ribs of left side were separated from their attachments to the corresponding vertebrae. We now turned the body round upon its belly in box, and again ripped clothes as in front, but found nothing unusual here except a hole in the fleshy part of left buttock. This hole was 3 inches long, 2 inches wide, and about 2 inches deep in its deepest part. This destruction of fleshy tissues, as well as that over left shoulder, corresponds to the holes in clothing previously mentioned, and from their appearances were probably caused by rats. From the examination of the body made by us, and from the nature of the injuries there present, we are of opinion that death was caused by repeated blows on the left side of the head, and that these blows were inflicted by some heavy, blunt instrument.''

By the COURT—Tell us in plain English what all this means?—I made my report in as plain language as I could write it. I did not use scientific terms.

The LORD JUSTICE-CLERK—Then we shall get it from Dr. Fullarton.

Examination continued—Well now, the important part of this report is as to the portions of the skull which you say were put back into the interior of the brain-box and were found in it?—Yes. They were nearly in the same position. I also had handed to me by one of the men present some portions of bone which were picked up on the ground afterwards.

Cross-examined by the DEAN OF FACULTY—When you first saw the body, were there some pieces of bone, of what you no doubt thought to be the skull, lying loose on the ground? —I did not observe them.

Would it be correct to say that there were such pieces

Evidence for Prosecution.

Dr Andrew Gilmour

before the body was touched?—It is probable, but I cannot speak to it.

Can you say whether, while the body was still under the boulder, and before it was disturbed, certain loose pieces of the skull were lying on the ground?—I cannot say. I did not see them.

You have described to us the condition of the face. Was it plain that from decomposition the soft tissues had gradually disappeared?—The greater part of them had practically disappeared.

Then you have no doubt that the denuded aspect of the face was due to decomposition; that would release the bones and they would fall as has been described?—Yes.

In your joint report you say : " The line of fracture began on the left side." You have described that in your report as a " line of fracture." Is that a correct description?— Well, it is as near the facts and the state of the brain-box as could be got at.

It was a continuous fracture, was it not?—I would not like to say that.

> [The Dean of Faculty then produced a human skull, which was handed to witness in order that he might trace upon it the line of fractures on the head of deceased alluded to in the report. Witness traced with his finger the line of the fracture, beginning at the left side and going round the back of the head, and pointed out in a similar way the lesser fracture across the base of the skull.]

Would you point to any other fracture that you desire to call attention to?—You could not have a skull broken into eight or nine pieces without numerous fractures.

There were a dozen fractures on the head?—Of course.

What I am asking you to do is to point to any other important fracture to which you desire to call attention?— There was a fracture described as extending to the upper part of the frontal bone.

Will you point to any other important fracture on the

John Watson Laurie.

Dr Andrew Gilmour

upper part of the head?—The left parietal bone was broken into at least five or six pieces, and therefore that embraces five or six different fractures.

Did you observe, on the occasion of the finding of the body, what was the condition of the back-bone? Was there any detachment of the highest vertebra from what was above it? —It was lying loose.

That is, the uppermost joint of the back-bone was lying loose?—Yes, that was the condition before I turned the body round.

From that I take it the head was separated from the trunk as far as the backbone was concerned?—The twelve bones of the neck, which join the head to the spine, are held together by strong ligaments. When the flesh is removed from these by injury, they soon decay. In this case decay must have set in and destroyed the ligaments which held the small bones connecting the upper part of the spinal column to the brain-box.

How was the head held on the body then?—Before I and the constable turned the body round at the boulder, the head was attached to the spinal column, but the detachment was so slight and loose from decay that when we turned the body round, although we brought the brain-box round with it, the upper bone or atlas got quite loose and fell under the force of the spinal column.

By the COURT—There was no injury to the neck by violence?—No.

Cross-examination continued—Were the soft parts of the neck much decomposed?—Yes.

Were they in such a condition that you could not say whether there might or might not have been violence before death?—I could not say one way or the other.

By the COURT—I am referring more to the bones of the spinal column. Was there any trace of violence to them?— I took out the atlas-bone and examined it and could find no trace of anything.

Cross-examination continued—But whether there had been dislocation of these before death, you could not tell?—No; no person could.

Evidence for Prosecution.

Dr Andrew Gilmour

Can you say where the white handkerchief, referred to in your second report, came from?—No.

Did you find it in the pocket of the deceased?—No. Some of the pockets were, however, searched by a constable.

It is described in your report as a stained white linen pocket-handkerchief. In what, way was it stained?—The stains on the handkerchief were dark. That is all I can say of them.

When the body was put into the box on the hill, was this handkerchief put in with it?—Very likely, but I am not certain. My attention was taken up with other matters.

I see in one of the passages in Dr. Fullarton's and your report you say that the facial part of the skull was awanting, as well as other parts enumerated. Then you say later : " The whole of that part of the face comprising the upper jaw was detached in one piece." Will you explain that?—If you will give me the skull I will be very happy to explain.

[The witness demonstrated the nature of the injury in question.]

What was the one piece in which the whole was detached?— The upper jaw was not fractured, but it was detached from the cheek-bone. It was quite loose and could be removed by the hand.

No part of that portion of the face, which you describe as detached in one piece, had been driven into the skull?—No. The pieces of bone found in the skull were from the back part.

Would it be correct to say that what you describe in your report as " one piece " seemed to have been driven down in one piece?—It must have been driven down.

In one piece?—Quite so, because there was no breaking in the centre.

Did you, in making your examination—I do not know whether the condition of the subject would be such as to let you know—see any bruised blood about the head?—I did not.

Did you look into the cavities of the ears in so far as they remained?—So far as I could see, there was no sign of blood in the external ear. The ear was very nearly all decayed.

Did you look for the purpose of seeing whether there was

John Watson Laurie.

Dr Andrew Gilmour

any blood in the pharynx?—I did not consider that looking into the mouth would be of any use owing to the amount of decay that had taken place in the external parts—I did not think I would find evidence of blood one way or another.

Did you look for blood towards the base of the brain where the spinal column enters?—No, it was full of maggots. Had there been any blood there at the time it would all have been changed. It would have taken better eyes than mine to have traced blood.

By the COURT—Maggots would very soon remove any mark of blood.

Cross-examination continued—I see your report says that Rose had been wearing a white shirt. Did you see any blood on his shirt?—There were dark stains upon the front of the shirt, but I could not say what they were.

Would you indicate what part of the shirt the stains were on?—There were dark stains—what I would call dirty stains —both on the collar and also on the front of the shirt.

Do you mean it was simply soiled linen?—I cannot say. If there was a drop of decayed blood it would be difficult to discover it—or any other stain—after three or four weeks. I did not observe any stains on any other part of the shirt.

He was lying on his face?—Yes.

There was nothing to suggest that the upper part of the shirt had been drenched in blood?—No appearance of that.

And no appearance of the soaking of the coat and waistcoat, or any part of his clothing?—No. There were dark stains, but what these were I could not say.

I see you say that he had on a knitted semmit. Did you see any traces of blood on it?—I would not swear I saw traces of blood, but there were dark stains. [Part of the shirt and the collar (Nos. 19 and 20) were here produced and examined by the witness.] Certain stains on these articles appear to me as though they were due to the effects of damp.

The injury to the shoulder-blade extended across and backwards?—Yes.

Did you dissect the soft tissues?—There was an external wound, and we could trace it without dissection.

110

Evidence for Prosecution.

You did not dissect it to see if there was extravasation of blood?—I did not think it was necessary. Two of the ribs were detached from the back-bone. I do not think they were detached from the breast-bone.

Could you determine that without dissection?—Perfectly.

Are you speaking from recollection?—From recollection.

Re-examined by the SOLICITOR-GENERAL—With reference to this long line of fracture, popularly speaking, it comes to this, that the fracture started at the left side of the head and ran downwards to the base of the skull, then ran up to the head and across, rather curving to the right, and then downwards. All bones to the left of the fracture were broken into fragments?—That is so.

All to the left of the fracture was broken into pieces?—The whole was broken into pieces.

With reference to the fracture which you describe on the head, it was a fissure on the head, the bones remaining intact? —There was a fracture, but the bones were not loose; you could not pick them out as you could the other parts on the left side.

In addition to the bones of the face, including the upper jaw, the nasal bone, the cheek-bone, and others were separately broken?—They were detached from their adhesions to the face-bone and from each other. The upper jaw-bone is one of the strongest bones in the body.

By the COURT—Do I understand that you could put your hand into the man's head until you got to the other side?— Right to the other side.

There was no skin?—No skin.

Re-examination continued—Portions in the reading of your report were left out. You said: " The left shoulder-blade near the top, where it forms the upper and outer boundary of the shoulder joint, was broken off "—and here is the passage that was omitted: " probably by a blow aimed at the head, striking it in a slanting direction." And then just at the end: " I have no hesitation in certifying that these fractures were not produced by a fall down a cliff or steep incline, but by a number of blows inflicted by a hard, blunt instrument, such as a large boulder; that these blows

111

John Watson Laurie.

Dr Andrew Gilmour

produced the fractures to the skull and injury to the brain-matter, which, in my opinion, was the cause of death." Then in the joint report, the concluding paragraph is: "From the examination of the body made by us, and from the nature of the injuries there present, we are of opinion that death was caused by repeated blows on the left side of head, and these blows were inflicted by some heavy instrument." Did your examination of the body with Dr. Fullarton confirm the impression made on you when you examined it on the hillside?—It did.

In the case of the injury to the shoulder blade, that was near enough to the head to suggest that a blow aimed at the head "missed it" and came down on the shoulder-blade?—That was the impression I formed at the time I examined the body in Glen Sannox.

Do you think it could have been caused by an accidental fall?—It is possible. The shoulder-blade is often broken by a fall.

All you can say about it is that it is possible it might have been caused by a fall, but your own opinion is that it was caused by a blow?—My own opinion is that it was caused by a blow from above downwards.

Would it take a fall from a great height to produce an injury like that?—Yes; it is a strong bone.

With reference to the injuries to the head and face, there again your opinion is in favour of a blow or blows as against a fall?—Yes.

Tell us in your own way what that is founded on?—It is founded on the whole of the injuries being confined to the left side of the head. Had the man fallen, there would have been other parts of the head injured besides the left side. A fall could not have produced such severe extensive fractures as were on the head.

You have had experience of injuries to the head caused by falls?—Yes, and by blows too.

And have you ever seen injuries to the head so extensive and so severe which had resulted from a fall?—Never; I never saw a skull so severely fractured.

Is it possible that all these injuries could have been caused by one impact of the body upon anything?—Impossible.

112

The Gully of Coire=na=Fuhren.

C. Spot where cap was found.   K. & P. Where knife and pencil were found.   W. Where waterproof was found.   S. Where walking stick was found.   B. Boulder under which body was found.

From the photograph produced in Court.

Evidence for Prosecution.

Dr Andrew Gilmour

Then there must have been repeated impacts, whether by blows or by falls, in order to produce these injuries?—Whether by blows or falls there must have been a number, owing to the nature of the injuries.

Is that opinion confirmed by the state of the rest of the body?—Yes, in my opinion, it is.

In what way?—Because the limbs were found free from fractures and dislocations. The clothing was entirely free from breaks. That could not have been the case had Rose fallen down the cliff.

If there had been continual and repeated concussions of the body upon rock or other hard substance, you would have expected injury to the other parts of the body?—Yes.

If, on the other hand, there was a fall down a sheer cliff, and only one impact, that could not account for the number of injuries, in your opinion?—Scarcely.

Have you any doubt about it?—There is a possibility that, if the body had fallen from a considerable height perpendicularly, fractures very similar might have been caused. There was, however, no precipice there.

We may take it that it would require a sheer fall from a great height?—Yes.

In your opinion, you have seen no such injuries as these caused by a fall?—None.

Does the fact of the attachment of the upper jaw being broken strengthen your opinion that the injuries must have been caused by blows as opposed to a fall?—Yes. The jawbone has a strong attachment to the other bones forming the face and could not have been loosened without a considerable amount of force.

Does the condition of the trunk confirm your view?—Yes.

If there had been a fall or succession of falls, would not you rather have expected the abdominal organs to be injured?—It is possible.

So that if they were found in a good state of preservation, and uninjured, that would rather confirm your view that it was a blow and not a fall?—That is so.

Were the injuries to the face in particular consistent with repeated blows by a hard instrument made for the purpose

John Watson Laurie.

of disfiguring and preventing recognition of it?—Well, I could not say.

Were they consistent with repeated blows upon the face with a hard instrument?—There must have been more than one blow inflicted on the face, and these blows were such as to reduce the flesh to a condition of pulp, but without cutting the skin.

That would account for the absence of hæmorrhage?—There is very little hæmorrhage from blows inflicted by a blunt instrument.

You have told us that decomposition had attacked the upper part of the face and body first, and that would be accounted for by that portion of the body being severely bruised?—That is how I account for so much decay on the side of the head.

You would never expect decomposition to begin there, but rather in the more fleshy parts of the body?—Yes.

Had there been any injury to the head, then decomposition would have advanced downwards into the cavity of the body, and that is exactly what happened?—Yes, the parts of the body that were exposed to the atmosphere, where the skin was broken, underwent rapid decay.

When you were on the spot you looked about you. You know where the articles of clothing were found?—That was pointed out to me by those who found them.

Did you see any rocks about those places where the various things were found, a fall from which would account for such injuries?—I did not.

Further cross-examined by the DEAN OF FACULTY—In expressing the opinion you did to the Solicitor-General that the injuries had been caused from above downwards, I suppose you mean from above downwards in relation to the body?—Yes.

Of course, an injury which is from above downwards, if the body is standing in its normal position, would be from below upwards if the body is pitched down, so that all you mean is that they were injuries beginning with the head and going towards the extremities?—I took it the body would be standing in a normal position.

But if the body were pitched down head first, the injuries

114

Evidence for Prosecution.

Dr Andrew Gilmour

would be from below upwards?—No such effect could take place.

We will come to that. Did you speak in relation to the upright state of the body?—Yes, I have never seen a head so severely fractured from any cause as this one was. It is quite certain that the injuries would be quickly fatal, and insensibility would take place almost instantaneously.

Would it be correct to say in this case that you consider the upper part of the head, as regards its left side, was very largely involved?—Certainly.

And also the base of the brain, or the lower part in the manner you have also described?—Yes.

Supposing a person pitched on his head from a great height, the vertex of the head would strike first, and might cause a fracture at a point opposite where the injury took place?—It is possible that that would happen.

So that if the fall were of such a nature as to involve a large part of the upper head, you would expect a correspondingly large part at the base to be involved?—There is no doubt of that.

And these features were present here?—Yes.

I suppose, in determining the effects of any fall in the head, it would be necessary to know the height from which a fall took place and the kind of substance the unfortunate person alighted upon?—It depends upon that to produce a certain amount of injury. The greater the height the vaster would be the ratio of the increase of the injuries. The effect upon the skull would largely depend upon whether it was a rough or smooth surface the head alighted upon. If it were a rough surface like a jagged stone, there might be a number of points of fracture just as if caused by blows from above.

Have you ever had any experience of a human body falling head-foremost from a height of, say, 32 feet upon a hard stone? You have never seen what that would do?—No.

Not even from a height of 19 feet?—No.

Have you any doubt that if a human body had fallen from either 32 feet or 19 feet the covering of the head would probably be a bag of broken bones?—It depends upon the nature of the resistance.

John Watson Laurie.

Dr Andrew Gilmour

Supposing a body fell head-foremost from a height of that kind upon granite or similar hard substance, have you any doubt that the covering of the head would only contain a mass of broken bones?—It is quite possible.

With a sudden impact of that sort would you expect very general fractures?—That would be according to the character of the stone.

In answer to the Solicitor-General you said that the injuries on the left side could not have been caused by a fall?—No, because there was no rock near where the deceased was found which could have caused the injuries.

Does your evidence and the whole tenor of your report not assume that the deceased met his death near to the boulder where the body was found?—No.

Did you not give that opinion?—I gave that opinion with reference to a question as to the *locus* in which the body was found, and not with regard to the nature of the injuries.

And you said that there was no appearance of injuries on other parts of the body and no appearance of interference with the clothes. You would have expected that if it had rolled over a considerable distance of rough ground?—Certainly.

I ask you to answer this—if a person pitched head-fore-most down a cliff, 19 feet or 32 feet in height, and remained there, would there necessarily be any interference with the clothes or any parts of the body except those nearest to the part which struck? You see what I mean?—There is no doubt that if a person were to be pitched perpendicularly upon a granite boulder, serious fractures would be produced if the head first came in contact with the rock.

Supposing a body were falling as I have described to you, the next place which we might expect to be injured would be the next protuberance—the shoulder or shoulders?—Certainly.

You have here a very strong bone in the shoulder broken?—Yes.

You suppose that that was done by a blow. What I ask you is, whether such an injury as that would not readily have been produced by a body being pitched down and

116

Evidence for Prosecution.

Dr Andrew Gilmour

alighting heavily, partly on the head and partly on the shoulder?—Possibly it might have been so produced.

I ask you to consider that if there was no rolling after alightment, is there any reason why any other part of the body should have been implicated in the injury?—If there was no rolling there would be no injury inflicted on the other parts of the body.

Did you find the thoracic cavity empty?—I did not examine it. I thought it was useless, after tracing the distinct cause of death, to enter into secondary matters.

Is your opinion as to the cause of death founded on the fact that there is nothing in that neighbourhood competent to produce such results by a fall?—That may perhaps be one reason for forming my opinion with regard to the fall, but, independent of the nature of the ground and of the height of the cliff and the slope, I formed my opinion on the spot from the nature of the fractures. I formed the opinion that they were inflicted by direct blows. My opinion was based upon medical observation.

You did not take any pains to ascertain whether there had been extravasation of blood?—I did not.

Is it not the case that if the death is due to serious injuries by blows, and if there is survival for a short period of time, there would be greater bleeding?—You can have fracture at the base of the skull without great extravasation of blood.

When there were such injuries about the base of the skull, is it not plain that there must have been a large amount of bleeding? Is it the fact that if a severe blow on the skull was struck, you would expect to find an injury on the opposite part of the skull from where the blow was administered?—Certainly.

Suppose a man is struck on the right side of the head, there would probably be injury on the other side?—I have known one side of the skull severely fractured and the other side perfectly sound.

Your first report was dated on the 6th, although your examination took place on the 4th, and the second report is dated on the 5th. Did you write your first report after the second?—I took notes at my first examination.

John Watson Laurie.

Dr Andrew Gilmour

Did you take any notes on the spot of what you observed?
—Some.

This is what you thought of the first inspection : " I have
no hesitation in certifying that these fractures were not
produced by a fall down a cliff or steep incline, but by a
number of blows inflicted by a hard, blunt instrument, such
as a large boulder." You have, I think, admitted that
under the conditions I have put to you it was possible that
the results might be produced by a fall?—That it was possible,
but not likely.

Do you not think this was rather confident language for
a first examination : " I have no hesitation in certifying,"
and so on? You would modify it a little now?—I do not
think I would.

May I ask to what you refer when you say " a number
of blows inflicted by a hard, blunt instrument, such as a
large boulder." How would a man hold a large boulder
in his hand?—I do not know how he would hold it.

No more do I?—He would get it by his thumb and
fingers.

" A large boulder " is your expression. Do you seriously
mean that?—A boulder might be a pebble of not half an
inch. A stone of 2 or 3 lb. I would call a large boulder.

What time was it when you went up the hill on the
Sunday night?—Close upon eight o'clock.

And what journey had you home?—A long, weary journey.

Were you not rather in a hurry to get home?—Yes.

Now, would it be correct to say that the first examination
was necessarily a hurried one?—It was, to a certain extent.

Have you been back at the place since?—I was close to
it afterwards, before I left the island.

Re-examined by the SOLICITOR-GENERAL—Of course, a fall
might be either a sheer fall or by rolls or bounds till the
body reached the bottom. It is the latter kind of fall you
think is excluded by the state of the body other than the
head, and the state of the limbs particularly?—From the
nature of the injuries I can come to no other conclusion
than that no fall could have produced those injuries.

What do you say would be the case in a fall where the

Evidence for Prosecution.

Dr Andrew Gilmour

body rolls or bounds from one place to another? In the case of a body alighting on the top of the head, could there be such injuries as you saw to the lower part of the face?—Certainly not.

You are clear about that. A fall of that kind could not both produce the injuries on the head and the fracture of the upper jaw?—That is my opinion.

Do you think it probable that such a fall as that could produce both the injury to the head and the injury to the shoulder-blade—one and the same fall?—It is possible, but not likely.

Dr. NEIL FULLARTON, examined by the SOLICITOR-GENERAL —I am a physician and surgeon, of Lamlash, Arran. I was called in to view the body of the deceased Edwin Robert Rose on the 4th of August, but I did not examine it until next day, when I assisted Dr. Gilmour. The report which has been produced and read [Production No. 4] and which was signed by me, is a true report. In that report mention is made of a pocket-handkerchief. That must have come out of a pocket of the clothes of the body. It was found lying outside the clothing, as though somebody had taken it out of a pocket. It was stained in such a way as to indicate that it must have been lying on the body during the whole time that decomposition had been going on. I know this part of the mountain, and I have gone over it both before and after this occurrence. I have examined it particularly since.

[Shown Production No. 10.] Is there, from the point marked on that photograph with a cross, a road down to Glen Sannox past the boulder, which can be taken by a person of ordinary activity in safety?—Yes, there are various ways of going down; but I know that people have come down there. I fancy the line to take would be, not down the actual watercourse, but to the right or left of it. At the letter C there is a rock which slopes in at the right-hand side, looking down to Glen Sannox. I do not think it can be higher than 10 feet.

But that is not in the line which anybody going from the ridge going down into Glen Sannox would naturally take?

John Watson Laurie.

Dr Neil Fullarton

—A few yards on either side of the track you pass it. The rocks in the gully are interspersed with vegetation to the right and left. In some parts there are rough granite rocks, hard and bare, and in places there is a kind of disintegrated granite between the boulders. There is a sheer drop of about 20 feet on the right-hand side at the point where the rock is shown in the photograph as overhanging.

That is a long distance below where the cap was found; no man whose cap was found where this one was could possibly have fallen over that rock?—No; unless some person had gone and deposited the cap where it was found.

Cross-examined by the DEAN OF FACULTY—I could not say whether the handkerchief, previously spoken of, was taken out of the pockets of the deceased. The average slope of the ground to the point where the cap was found forms an angle of about 45 degrees. Some of the breaks in the slope are of a slippery character, formed of disintegrated granite; there are some other slopes of polished granite at the right-hand side. There is a space of about 2 or 3 yards, just about where the waterproof was found, where a person would be apt to slip.

The ordinary way of coming down from the top is by The Saddle?—If you want to run into more danger you would go by The Saddle.

Which way do most people go?—By The Saddle, because they want to see the hills.

But they are wrong, from the safety point of view? People go there not caring for the slopes?—They look to that too.

A person might, of course, take a step or two out of their way. Did you see a place not far from where the cap was found, on the right side going down, where there is a sheer drop of 20 feet?—That is where the ledge runs into the projecting slope.

Then there is a place farther down about 32 feet?—Yes.

Re-examined by the SOLICITOR-GENERAL—I have never gone by The Saddle route. I just know about it from looking at it from the top of the ridge. It looks like a place where a false step on either side might precipitate one a long distance.

120

Evidence for Prosecution.

Dr Neil Fullarton

[At this stage the witness was handed the skull, on which he traced the lines of the fractures over the vault and base, describing them as being continuous.]

There were a number of fractures on the skull. There was a fissure extending from the line of fractures down to the middle of the forehead. That, so far as I saw, was the only injury to the right side of the head, but the left side was smashed into fragments.

Within the lines of fracture you have described, was there anything in what you saw which suggested that the injury to the upper jaw-bone was anything other than the result of violence?—No, because the upper jaw-bone offers most resistance to violence. I examined the body again along with Dr. Littlejohn on the 27th of September and prepared a joint report with him. [Production No. 5]. My opinion, as expressed in the report signed by Dr. Gilmour and myself, is that the injuries to the head were the result of repeated blows inflicted by a heavy, blunt instrument.

What led you to that conclusion?—The extent and severity of the fractures, as well as the general outline of them.

The fractures were very severe?—I have never seen a head smashed like it, unless by a machinery accident; and then the person was mangled otherwise as well.

Was there anything in the nature of the injuries themselves which led you to the opinion that they could not have resulted from one impact of the head upon any hard substance?—The curvature as described on the outside of the skull by the fracture leads one to the opinion that it was the result of repeated blows.

The injuries were quite consistent with that?—Yes.

Take a sheer fall down a rock, without the body touching anything till it reached the bottom—could that produce the injuries to the head and the fractures on the face?—It is not at all likely.

Does the existence of the injury to the shoulder-blade also render it more difficult to believe that all those injuries could have been caused by one fall?—The situation of the injury on the shoulder led us to believe it must have been from blows.

121

John Watson Laurie.

Dr Neil Fullarton

The position of the fracture of the shoulder seemed to indicate that it was not caused by a fall, unless in an unconscious person?—Any conscious person, falling, would have had his hands out before him. A person might get such an injury walking carelessly with his hands in his pockets on the level, if he had no time to put out his hands before he reached the ground.

By the COURT—Is it a recognised thing that a person falling over a height of that kind stretches out his hands?—There is always an effort made to save one's head.

Is it an unconscious action?—It is almost unconscious. From childhood to old age you see a falling person put out his hands.

Re-examination continued—If the body in falling were to roll or bound from one point to another, that would increase the likelihood of there being injuries to other parts of the person?—It would. The injury to the shoulder might possibly have been inflicted in that way, but in that case there would have been no other injuries. Taking the injuries as they actually existed, I entirely excluded from my view the idea of a fall of that sort. The injuries are quite consistent with repeated blows with a stone or other blunt instrument. The injury to the shoulder-blade was such as might have been caused by a severe blow from above downwards, and a little from behind, missing the head and striking the shoulder.

Further cross-examined by the DEAN OF FACULTY—I think the first reason you gave for the opinion that these injuries resulted from repeated blows was the severity and extent of the lines of fracture?—Severity of the fractures and extent.

Let us first take the severity. Do you think that, if a person fell over either 19 feet or 32 feet and pitched on to a granite rock, the severity of the blow would not be as great as any inflicted by the hand?—It would be, but it would not cause so many fractures.

We will speak about that directly. Would not a sheer fall on the vertex of the head upon a hard object be more severe than a blow from a stone in a man's hand?—It would

122

Evidence for Prosecution.

Dr Neil Fullarton

be, from a sufficient height; but it would end in only one smash. And you cannot compare the severity in that way.

Would there be, apart from direction, a kind of proportion between the severity of the blow and the extent of the resulting injuries? Could you imagine anything more likely to shatter a man's head than a fall down a cliff of 19 feet?—I could not, and that is the reason why I think it was due to blows. The injury was localised.

Do the lines of fracture you have indicated not implicate the whole of the top of the head?—Yes.

Did you find that there were fractures extending practically over the whole base of the skull?—There was a line of fracture which indicated the separation of the front from all behind.

Is that not the sort of thing that would only happen if a person had pitched on the top of his head, the whole upper and lower cranium being implicated?—I should not have expected it.

If there had been such a series of local blows, as you have described, on the left side of the head, do you think you would have had such a result on the right side?—I do not know if the blows were confined to the left side.

We do not know if there were blows at all, but what I am asking is, would you not have expected that a series of local blows would have led to a corresponding number of local lesions on the opposite side of the head?—It depends upon how the blows were applied.

That you do not know?—No; but from their appearance they were inflicted from above downwards.

You mean with reference to a body in an erect posture?—I mean with reference to a body in a natural position. If you turn a body round, an injury from above downwards becomes an injury from below upwards.

If there was an injury to the skull implicating the larger part of the upper head of a man on the left side, would not such injury produce the result of implicating the skull in its lower base?—Yes.

Whereas would not serious local injuries by blows have led to serious local lesions on the opposite side of the head?—Sometimes; not always.

John Watson Laurie.

Dr Neil Fullarton

Would not a person falling on the head downwards, pitch also on the left shoulder?—I do not see why he should not dislocate or break his arms.

By the COURT—That is supposing him to have stretched out both his hands?—Yes, in attempting to save himself.

Cross-examination continued—That is exactly what I would have expected. I suppose there may be various conditions under which a person may not have time to stretch out his hands if he slipped and came down suddenly?—Here, he would anticipate slipping.

Don't you think, if he could anticipate slipping, he would keep away altogether?—I do. That is the reason why I believe he did not fall.

But it is impossible, without having seen the occurrence, to tell what happened. Did you observe whether there was an external lesion occurring in the region of the left scapula? —I did; it was denuded of soft tissues.

There was also a hole in the clothing there?—Yes.

Did you observe that two ribs on the left side were detached from the vertebræ?—They were.

But not on the right side?—No.

Would not these left ribs, after the head and the shoulder, have been the parts on which stress would have come if the man had pitched on his head?—The collar-bone would have been broken.

Re-examined by the SOLICITOR-GENERAL—Whatever the cause of the injuries, those fractures on the left side of the head were not followed by the counterstrokes which sometimes occur?—They were not.

Whatever was the cause, was there any case of counter-strokes or what seemed to you like counterstrokes at all?— Nothing whatever.

What conclusion did you draw with regard to the injuries to the base of the skull?—The conclusion I drew was that the injury must have been inflicted by repeated blows from above downwards.

Is it your opinion that there must have been several blows inflicted in different positions?—There may have been only

Evidence for Prosecution.

one blow when the man was standing, the others being inflicted when he was down.

It is not only that they may have been so inflicted, but that is what they suggest to your mind?—Yes.

And you conclude that the injuries to the face were inflicted when he was standing or when he was down?—I cannot see how such injuries would be inflicted on the face by one blow; they must have been done by a series of blows. Therefore, as I did not consider it probable that these facial injuries were all inflicted at one time, I would conclude that they were inflicted when he was down.

Further cross-examined by the DEAN OF FACULTY—On examining the body, did the possibility of heart disease suggest itself to you?—Yes; but after seeing the place where the body was found, I satisfied myself that any idea of heart disease was out of the question.

By the COURT—What did you mean when you said that one of the fractures ran into another?—What I meant was that, at the left side of the base of the skull, one fracture came up to another and stopped there. That led me to the conclusion that one of the fractures was inflicted before the other.

Dr. HENRY LITTLEJOHN, examined by the SOLICITOR-GENERAL —I am medical officer of health and surgeon of police for Edinburgh. On 27th September Dr. Fullarton, the previous witness, and I examined the body of Edwin Robert Rose which was exhumed in our presence and identified as the body of the deceased by Dr. Fullarton and Constable Munro. We prepared a report [Production No. 5] which reads as follows :—

"30th September, 1889.

" We hereby certify, upon soul and conscience, that, on Friday, 27th September, 1889, by warrant granted by the Sheriff-Substitute of Bute, we examined in Sannox Church-yard, Arran, the body of Edwin Rose, which was exhumed, in our presence, the grave and coffin being identified by Alexander M'Killop, undertaker, and William Munro, police constable, and the body of deceased by P.C. William Munro and by one of ourselves, Dr. Fullarton. We examined more

125

John Watson Laurie.

Dr Henry Littlejohn

particularly the contents of the great cavities of the body.
The brain was totally destroyed and so were the soft structures
of the neck, including the windpipe and gullet. The cavity
of the chest was empty, and no portion of the heart, great
vessels, or lungs could be discovered. It was otherwise with
the abdomen, the skin of which was remarkably well preserved.
On making a free incision and exposing the abdominal cavity,
the following was the condition of the organs:—The diaphragm or midriff was intact and deeply stained of a dark
colour which had apparently come from the liver which presented a similar appearance. This organ was normal in size
and appearance. It was intact and uninjured. The stomach
was empty or almost so, its internal or mucus surface being
covered here and there with a few granules of semi-digested
food. This organ was healthy and presented no particular
odour. The intestines—both large and small—were normal,
and contained a moderate quantity of fæces. The spleen,
kidneys, and bladder were also normal. All these organs were
uninjured and presented a remarkably fresh appearance. The
whole of the walls of the abdomen was examined without
detecting any bruise or effusion of blood.

> " NEIL FULLARTON, M.B.
> " HENRY D. LITTLEJOHN, M.D."

That is a true report.

You have heard the evidence given and the report of the
other doctors. Judging from these and your own examination
of the body, what is your opinion as to the cause of death?—
The condition of the cranium, as I saw it in the coffin, was
at once suggestive of direct violence, such as blows.

One blow could not have produced the injuries to the skull?
—Quite impossible.

What do you say to the explanation of a fall?—A fall, in
my opinion, would not have inflicted such localised violence
as I saw in the head and face of the deceased, without producing severe injuries to the extremities and to the internal
organs of the abdomen.

So that the state of the abdomen confirms the view that
the injuries were the result of blows and not of a fall?—It
does. In any fall from a height the liver is especially apt

Evidence for Prosecution.

Dr Henry Littlejohn

to suffer. If it does not suffer, we find effusions of blood in the abdominal walls, and also covering the organs of the abdomen, whereas here the abdominal organs were quite uninjured and remarkably well preserved.

They were distinguished in that respect from the organs of the chest or lungs?—They were. I saw no vestige of these organs.

How do you explain the fact of decomposition having attacked the head, heart, and lungs first?—I explain it in consequence of the injuries to the body being chiefly located in the upper portions, namely, the head and face. When once maggots attack that part of the body, they gain ready access to the chest, and remarkably quickly destroy organs like the lungs and heart, which contain a large amount of blood.

These are the organs they would attack first?—Yes.

Why, in this case, should they have begun with the face?— Decomposition always attacks organs or parts of the body which have undergone injury, especially by blows. The soft parts, such as the skin, are reduced to a pulp, which becomes a ready prey to maggots. If the skin of the face and head had been uninjured, decomposition would not have attacked it so soon as the organs of the chest.

Confining ourselves to the injuries to the head and face, what do you say to the theory that all of these were caused by a single sheer fall from a height?—From my own experience, I should say it is quite impossible that a single fall from a height could inflict such large damage to the head and face.

You have had experience of such falls?—I have had considerable experience of falls from great heights, such as the Dean Bridge, the Castle Rock, and other places in the neighbourhood of Edinburgh.

In all your experience, did you ever see injuries like these caused by a fall from a height?—I have observed extensive fractures of the skull, but I have never seen dislodgment of the upper jaw, which existed in this case.

Is that dislodgment of the upper jaw, in your view, an important feature of the case?—In my opinion, because

John Watson Laurie.

Dr Henry Littlejohn

the connections of this bone are the firmest and strongest in the body.

A dislodgment of that sort could not be the result, could it, of a fall on the top of the head?—I should say, from my own experience, no.

But dislodgment was quite consistent with a blow or blows with a blunt instrument?—That was the explanation which presented itself to me when I examined carefully the head and face. A heavy stone, held in the hand, would be such an instrument as would cause the injuries.

There was direct violence of some kind?—I noticed the fracture across the base of the skull.

Did that suggest to you any view as to whether it was caused at the same time or after the fracture on the upper part?—I have found that fractures on the vertex of the head often cause fractures at the base of the cranium.

That is called a counterstroke, but it can be produced by direct violence also?—I observed no sign of counterstroke here.

Was that at all surprising?—In direct violence we do not expect to find such evidence of counterstroke, because the violence is so severe as at once to knock in the bone. It is when a bone is not knocked in that force is propagated round the cranium and takes effect on the part opposite. The counterstroke is caused by transmission from the stronger to the weaker parts.

Did the absence of fractures or injuries of any kind to the upper parts of the body seem to you to be an important element?—I was struck by the absence of injury to the spine and to the extremities. I should have expected in a fall that injuries would have been found at these parts of the body.

You saw the injury to the left shoulder-blade?—Yes. That is a remarkably strong bone, and well covered below with muscle, but not so much above.

In the case of severe falls have you known that bone to be fractured?—I have found it fractured as spoken of to-day.

It is often broken in the hunting field?—That is a case where the body alights upon the shoulder and receives no other injury.

128

The Boulder.

The walking stick indicates the space towards which Rose's head was lying.

From the photograph produced in Court.

Evidence for Prosecution.

Dr Henry Littlejohn

Do you think there is probability in the view that the same fall could have caused that injury to the shoulder-blade and also to the head?—No. A succession of falls from a considerable height would be required to break up the shoulder-blade and the face.

If the injury to the shoulder-blade had been the result of a fall, would you not have expected the collar-bone to have been fractured also?—It depends on the angle at which the body reaches the ground. But if the shoulder is broken in the way spoken of, that would save the head and *vice versa*, so that the occurrence of both injuries seems to preclude the idea of the injuries being caused by a single fall. If the shoulder reached the ground first, there would be little force expended on the head, while, if the head was first fractured, there would be little effect on the shoulder when it reached the ground.

Was the injury to the shoulder such as might have been caused by a blow downwards?—Quite possible.

Would you expect in that case that it must have been from behind?—It seemed to me as if the blow must have been from behind.

A blunt instrument, such as a stone, might have caused such a fracture?—That is just the kind of instrument that would have been likely to have caused the injury.

Did you see any marks of blood upon the clothes of the deceased?—No.

Did that surprise you?—Not when I looked at the injuries. In all bruises caused by direct violence the vessels themselves are bruised and closed. In cases of incisions the vessels bleed most freely.

If the face was reduced to a soft pulp, would that account for the decomposition?—Yes.

What was your final conclusion regarding these injuries?—It seemed to me as if the injuries on the face must have been caused by striking the face with some hard substance.

Cross-examined by the DEAN OF FACULTY—My first examination was on 27th September. The parts of the left side of the skull were separated from the skull by the time I arrived —they were packed into the skull. I had not the advantage

K   129

John Watson Laurie.

Dr Henry Littlejohn

of seeing them in position. The nasal bones were lying loose in the coffin. By this time the body had been subjected to a great deal of handling.

Apparently the upper parts of the head on both sides and in front were more or less implicated in the injury?—They were. The right side was comparatively intact, with the exception of the fissure passing down towards the ear. The whole of the left side of the skull was gone.

Is it not the case that, in the event of a fall, and a person pitching on his head, you would have very much the same injuries as appear to be inflicted on the upper part of the head?—Quite consistent with a heavy fall on the left side of the head.

I think you found that the base of the skull was very much broken up?—I saw that, and that the parts from side to side were more or less implicated.

Is it a common thing in the case of a fall or severe blow of any kind that you find corresponding fractures on the opposite side?—That is the rule if you have implication of the vault of the cranium, and that would be true of an injury to the vault arising from a heavy fall.

The momentum of a fall of 19 feet or 32 feet would be very great?—Yes.

What would you say would be the effect of such a direct fall upon the bones of the head?—The skull would give way in numerous places unless the arch remained, when the body would rebound.

Where such a heavy impact was made on the head, would that not tend, with the weight of the body, to break the upper jaw-bones?—No; it is not in the line of the momentum. The line of the momentum passes down the spine.

May it not be considered a possibility that there might be injuries in the anterior part of the skull?—It is within the bounds of possibility.

Would it not be extremely difficult to say how, in a smashing fall, the bones of the skull might be knocked about?—I allow that; but I never knew a case in which such injuries involved the bones of the face.

It would depend on the direction in which the force would act?—The force would act down the spine.

130

Evidence for Prosecution.

Dr Henry Littlejohn

Might it not to some extent depend upon the kind of stone the head struck?—It is impossible to dogmatise; it might be so struck as to bring into contact with any rough, hard substance any parts of the head.

You have told us you would have expected lesions on other parts of the body. Now, you have a lesion, and an important lesion, on the left shoulder?—Yes.

You referred us to the hunting field, and the shoulder acting as a buffer; but is it not conceivable that a man might fall downwards from a height, and might so fall to the bottom as to strike with force on the top of his head and shoulder?—Rebounding from crag to crag, he might do so.

What I put to you is this: suppose a hard substance, struck at the bottom, is of such configuration that it simultaneously hits head and shoulder, it would affect both. That is possible?—Yes.

And if it did so strike, it would cause a fracture of both? —If the body fell, and was wedged in between two masses of rock, the injuries might be explained.

Now, you said something in regard to other parts of the body. You were not in a position to know what state the vertebrae were in when the body was discovered. If you were told that the higher cervical vertebra was detached when the body was discovered, would you take special notice of the fact? Would such detachment be consistent either with dislocation or decay of the tissues?—With either.

If the question was between direct blows and a fall, and you found the higher cervical vertebra dislocated, you would have examined whether that was due to decay or stretching of ligaments?—Undoubtedly; but I had no means of doing either.

You did not find anything in the cavity of the chest? The organs were entirely destroyed. Would not the fact of that decay having taken place about six weeks after death rather point to the fact that they had suffered in some way? —Quite possibly. I have already explained why, in my opinion, these organs were entirely destroyed.

You spoke of the abdominal viscera, and particularly the liver. Do you mean that the liver is sometimes ruptured by a heavy fall?—Always.

John Watson Laurie.

Dr Henry Littlejohn

But I suppose you could hardly, without entering into all the conditions of the fall, say what proportion there should be between head damage and other damage in the abdominal viscera?—No, but we assume, when we find such violence to the head, that the liver must necessarily be implicated.

I think you said that one of the points which led you to a conclusion was the absence of injury to the spine?—Yes; with the single exception of the upper vertebra, which was pointed out to me by Dr. Fullarton.

Re-examined by the SOLICITOR-GENERAL—We have been speaking of falls from great heights. What about the case of a fall from 19 feet or thereabouts? Would such a fall as that be at all likely to cause injuries such as you have here—to head, face, and shoulder, all by one impact?—I should say not, unless there was superadded the elasticity by which the body would be lifted up and thrown down again.

In a natural fall, would not there be an effort to save oneself by throwing out the arms?—Undoubtedly, I should expect so.

And therefore the body would be most unlikely to alight on the shoulder or even on the head?—Yes. In the circumstances you would naturally find some injury to the arms. I think a fall from crag to crag must be excluded; because if there had been such a fall, I would have expected injury to the rest of the limbs.

Within 19 feet there is not time for a body to turn round?—Hardly, I think.

[Shown Label No. 13.] Did you remove these pieces of clothing from the body at the instigation of the chief constable of the county?—Yes.

Further cross-examined by the DEAN OF FACULTY—You have said that you would expect that a person falling would try to save himself. No doubt that would be the natural course if the man had a chance to do it—if he had noticed he was going to fall; but if he had slipped down a smooth or slippery rock, he might not readily have a chance of saving himself?—That is possible, but the instinct of self-preservation . . .

Evidence for Prosecution.

Dr Henry Littlejohn

If you are going down frontwise, yes; but you observe the injuries are mainly on one side?—Yes.

He might not very readily turn sidewards or backwards?—No.

By the COURT—In putting out his hands, if there is injury to the head, there must be injury to the arms as well?—Undoubtedly, my Lord.

Have you ever known injuries, of the extent here exhibited, to happen to a person falling on his head?—Rarely, if ever.

JANE VANNEN, examined by Mr. M'KECHNIE—I reside at 3 Commercial Road, Glasgow. I am employed in a broker's shop in the Saltmarket, Glasgow. On 31st July, at four o'clock in the afternoon, I remember a man coming into my shop. I recognise the accused as that man. He offered to sell me a chest of pattern-maker's tools, which a man along with him was carrying. I gave him 25s. for the tools. He gave me no reason for selling them.

Cross-examined by Mr. SCOTT DICKSON—Twenty-five shillings was their full value?—They were in good condition, and I would not have given any more than £1 for them had they not been clean.

ELIZABETH ENNITT, examined by Mr. M'KECHNIE—I am a widow and reside at No. 10 Greek Street, Liverpool, where I keep lodgings. I identify the accused as having come to my house and taken rooms from me on the first Tuesday in August. He had then nothing with him in the way of luggage. He took a room, and later came and brought the trunk now produced [Label No. 22]. He took the room as a permanent lodger, and next morning he paid me 5s. in advance as a week's rent. That was on Sunday morning. On Thursday morning he knocked at my door and said he was going to leave. I said: "I thought you were here permanently." He said he was going to Manchester, where he had a situation and letters at the post office waiting for him, and that he would leave his box. I asked him what he was, and he said he was a commercial traveller in the cotton trade. I saw a description of his box in the newspapers, and informed the police. A policeman came from Scotland and took the box away.

133

John Watson Laurie.

Sydney Alfred Newman

Sydney Alfred Newman, examined by Mr. Graham Murray—I am a tailor and hatter and reside at 379 Brixton Road, London. [Shown Label No. 9.] The soft felt hat now produced is of my manufacture. I know by the private mark that it was sold some time last summer from my shop. I could not swear to the customer, but it was sold in London. I have not exported any of that sort to Scotland.

John Silverman, examined by Mr. Graham Murray—I reside at Olive House, High Road, Balham, London, and I am a partner of the firm of Silverman & Chick, tailors and clothiers, London. I knew the deceased Edwin R. Rose, who was a customer of mine for some years. In June last Mr. Rose ordered a tweed suit with a cap, all of the same material. [Shown Label No. 3.] That is the cap I made for Mr. Rose. [Shown Label No. 7.] That is the stuff of which Mr. Rose's suit was made. [Shown Label No. 2.] These are my firm's buttons, and such as I put on Mr. Rose's suit.

James Baldwin, examined by Mr. Graham Murray—I am a boot and shoemaker in Spring Terrace, Beechcroft Road, Upper Tooting, London. I did not know the deceased, but I knew that a gentleman of that name was a customer of mine. Shoes came from him for repair. [Shown Label No. 11.] These are shoes which belonged to Mr. Rose and which I have repaired. I am certain of them, from the way the heels are nailed on. I recognise my own work.

James Goodman, examined by Mr. Graham Murray—I am a builder, of Mostyn Road, Brixton, London, and Mr. Rose was my clerk. I knew him nearly twenty years. He was a most trustworthy young man, upright and righteous in all his conduct. He enjoyed fairly good health. He went for a fortnight's holiday every year. I did not know that he was going to Scotland last summer, but I afterwards heard about his having been missed, and about the body having been discovered. His cash was balanced before he left, and his books have been through my hands and examined since. They are correct.

134

Evidence for Prosecution.

JOHN PYPER, examined by Mr. M'KECHNIE—I am a criminal officer of the Western District, Glasgow Police. On 14th August I went to Liverpool and brought a trunk belonging to the accused to Glasgow and thence to Rothesay, where it was handed over to the chief constable. [Witness identified a number of articles found in the trunk, Labels Nos. 14 to 21 inclusive.]

MARY REBECCA ALICE ROSE, examined by Mr. GRAHAM MURRAY—I reside at Wisset Lodge, Upper Tooting, London, and I am a sister of the deceased Edwin R. Rose. My brother was a person of cheerful spirits, and he enjoyed very good health. He played lawn tennis and cricket, and was accustomed to walking and running. He was on good terms with all his family, and had no particular troubles to contend with. I knew of his going to Arran for his holidays. On the 18th my brother went to the station to meet him, and when he did not arrive we got alarmed and communicated with Mr. Goodman, who we knew was in Rothesay. [Shown Labels Nos. 3, 9, and 11.] These are similar to the cap, hat, and shoes belonging to my brother. [Shown Label No. 12.] That is my brother's tennis racket, I am sure.

LOUISE ROSE, examined by Mr. GRAHAM MURRAY—I reside at Wisset Lodge, Upper Tooting, London, and I am a sister of the deceased. My brother took part in athletic games, was cheerful, and enjoyed good health and spirits. He was in full possession not only of his mental faculties, but of his bodily powers. [The witness identified the sachet, brush and comb bag, and shirt, Labels Nos. 14, 15, and 18, as belonging to her brother.] With regard to the white shirt, I recognise the laundry mark " 48 T." I find on that shirt a stamped impression of the name " John W. Laurie " —such a stamped impression as might be put on with an impress stamp. My brother's shirts, when last I saw them, had no " John W. Laurie " on them.

ALICE BARNES, examined by Mr. GRAHAM MURRAY—I reside at South Lambeth Road, London, and I am in the employment of Robert Cook & Company. We do the washing of

135

John Watson Laurie.

the Rose family. [Shown Label No. 18.] I recognise the washing mark " 48 T " on this shirt shown to me. It belonged to the deceased Mr. Rose. I put it there to distinguish the Rose family. I also see a stamped impression " John W. Laurie." That was not on it when I washed the shirt. [Shown Label No. 19.] I recognise the washing mark " 48 T " on that shirt, which bears also the stamp " John W. Laurie."

The LORD JUSTICE-CLERK—It is exceedingly desirable that this case should not be carried over Sunday. I wish it to be distinctly understood—and I am sure the jury will be with me—this case must be finished to-morrow night.

[The Court adjourned.]

Evidence for Prosecution.

Second Day—Saturday, 9th November, 1889.

Mrs. MARY CURRIE, examined by the SOLICITOR-GENERAL—I am the wife of John Currie, Iona Place, Port Bannatyne, Buteshire, and I am in the habit of letting my house to summer visitors. I know the accused. He came and asked me for a room in July last. He took the room at a rent of £1 a week. That was on Saturday, 6th July. He had with him, when he came, a small brown leather bag and an umbrella. One day in the following week he went to Glasgow and returned to my house the next day. He left my house again on Friday, the 12th, and said he was going to Arran for a trip. He did not sleep in my house that night. When he came to my house the name he gave was " John Annandale." He had in his possession when he arrived a brown felt hat and a straw hat. When he went to Arran he took the straw hat with him, leaving the other one in the house. I remember seeing one of his calling cards on the table, bearing the name " John Annandale." He returned to my house on Tuesday, 16th July. He was then wearing an overcoat. He had a small paper parcel with him, and he wore a grey felt hat. [Shown Label No. 9.] That is similar to the hat he was wearing. When he finally left my house he left the grey felt hat and took the brown hat away. I saw what the paper parcel contained; it contained a white serge cap and a tennis coat with chocolate-brown and white stripes. [Witness identified Label No. 10.] That was all that was in the parcel. I saw under the washing-stand a pair of tennis shoes. [Shown Label No. 11.] These are the shoes I saw. These shoes were not there before the accused returned from Arran, and he left them in my house when he went away. I saw him wearing the cap on his head. He remained with me from the Tuesday till the following Saturday, the 20th. His time was up on the Saturday, and in the morning he said he was going away. I was to have his dinner and bill ready at one o'clock, as he had to start immediately after that. He did not return for

John Watson Laurie.

his dinner and bill, and I never saw him again; I never saw him after he went out in the morning. The amount of his bill was £3 3s. 8d., and it remains unpaid. Besides the articles mentioned which he left in my house, the accused also left a small hairbrush and a pair of white flannel trousers. He had the trousers on when he first came. In conversation with me he referred to his visit to Arran. He said he was going there with a gentleman friend. When he returned I asked him if he had enjoyed his trip, and he said "Yes."

Cross-examined by Mr. SCOTT DICKSON—Did you ask him whether he had been up Goatfell?—Yes. He said "Yes," and talked quite pleasantly about it.

Was he pleasant and agreeable in his manner?—Yes.

Did you notice anything different in his manner when he came back?—He was as pleasant and chatty and agreeable as before.

He was quite willing to tell about his visit to Arran?—Yes.

FLORA CURRIE, a daughter of the last witness, in answer to the Solicitor-General, gave corroborative evidence as to the accused taking lodgings in her mother's house. He occupied these under the name of "John Annandale." He went to Arran, returned, and finally left on Saturday, 20th July.

FRANCIS ORD MICKEL, examined by the SOLICITOR-GENERAL —I am a wood merchant and reside at Friarsbrae, Linlithgow. During my holidays last summer I stayed for some time in the Glenburn Hydropathic, at Rothesay. I arrived there on 8th July. My companion was Mr. Thom, Linlithgow. The first night I was there I made the acquaintance of a young English gentleman, Edwin Robert Rose, who was staying there. We "chummed" with him a good deal during the rest of our stay. He struck me as a person of agreeable manners, frank, open, and ready to take up with strangers. I remember him wearing a light, slate-coloured felt hat, a tweed suit, light coat, and white vest. He also wore a grey felt hat. [Shown Label No. 9.] That is similar to the hat he wore, but I could not swear to it.

138

Evidence for Prosecution.

Francis Ord Mickel

He also wore a brown pair of shoes and a chocolate-and-white tennis coat. He had a black waterproof coat, white inside. [Witness identified Labels Nos. 1 and 10 as belonging to deceased.] I saw a small pocket-book in his possession, and he said it contained a half-return ticket to London. He gave me a leaf out of that book, in which he had written his name. He had a Gladstone bag with a strap at both ends. While we were going about, and sharing expenses, the deceased seemed to have a sufficiency of money in his possession, and he paid his way. He wore a watch and chain—I cannot remember what the chain was like. I remember a picnic party going from the Hydropathic to Arran on 12th July. The deceased, Thom, and myself were in the party, and it was on that occasion that Rose made the acquaintance of the accused. I recognise the accused as the man with whom Rose struck up an acquaintance on board the *Ivanhoe;* I did not know him before that. I did not see them speaking, but Rose told me that he had made his acquaintance. He said he had met with a man named "Annandale" on board the boat. That was all he told me on the Friday night. On Saturday I told Rose I proposed going to Arran to stay from Saturday till Monday, and he said that he also was going and had arranged with the young man "Annandale" to share his rooms.

By the COURT—He was going to live with "Annandale."

Examination continued—Thom and I started the next day for Brodick on board the *Ivanhoe*. Rose and the accused came also.

Did they come together?—Not together. They joined each other on board the *Ivanhoe*. The deceased introduced me to the accused on board the steamer, and when we arrived at Arran we were together the most of the day. When we arrived at Brodick, about 2.30 on the Saturday, we disposed of our bags. After putting our things away, Thom and I went a short walk, came back, had some refreshments, and met "Annandale" and Rose. Rose and the accused each had a bag. I saw them again on the Sunday. We were not a great deal in their company during the day. We walked across to Lamlash and they left us. We saw them at night, as they were returning from Glen Rosa. On

John Watson Laurie.

Francis Ord Mickel

Monday, 15th July, I saw Rose at breakfast in Wooley's about ten o'clock. The accused was not with him then. He came in before we left. The deceased had white flannel trousers on, and I advised him to change them for his tweeds, if he intended climbing Goatfell. He did so. "Annandale" complained of toothache, and he left us to get some quinine powder. Before they left to climb Goatfell we had a row in the bay with them. The last I saw of Rose was on the pier when Mr. Thom and I were preparing to leave.

Had you any conversation with Rose on that occasion?—Yes. I took him aside and told him that I did not care for "Annandale's" manner. His appearing and disappearing were extremely peculiar, and I strongly advised the deceased to get rid of him as soon as possible, even if he had to leave his lodgings, and not to climb Goatfell.

What did the deceased say in answer to you?—He said that, as I had spoken to him so often of trying to get rid of "Annandale," he would not climb Goatfell, and promised to try and get rid of him. I had spoken to him to the same effect before—on the Saturday night and on the Sunday morning.

Then you had early formed an unfavourable opinion of "Annandale"?—Yes. He was very silent and uncommunicative.

Did you know anything about him?—I did not ask any direct questions; but I hinted, and tried to find out where he came from and what he was. I could not get a satisfactory answer.

When you last saw Rose he was wearing a tweed suit and had a stick?—He had a stick in his hand.

Just tell us what he had on at the time when you saw him last on the pier?—He had on a tweed suit and a cap to match, a pair of small leggings and leather boots, with his waterproof under his arm. I did not notice if he was wearing his watch. I do not remember that I noticed anything else about him. [Shown Label No. 3.] That is the cap Rose was wearing; it corresponds with the suit.

Cross-examined by the DEAN OF FACULTY—You made Rose's

Evidence for Prosecution.

acquaintance casually at Rothesay, and he just met "Annandale" casually in the same way, so that you were both casual acquaintances?—Yes.

You apparently had some conversation with "Annandale." You asked him some questions?—I did not ask him any direct questions. I did not care about going about with him unless I knew something about him.

You did not need to go about with him unless you liked?—Rose was going about with him.

You thought he was rather silent and uncommunicative?—Very.

Did you know that he was suffering from toothache?—Yes, on the Monday.

You did not know whether he was troubled with it before or not?—No.

Had you seen "Annandale" at the Hydropathic on the Friday evening?—I had.

Re-examined by the SOLICITOR-GENERAL—You had formed an acquaintance with Rose and a liking for him?—Yes.

Was it your interest in him that led to your warning him the way you did?—Certainly.

By the COURT—You spoke about "Annandale" appearing and disappearing. What do you mean by that?—While Rose, "Annandale," and I were standing together, "Annandale" would suddenly go away without saying where he was going or what he was about.

That raised a feeling of doubt in your mind?—Yes.

WILLIAM THOM, examined by the SOLICITOR-GENERAL—I am a commercial traveller and reside at Linlithgow. I was with Mr. Mickel at the Hydropathic in Rothesay last July. I there made the acquaintance of the deceased, and he was a good deal in my company afterwards. I remember going to Arran with him. I went first on Friday, 12th July, and we returned again to Rothesay. On the Saturday we went again to Arran on the *Ivanhoe*. The deceased had by that time formed the acquaintance of the accused. He told me he had met "Annandale" and introduced him to me. I know that Rose occupied the same room with the accused in Arran from the Saturday to the Monday. I saw a good deal of

141

them on the Saturday and Sunday. On the Monday I saw very little of Rose or " Annandale " till about one o'clock. We then had a walk about for some time, and afterwards had something to eat in Wooley's before leaving. We left at half-past three by the *Ivanhoe*, and we left " Annandale " and Rose standing on the pier. Rose was then wearing a tweed suit with a cap to match. He wore a pair of short leggings, but I could not say whether he had a waterproof. [Shown Label No. 3.] I identify the cap now shown me as the cap deceased was wearing. Whilst I knew the deceased he had a watch and chain.

When you left them on the pier, were they preparing to ascend Goatfell?—No. They said nothing at that time about going up the mountain. The deceased had spoken about it on the previous day, remarking that he intended to ascend Goatfell with " Annandale."

When you last saw them, did you think they had given up the idea?—Oh, no. [Witness was shown Labels Nos. 9, 10, and 11, all of which articles he said were very like those worn by Rose.]

Cross-examined by the DEAN OF FACULTY—Do you remember, on the Friday evening, at the Hydropathic, Rose asking you to show " Annandale " round the place?—Yes. I did so, and left him in the recreation room. This was while Mr. Rose was changing his clothes.

Did you and Mr. Mickel try to get rooms in Arran?—We expected to stay with some friends, but they were full up on the Saturday, and we could not get rooms; so we had to sleep on a friend's yacht.

Did you know that " Annandale " had got a room?—Yes.

Do you know that it was to give accommodation to Rose that he allowed him to share it?—Yes.

Do you remember Rose bringing out " Annandale " to your friend's yacht along with Mickel on the Monday?—Yes.

Do you also remember Rose, " Annandale," Mickel, and yourself being in Wooley's shop together on the Saturday?—Yes.

Had you some friends named Gilmour at Corrie?—Yes.

Did you ask the three gentlemen to visit them?—Yes.

Evidence for Prosecution.

And you all had tea there?—We had.

Was not "Annandale" being taken about and introduced, not only by Rose but by mutual friends, as Rose's friend?—Yes.

Mrs. ESTHER WALKER, examined by Mr. GRAHAM MURRAY—I am the wife of William Walker, shoemaker, Invercloy, Brodick, Arran. I remember on Friday, 12th July, Mrs. Shaw brought a young man to my house for a room. He did not tell me his name, but he handed me a card with the name "John Annandale" on it. The accused is the man. He came between one and two o'clock the next day, after the steamer came in from Bute, and took possession. He was accompanied by another gentleman, whom he did not introduce to me. He said his friend would share his bedroom and take his meals outside. Mr. "Annandale" himself was to take his food in his room. I have since seen a photograph of the deceased Mr. Rose, and I recognise him as the gentleman who was with Mr. "Annandale." They were very little in the house at that time. At the same time I had also in the house a brother and a brother-in-law, Alexander Morrison and Thomas Purdon. The room occupied by "Annandale" and Rose was situated at the end of the house outside, so that one could only get into it from the outside. The young men occupied that room on the nights of Saturday and Sunday. On the Monday they went out in the morning, and I heard they had gone somewhere. That night we went to bed about twelve o'clock. At that time I could not say whether either of the lodgers had returned. It was possible, however, that they might have returned without my knowing it. Next morning I went to their room about eleven o'clock. I did not want to disturb them early, because I thought they had been out late. I knocked and got no answer. I then looked into the room and found both the gentlemen and the bags were gone. I found a straw hat, a pair of slippers, a waterproof coat, and a tennis racket, all belonging to the occupants of the room. [Shown Label No. 12.] I identify the racket produced as the racket which was left in my house. I handed these articles to the police. The lodgers had two bags. One was a pretty large bag,

143

John Watson Laurie.

black in colour. As to the colour of the other I could not be certain. Neither " Annandale " nor Rose ever came back, and my bill was never paid. " Annandale " had taken the room for a week.

Did he say anything about his movements or his friend's? —He said his friend would not stay longer than the Tuesday or the Wednesday.

Did he say he came from Tighnabruaich?—Yes.

Did he say anything about coming from Rothesay or Port Bannatyne?—No.

Cross-examined by the DEAN OF FACULTY—Is Tighna-bruaich on the way from Rothesay?—Yes.

Do you let your rooms by the week?—Yes.

Is it a little " lie-to " at the end of the house, to meet the demand there is in summer at a time like the Fair holidays? —Yes; swarms of people come down, and many of them sleep out.

Would you let your room for less than a week?—I would not think of letting it for less than a week.

How much was " Annandale " to pay?—Seventeen shillings for the week; and when he mentioned that his friend was coming, he said he would give me 3s. extra.

How many beds are there in the room?—There is just one bed in the room.

Did " Annandale " complain of toothache on the Monday afternoon at dinner time?—Yes, he said he could not eat for it.

Re-examined by Mr. GRAHAM MURRAY—When did he dine on that Monday afternoon?—At two o'clock.

Mrs. ISABELLA WOOLEY, examined by Mr. GRAHAM MURRAY —I am the wife of Alexander Wooley, baker, Brodick. Attached to my shop is a tearoom. In July last a young gentleman named Rose came and took his meals there on a Sunday. He did not know the name of his landlady. He told me, however, that he was lodging quite close at hand. He also told me he had a friend with him, called Mr. " Annandale," and that he had newly made his acquaintance since he came to Scotland. He told me he had been with him

144

Evidence for Prosecution.

at the Hydropathic at Rothesay. He told me also that he was going home on Thursday to London. On the Sunday, when he took his meal, he asked for writing materials, saying he had several letters to write, and he wrote them. He told me that on Monday he intended to ascend Goatfell. [Shown Labels Nos. 9 and 10.] I saw him wearing the soft hat and the yachting cap now shown to me.

ALEXANDER MORRISON, examined by Mr. GRAHAM MURRAY— I am a shoemaker and I reside at 14 Carfin Street, Govanhill, Glasgow. I am a brother of the last witness, Mrs. Walker. On Saturday, 13th July, I paid a visit to my sister at Brodick. I had along with me my brother-in-law, Thomas Purdon. We lived in my sister's house and stayed there till the 18th. On Sunday, the 14th, I remember seeing two young gentlemen in the house. In particular, I saw a gentleman named Rose. I knew at that time of a Mr. "Annandale" being in his company, and saw him going about. On Monday Purdon and I went up Goatfell. As we were coming down, we met these two gentlemen I have spoken of, going in the opposite direction. The deceased was one of them, and the other was, as I understood, Mr. "Annandale." The place at which we met them was in the Castle grounds. We got home at five minutes to five. From the point at which we met them to the house, it would take about fifty minutes. They were walking at a pretty sharp pace and were going straight in the direction of Goatfell. I never saw them again. I heard next morning that my sister's lodgers had gone.

Cross-examined by Mr. SCOTT DICKSON—When you were coming down, did you meet a good many people going up? —Yes.

Did you know any of the other people except the two you have mentioned?—No.

How many people did you meet in all?—About seven.

THOMAS PURDON, examined by Mr. GRAHAM MURRAY—I am a sailmaker, and I reside at 33 Marlow Street, Kinning Park, Glasgow. I was staying with my sister-in-law at Brodick on 13th July of this year, and I remained there till

L

John Watson Laurie.

the following Thursday. I knew that " Annandale," whom I now recognise as the accused, was staying there, and that he had a friend with him. On Monday, the 15th, I went up Goatfell with the last witness, Morrison. On coming down, we met " Annandale " and another young gentleman. That would be about five minutes past four. They were going at a good pace in the direction which people would take going up to Goatfell. " Annandale's " companion had on a light suit, all the things being made in the same style. I noticed he was wearing a watch chain. I never saw them again.

Cross-examined by Mr. Scott Dickson—Could you swear to the chain if you saw it again ?—No, but I remember seeing it at the time I passed.

Did you meet a good many people going up ?—Yes.

It was a day when a good many people were going up and down ?—Yes.

Rev. Robert Hind, examined by the Solicitor-General— I reside at the Manse, St. James Street, Paisley, and in July last I was staying in Lamlash from the 10th to the 18th. With me was a Mr. M'Cabe, from Hamilton. On Monday, 15th July, Mr. M'Cabe, the Rev. Joseph Ritson, from Motherwell, and myself went from Lamlash to Brodick and ascended Goatfell. We started from Brodick about three o'clock. We took the ordinary route through the Castle woods, past the keeper's house, into the open, and up the usual well-defined path.

Do you remember being overtaken by two young men after you got some distance beyond the Castle woods ?—Yes, when we were out on the open hill.

About what time did these two young men overtake you ?— Possibly about four o'clock, or perhaps a little later.

Just look at the accused. Do you think he is one of them ? —I think he is exceedingly like one of them.

You cannot say more than that ?—No.

What was the other like ?—He was a much more slenderly built young man. He was of dark complexion and had, I think, black hair and a black moustache.

146

Evidence for Prosecution.

Rev. Robert Hind

In what kind of clothes was he dressed?—The suit of clothes was not one that made any definite impression on my mind. I could hardly define the suit of clothes, because it was not striking.

Tweeds, I suppose?—I think they would be.

When the two men overtook you first, did they join you or pass you?—They went immediately past us.

Did you say anything to them at that time?—I think not.

When did you see them next?—Almost immediately afterwards we overtook them, and, still going up the hill, we walked together for twenty minutes or half an hour.

On that occasion you had conversation with them, of course?—We had conversation with the dark young man.

As much as the ascent of the hill allowed?—Yes.

In what order were you going? In Indian file or all together?—For the most part we were in Indian file, but I should say we sometimes changed places, that is, we were not always in one order. For instance, I was sometimes last and sometimes second.

Who led as a rule?—The light-complexioned young man whom we had joined.

The man whom you think is like the accused?—Yes.

Had you any conversation with him?—None whatever.

Did he, as a rule, keep ahead of the party?—He kept steadily 5 or 6 yards ahead.

I suppose your conversation with the dark young man was about casual subjects?—I think it began between Mr. M'Cabe and him.

You had no particular conversation with the dark young man?—After he had said that he had come from much farther south than Hamilton, where Mr. M'Cabe came from, I think I remember asking him if he came from very far south, because I thought he might be from the north of England, where I have frequently lived. He then said he came from London.

After you had been in their company for half an hour what happened?—A shower of rain came on; and as our party had no overcoats we went to shelter behind boulders, and the other two went on.

John Watson Laurie.

Rev. Robert Hind

Did you notice if they put on their waterproofs?—I did not notice; but they had them.

How long did you remain in shelter?—For about ten minutes. It was just a passing shower. Then at a point farther up the hill we took shelter for perhaps other ten minutes.

When did you see the two young men next?—We saw them a good distance on before us as we went up, and I also saw them on the top of Goatfell.

When did you reach the top of Goatfell?—About six o'clock.

How long did you remain there?—About a quarter of an hour or so. We got down to Brodick in time for the 8.30 boat from Lamlash.

Did you take any particular notice of the two men when you saw them at the top?—No. I only saw them for a minute or two, because I was taken up pretty much by the scenery. I saw the young men on the farther edge of the summit of the fell from the point where we reached the top.

Were the young men standing when you saw them?—I think so.

Were they on the edge of the mountain nearest Brodick, or on the edge nearest Glen Sannox?—I am not sufficiently acquainted with the mountain to say that.

You were not within speaking distance?—No.

Did you see them again?—No.

By the COURT—Did they get out of your sight a minute or two after you saw them?—Yes.

Examination continued—Did you descend by the same way as you had gone up?—Yes.

And did you see them on the way?—No.

Was anything said about that at the time?—I remember I mentioned to my friends that I had seen the young men on the top, and as they were not on the road before us— and we could see, I should think, quite 2 miles down—I wondered what had become of them. Mr. M'Cabe, who had been on Goatfell before and who had gone back on the former occasion by way of Glen Sannox, said they had probably gone by the Glen Sannox route, and that if they had done so they had undertaken rather a difficult task. On the top I saw two other young men with photographic apparatus.

148

Evidence for Prosecution.

Rev. Robert Hind

[Shown witnesses Frederick and Edward Francis.] I think these are the two young men I saw, but I took so little notice of them that I could not really say definitely.

By the COURT—You are not supposed to identify them?—I think they are the gentlemen.

Examination continued—These men are not the two men I saw on the farther ridge. The young gentlemen with the photographic apparatus came down by the route we went up.

Cross-examined by Mr. SCOTT DICKSON—Did you see several other parties on the hill besides these young gentlemen?—Yes.

You saw one gentleman trying to break the record?—He was going at a tremendous rate for the top.

Was there a mist when you reached the top?—Only on the side opposite that which we came up. We had a splendid view on the other three sides.

For the summit of a mountain, is the top of Goatfell very broad?—No, not very broad.

Were you the last person to leave the summit?—Yes.

You seem to have expected that the young men you saw on the farther ridge would have been on the road before you to Brodick?—Yes.

Could they have got over to that side without you observing them?—Certainly not.

Why did you expect to find them?—Because on looking round, before leaving the summit, there was no one there.

They might have got behind a boulder unseen by you?—Yes.

Re-examined by the SOLICITOR-GENERAL—Was the mist such as to interfere with your descent?—No, it was on the farther side.

JOHN M'CABE, examined by the SOLICITOR-GENERAL—I reside at Cramlington Cottage, Leechlea, Hamilton. On Monday, 15th July last, I ascended Goatfell along with Mr. Hind and Mr. Ritson. I remember being overtaken by two young men. In general appearance the accused is like one of the men, but I cannot absolutely identify him. The other gentleman was somewhat taller and dressed in a tweed suit. I think he was somewhat thinner. I cannot say if he had

John M'Cabe

dark hair. They first passed us, and then we came up with them and continued with them for some distance up the hill, walking in Indian file. For the greater part of the way the man who resembled the accused was in front. He never spoke. I had, however, some conversation with the other young man, and he told me that he came from London.

Did he give you any other particulars about himself?— He referred to the other young man, and said he was his guide, and he also told me that he had been staying at Rothesay, although he did not say he was on holiday. We stopped for shelter, and the other two went on; we could see them going before us for a very long time until we came to the steepest part of the hill, when I lost sight of them. We reached the summit about twenty minutes past six, and remained upon it for ten minutes or a quarter of an hour. I saw two other young men who were carrying photographic apparatus, but I had no conversation with them, and I do not think I should know them again if I saw them. I saw them going down in front of us.

Cross-examined by Mr. SCOTT DICKSON—How far in front? —Only a few yards.

Rev. JOSEPH RITSON, examined by the SOLICITOR-GENERAL —I reside at Avon Street, Motherwell, and I am minister of the Primitive Methodist congregation in Motherwell. On 15th July last I ascended Goatfell with Mr. Hind and Mr. M'Cabe. I remember two young men overtaking us and passing us. We subsequently came up with them again, and went some distance up the hill with them.

Look at the accused: do you think he was one of the men?— The accused has a very striking resemblance to one of the men I saw.

As regards the other, were you afterwards shown a photograph of Mr. Rose, and did you recognise it as that of the young gentleman who said he was from London, and who was along with the man whom the accused resembles?—Yes.

Did you see these two men on the top of the hill?—No. The last I saw of them was when they were ascending the highest ridge ahead of us, after the shower which compelled us to seek shelter. In coming down we wondered what had

150

Evidence for Prosecution.

become of them, because we were unable to see them either in front of us or behind us.

Had you any conversation with the man like the accused?—He never spoke to any of us. He was generally ahead.

Was there a mist?—The mist was on the very summit, and on the west and south-west.

Was there any mist in the direction of Glen Sannox?—The mist was away from the glen, I think. Glen Sannox, I should say, is to the north-east.

FREDERICK WILLIAM FRANCIS, examined by the SOLICITOR-GENERAL—I am an electrician and reside with my father at 262 Brockley Road, Brockley, London, S.E. My brother Edward and I were in Brodick on Monday, 15th July last, and on that day we ascended Goatfell, starting about three o'clock in the afternoon. I had my photographic apparatus with me, and took a few photographs on the way. Some distance from the top my brother became tired and decided to rest, and I went on, and reached the summit about twenty minutes before him. When I saw him coming up the last ascent two young men were with him.

Do you think the accused is like one of the two?—He is somewhat like one of them. The other was of dark complexion and had a black moustache. He seemed to be an Englishman, so far as I could judge from his tongue. He was wearing a black mackintosh. [Shown Label No. 6.] His mackintosh was similar to the one I see before me, but it was apparently a new one, and not in the split condition in which I see this one. When I saw my brother and the others ascending the hill, they were in single file—the man resembling the accused being first, the Englishman second, and my brother last. We had some conversation on the top about the scenery. I do not remember the Englishman asking any questions about the way down. The two men afterwards jumped on to a large boulder and looked towards Ailsa Craig. The man like the accused pointed it out. Both men seemed strong and active. I did not see them leaving the hill; the last I saw of them was on the top of the boulder, with their backs to Ailsa Craig, pointing in an opposite direction. They were apparently arranging about going down, and

John Watson Laurie.

Frederick W. Francis

the direction in which they pointed was not that by which they had ascended. I remember the three gentlemen, Messrs. Hind, Ritson, and M'Cabe, coming up on to the summit. When we left the summit it would be about twenty-five minutes past six. My brother and I came down a few yards with Mr. Ritson and then we went ahead.

Cross-examined by Mr. SCOTT DICKSON—The two young men, with whom your brother came up, were looking towards the right of the road by which you came up?—Yes.

Was that the last you saw of them?—Yes.

Did you and Mr. Ritson's party practically leave the summit together?—Yes.

You thought, when you saw them standing on the boulder, they were arranging about the direction in which they were to descend?—Yes.

That was purely inference on your part?—Yes.

Did the young men seem to be on friendly terms?—Oh yes, they appeared to be on good terms.

They were talking together?—Yes.

EDWARD JOHN FRANCIS, examined by the SOLICITOR-GENERAL, corroborated the evidence given by his brother, the previous witness, as to being on Goatfell on 15th July and seeing the accused and the deceased there. He identified the accused. He did not know in which direction the accused and Rose went after he left the summit with his brother.

DAVID M'KENZIE, examined by the SOLICITOR-GENERAL—I am a shepherd and reside at South High Corrie, Arran. On Monday, 15th July, I was near Sannox burying-ground. There is a distance of about 3 miles between the sea and the head of Glen Sannox. The burying-ground is about a quarter of a mile from the sea, and about a mile and a quarter from Corrie Hotel. A person coming out of Glen Sannox to Corrie Hotel would either pass the burying-ground or go through a neighbouring field for a short cut. On the day in question I was near the burying-ground between nine and half-past nine in the evening, and I noticed a man coming out of Glen Sannox. When I noticed him he was half-way between the main road and the burying-ground, coming through the

Evidence for Prosecution.

David M'Kenzie

field I have mentioned. He would be about 300 yards from the main road, taking the short cut through the field from Glen Sannox to Corrie.

Did anything attract your attention to him?—Well, I made a remark to two girls that I had passed a man, but that I did not know who he was; that he was awful tired and worn out like, and that he appeared to have had a heavy day's travelling on the hills.

Look at the accused : is that the man you saw coming out of Glen Sannox?—Yes, sir, that is the man.

Would a man standing at the top of Goatfell, with his back to Ailsa Craig, be facing in the direction of Glen Sannox?—Yes, in a north-east direction.

Does Glen Sannox lie to the north?—It lies to the north-east.

And the glen to the west is Glen Rosa?—Yes.

Cross-examined by the DEAN OF FACULTY—You did not mention the names of the two girls who were with you?—One of them is named Macdonald; I do not know the other. They were servant girls to some visitors, and were taking a walk.

What did you say to them?—I just merely said that I passed a man; that I did not know who he was; that he was awful tired and worn out like, and that he appeared to have had a heavy day's travelling on the hills.

That was all that passed?—Yes.

JAMES WILSON, examined by Mr. M'KECHNIE—I am a law clerk, of 2 Shaw Place, Greenock. On 15th July last I was holidaying in Arran, at Corrie. On that day I was away with a picnic party and returned to Corrie about ten o'clock at night. I felt cold and went into the hotel, where I ordered some refreshment at the bar, which is situated in the lobby. I saw the accused there—he was there before I arrived. He spoke to me, asking if I could get him something to drink. As far as I remember, he told me that he thought it was past the hour, and that he could not get it for himself. I suppose he took me for a guest in the hotel. I asked him what he wanted, and he said he would have a bottle of beer. I asked the girl at the bar to let him have it, and he got it and paid for it himself. After that I left him standing at the bar, and went into the smoking-room.

153

John Watson Laurie.

Cross-examined by the DEAN OF FACULTY—Is ten the closing hour of the hotel?—Yes.

And did he indicate to you that he would have difficulty in getting a drink?—That was what I understood.

Did he say anything as to where he was going?—He said he had a long walk—that he had to walk back to Brodick that night.

And so he had a glass of beer and walked off?—Yes.

What is the distance?—About 6 miles.

MARGARET LIVINGSTON, examined by Mr. M'KECHNIE—I am barmaid at the Corrie Hotel, Arran. I was in the bar on the night of 15th July, when Mr. Wilson, the previous witness, whom I know, came into the lobby and forward to the bar. I saw another man standing there at the time. This was about ten o'clock. Mr. Wilson asked for a drink for the other man, and he afterwards went into the smoking-room. The other man wished to purchase drink. I put some in a bottle and sold it to him. It was spirits; it might have been brandy or whisky. He said that he required spirits because he had to walk to Brodick. He then went away.

Look at the accused: is he like the man who came into the bar that night with Mr. Wilson?—I could not recognise the man.

I suppose you see a great many in the bar at that time?—Yes.

MARY ROBERTSON, examined by Mr. GRAHAM MURRAY—I live at 5 Hill Street, Kilmarnock. In July last I was staying at Invercloy, Arran, on a visit. On the morning of Tuesday, 16th July, I went to Brodick pier at seven o'clock in order to get a steamer. Between my lodgings and the pier I passed a man carrying two bags—one dark and the other a sort of yellow.

Look at the accused: is that the man you passed with the bags?—Yes, that is the man. He was seemingly going in the same direction as I was.

ANDREW FRANCIS CRAIG GILMOUR, examined by Mr. GRAHAM MURRAY—I am a student of medicine and I reside at High

154

Evidence for Prosecution.

Andrew F. C. Gilmour

Street, Linlithgow. Last July I was staying in Corrie for some days. On Saturday, the 13th, I met Mr. Mickel and Mr. Thom. They came in the *Ivanhoe*. When they arrived they introduced me to two other young men—Mr. Rose and Mr. " Annandale."

Look at the accused and tell me if that is the man introduced as Mr. " Annandale " ?—Yes, that is the man.

Did you notice what Rose was wearing?—No, I did not notice particularly.

Anything about his demeanour?—Yes, Rose was very talkative.

Was the other man quiet?—Very quiet.

On Tuesday, 16th July, I think you left Brodick for Ardrossan to go home?—I left by the steamer *Scotia* at ten minutes past seven in the morning. On going on board I saw " Annandale " and recognised him as the person to whom I had been introduced on the Saturday, and so I spoke to him. He said he was going to Glasgow.

Did you notice whether " Annandale " had any luggage? —Yes. I don't exactly remember what kind of luggage, but he had bags with him.

Are you sure that he had more than one?—I cannot remember.

Did you offer to help him to carry it?—Yes.

Do you think it would be likely you would have offered to help him if he had had only one bag?—No. [Shown Label No. 9.] The accused was wearing a slate-coloured hat on that occasion similar to the one which is now shown to me. We got into the same railway compartment. He took a black-coloured leather bag into the compartment with him. I saw it in the rack. We parted at Greenock Station.

Mrs. ELLEN KING, examined by Mr. GRAHAM MURRAY—I am a widow and reside at 106 North Frederick Street, Glasgow. I let lodgings. I knew the accused under the name of John Laurie. I first made his acquaintance on the 8th of June last when he came to my house with the view of taking lodgings. He took lodgings, sharing a bedroom and parlour with another gentleman, Mr. Matthew Eaglesome, who stayed with me until a fortnight ago. The accused told me that

155

John Watson Laurie.

Mrs Ellen King

he worked at Springburn; that he had come to that neighbourhood because he could not get the train up to his work.

Did he say what he worked at?—He said, I think, he was an engineer, but I could not understand it—a superior engineer. I went away to the coast in July. My lodgers went on as before, but I only saw Laurie once during the month.

But on the night of Friday, the 12th, you stayed at home?—Yes.

Was Laurie in the house then?—Well, he was; but he used to go out in the morning at six o'clock, and he did not come in till I was in bed at night.

Did you see him on the 12th?—No, I saw him on Friday, 26th July.

That was the only time you saw him in July?—Yes.

What time was this?—In the evening, about six or seven o'clock. He did not say anything to me regarding what he had been doing. He came in only for a second. He merely said to me, " You have got home," and I replied, " Yes." I got back for good to my house on the 1st of August and found that Laurie had left on the previous night. On the 3rd of the month I got a letter from Laurie. [Shown Production No. 6.] That is the letter I received from the accused. It is addressed to me in Glasgow, written on a scrap of paper, and reads : " Dear Madam,—I beg to enclose P.O.O. for my rent as I can't call for I have to go to Leith. There are some people trying to get me into trouble and I think you should give them no information at all, and I will prove to them how they are mistaken before very long.—Yours respectfully, John Laurie." I kept that letter and eventually gave it to the police, with whom I communicated in respect of what I saw in the papers, and on account of what Laurie left behind him at my house. I gave the police all the things he left. [Shown Label No. 22.] That is the trunk which Laurie brought to my house. He did not leave that behind; he took it away with him.

Cross-examined by the DEAN OF FACULTY—Was this P.O.O., which accompanied the letter, for the rent that was due?—Yes.

What was the amount?—Four shillings.

Evidence for Prosecution.

JANE M'LELLAN, examined by Mr. GRAHAM MURRAY—I am a domestic servant employed by Dr. Ronald Currie, Skelmorlie, Ayrshire. In July last I was employed in the service of Mrs. Ellen King. While I was there the accused lodged in Mrs. King's house, occupying a bedroom and parlour with Mr. Eaglesome. I remember the accused going away in July for holidays. He went away on the 6th and came back about the 19th. While he was away Mrs. King was at the coast. She was away when Laurie came back. Mrs. King returned for good on 1st August, the accused having left the night before she returned. He said he was going to Leith, where he had got a situation, and that he should have given longer notice that he was leaving. I never saw him again.

MATTHEW EAGLESOME, examined by Mr. GRAHAM MURRAY— I am a letter sorter, and I reside at 106 North Frederick Street, Glasgow, the house of Mrs. King. In July of last year the accused occupied a room with me at Mrs. King's. I was absent when he went away in July for his holidays. I came back and found he had gone. When he came back he did not say anything to me as to what he had been doing. We were not particularly intimate. I remember him leaving for good. He left suddenly, saying he had got a situation at Leith. I remember he did say he had been in Arran. I saw him with a light-brown bag, never with a black one.

Did the accused ever say anything to you about what he was going to do at the end of the season?—He expected to go to London.

Did he give you any reason why he expected to go there?— He said he had got a ticket for London.

What kind of ticket?—A return ticket.

Had he come from London at any time, so far as he told you?—No.

Did he explain to you how, not having come from London, he was in possession of a return ticket to London?—No.

JAMES GILLON AITKEN, examined by the SOLICITOR-GENERAL —I am a grain salesman, residing at 3 Lansdowne Place, Shawlands, Glasgow. On 6th July I went to Rothesay for a

John Watson Laurie.

James G. Aitken

holiday. On arriving there I saw the accused on the pier; I knew him from having met him in Rothesay the year before. In the week following the 6th I saw him two or three times. On Friday, the 12th, I was on board the *Ivanhoe*, bound for Arran, and the accused was there. I introduced him to some of my friends.

Shortly afterwards do you remember him saying to your friends and to you anything about a strange incident?—I recollect that he said a strange coincidence had happened to him. He said a gentleman had spoken to him, taking him for a man who was staying at the Hydropathic. The accused said he must have made a mistake, as he was not staying in the Hydropathic. The gentleman had said to him, "Nevertheless, I am glad to see you." The accused pointed out the gentleman who said this, and said his name was Rose. I afterwards saw Rose and the accused talking together on the boat. I went on to Whiting Bay and then returned with the steamer, which picked up Laurie and others at Brodick. I asked him if he had been successful in getting lodgings in Arran, and he replied that he had, and mentioned that Rose was likely to accompany him the next day. On the morning of the next day—Saturday—I saw the accused again on the pier at Rothesay. He was preparing, I understood, to go to Arran. I did not speak to him. I saw him again that day on the Esplanade before I went off. The next time I saw him was on Friday, 19th July—again at Rothesay. [Shown Label No. 10.] On that occasion he was wearing a white serge yachting cap, similar to that produced. When I saw him with it, the thought passed across my mind that it was very like the cap worn by Rose on board the steamer on the previous Friday. I had it on the tip of my tongue to say so. I saw the accused again on the 20th, when I had about fifteen minutes' conversation with him. I said, "How did you and your friend get on in Brodick?" and he said, "Oh, very well. We met in with a very nice set of fellows." He did not go into details and the subject was dropped. He told me then that he was going back to Glasgow, his holidays being over. I saw him next on the Saturday following, the 27th, probably between six and seven o'clock at night, in Rothesay.

158

Evidence for Prosecution.

James G. Aitken

I asked him what he was doing there, and he said he was down for the afternoon. He left Rothesay that night. I saw him next on Wednesday, 31st July, in Hope Street, Glasgow. That was a casual meeting.

Now, by that time, had you read in the papers about the disappearance of Mr. Rose?—I had. At the time I saw the accused in Hope Street, I was standing speaking with a customer at the office door, and we were talking of the strange disappearance of Rose. I wanted information, and when I saw Laurie coming down the street, I called to him to come over. He stood close by us until I had finished speaking to my customer. He then said, " Well, is this where you are? " And I said " Yes." I said in a blunt way, " What do you know about the Arran mystery? " He " hummed and hawed " and hesitated. I said, " Have you not been reading the papers? " and he said he had. I said, " Didn't you see there is a tourist amissing called Rose? " and he " hummed and hawed " again. I then said, " Was not that the name of the man you said you had intended to go to Brodick with? " He hesitated again. " That was the name you gave him," I said. He said, " I believe it is; but that must be a different Mr. Rose from the Mr. Rose who was with me, for he returned with me and then proceeded to Leeds."

What did you say to that?—Well, I said, " You had better go and do your duty, and tell the authorities what you have told me." He said, " Do you think so? " I said, " If you do not, I will have to do it myself." By that I meant, of course, that I would go to the authorities and mention his name as one who knew something about the whereabouts of Mr. Rose.

By the COURT—I advised him strongly to do it.

Examination continued—What next, Mr. Aitken?—I twitted him about the cap that he wore on the Friday night.

By the COURT—You spoke about the cap?—Yes. I asked him whose cap he was wearing on the Friday night. I said, " Whose cap were you wearing on yon Friday night? " He replied, " Surely you don't think I am a——," and then stopped short.

He did not add anything?—He may have, but I could not swear. He might have added the word " thief."

John Watson Laurie.

James G. Aitken

You took him to mean that?—Yes, I did.

Examination continued—Do you think you made any reply?—I do not think so.

Did you ask him to come into the office with you?—Yes.

What object had you in asking him that?—Well, to get further information about the matter.

Did he agree, or what did he do?—He said he would rather not.

How did the conversation end?—He promised to meet me again that evening and let me know further. He made a definite appointment with me, or at least I understood him to do so. He asked when I left the office, and I said about six o'clock. I expected him to come back at six, and I was waiting for him.

By the COURT—You proposed to meet him again?—He proposed. He asked when I left the office and I said about six o'clock.

Examination continued—He did not come, did he?—I never saw him again.

When he left you, did he say anything about seeing a person he knew on the opposite side of the street?—He spoke of a person he knew going down the same side of the street.

Yes, but I mean did he make that a reason for leaving at the moment?—He made that his reason for wanting to be off.

What did he say, so far as you can remember?—He said, " Oh, here is so-and-so coming; I think I had better go."

By the COURT—" Here is so-and-so "?—I think he mentioned the name.

Can you give us the exact words?—I believe he said, " Here is John Waddell." I know John Waddell by sight.

Examination continued—Was Mr. Waddell coming?—He was coming down the same side of the street.

Did he go off towards Mr. Waddell?—He did not. He went in the opposite direction.

And did not join him. Did you notice anything about his manner during that conversation?—He looked a little pale and tremulous. In the course of the conversation he said he was innocent of anything. That was in the middle of the interview.

This conversation was on 31st July, and a few days after-

Evidence for Prosecution.

James G. Aitken

wards I think you saw in the newspapers an account of Rose's body having been found?—I did. I then thought it my duty to inform the police authorities of what I knew.

Cross-examined by the DEAN OF FACULTY—You told us you knew Laurie before you saw him on the 6th of July at Rothesay?—I said so.

I suppose you addressed him by his name Laurie?—I knew him as Laurie.

Did you introduce him to your friends on board the boat as Laurie?—I did.

In describing your conversation with Laurie in Hope Street, Glasgow, you said that you began rather bluntly. I think you said, "What do you know about the Arran mystery," in rather a blunt manner?—Yes.

And then you twitted him about the cap he had worn?—Yes.

From your manner of twitting him about the cap, did you intend to convey that you suspected him?—I could not do otherwise.

Was it then that he said, "Surely you don't think I am a——?" You think he meant thief?—Yes.

Was it immediately afterwards that he spoke about being innocent?—It may have been; it was during the conversation.

Had there been any articles appearing by that time in the papers?—There were.

On that very day had there not been an article associating the name of "Annandale" with this business?—Yes.

At all events you did speak to him about what was appearing in the papers?—Yes. I had seen in a Monday evening paper an account of the missing tourist.

Monday would be the 29th and Wednesday the 31st, so that the papers had been at it three days?—Yes.

On 5th August, when you went to the police office, did you ask if they were certain the name was "Annandale"?—Yes, I asked Superintendent Orr. He said no, that it was Laurie.

The police knew quite well?—Yes.

JOHN ALEXANDER PORTER NAPIER, examined by Mr. M'KECHNIE—I reside at 518 Springburn Road, Glasgow, and

M   161

John Watson Laurie.

John A. P. Napier

I am a foreman patternmaker in Springburn Works. The accused was a patternmaker at our works last summer. On 31st July he asked to be paid for a few days that were due to him, giving as a reason that he was leaving to be a traveller in the grain trade. He said he had got a situation in Leith.

Cross-examined by the DEAN OF FACULTY—The accused's wages were about 30s. per week?—He often had overtime, and his average wage would be about £2 a week.

GEORGE M'MASTER, examined by Mr. M'KECHNIE—I am a patternmaker, and I reside at 294 Springburn Road, Glasgow. I know the accused. I worked at an adjoining bench to his at Springburn Works last summer. On 31st July I remember he said he was tired of working at Springburn, and he told me he was going to Leith to the works of Ramage & Ferguson, the engineers. I remember his going away for holidays in July. When he came back from Rothesay he told me that he had been with a friend in Arran, that he had been up Goatfell on the Monday with his friend, and that he had left him in Arran, where he was spending some time. He told me that he came back from Rothesay alone.

Did he say anything about going anywhere else?—He told me that if he had not got back his job on Monday he would have gone to London as he had got a ticket.

Did he say what kind of a ticket?—No, and I did not ask.

Cross-examined by the DEAN OF FACULTY—Did he say he had had the ticket since last year?—He told me he took it out in London about the end of last season.

JOHN MACKAY, examined by Mr. GRAHAM MURRAY—I am chief constable of Buteshire and I am stationed at Rothesay. [Shown Label No. 22.] I received that trunk from Detective John Pyper, of the Western District, Glasgow Police, who brought it from the accused's lodgings in Liverpool. [Shown Labels Nos. 14-21.] I found these articles in the trunk. Label No. 21 is a stamp by which you mark linen—an impress stamp. That stamp bears the name of J. W. Laurie, and,

162

Evidence for Prosecution.

if properly inked, will make such an impression as is found on the shirts produced. These shirts bear the impression " John W. Laurie." [Shown Productions Nos. 7 and 8.] These two letters were handed to me by Captain Boyd. They bear to have been written by " John W. Laurie." They are respectively addressed to the editors of the *Glasgow Herald* and the *Glasgow Mail* newspapers.

WILLIAM JOHNSTON, examined by Mr. GRAHAM MURRAY—I am a clerk and I live at 26 Sunnyside Road, Coatbridge. I have known the accused for about four years. We were members together of an athletic association, of which he was at one time treasurer. I succeeded him as treasurer and had frequent opportunities of seeing his handwriting in a set of books kept by him, which I took over. [Shown Productions Nos. 7 and 8.] These letters are in handwriting which bears a marked resemblance to that of Laurie.

Do you think it is the handwriting of the accused? Have you any doubt it is not his handwriting?—It certainly resembles his handwriting.

Are they like the handwriting in the treasurer's book?— Yes, they do resemble it.

Had the accused to sign his name in the treasurer's book? —No.

Have you seen him sign his name?—No.

So far as the body of the letter is concerned, is the hand-writing like that in the treasurer's book?—It does resemble the handwriting in the treasurer's book.

PETER M'LEAN, examined by Mr. GRAHAM MURRAY—I am a grocer and I stay at 150 Whifflet Street, Coatbridge. I have known the accused for some time, and I had occasion in my acquaintance with him to see statements of his hand-writing. [Shown Productions Nos. 7 and 8.] These letters, signed " John W. Laurie," are in the handwriting of the accused. I have no doubt about that.

The LORD JUSTICE-CLERK—Gentlemen of the jury, before these letters are read, there are certain passages in them which relate to other people, and it would be painful to have their names dragged into this trial, and the counsel

John Watson Laurie.

are agreed that the full import of the letters can be given to you without dragging in the names of those persons.

Mr. GRAHAM MURRAY—Gentlemen, as you have heard, one of the letters is addressed to the *Glasgow Mail* and bears the Liverpool postmark. It is dated 10th August, 1889, and is in the following terms :—

" Dear Editor,—I feel that I should write a long detailed letter to your paper, but I am in no mood to do so. I rather smile when I read that my arrest is hourly expected. If things go as I have designed them, I will soon have arrived at that country from whose bourne no traveller returns, and, since there has been so much said about me, it is only right that the public should know what are the real circumstances which has brought me to this. . . . Since then I have been perfectly careless about what I did, and my one thought was how to punish her enough for the cruel wrong she had done me, and it was to watch her audacious behaviour that I went to Rothesay this and last year. I may say that I became acquainted with another young lady whose good qualities I sincerely wish that I had learned to appreciate sooner, as if I had I would have been in a very different position to-day. As regards Mr. Rose, poor fellow, no one who knows me will believe for one moment that I had any complicity in his death. The morning I left for Arran I was in the company of two friends on Rothesay pier, when Mr. Rose came to me and said that he was going to spend a few days with me at Arran. I was very much surprised at this, as my friends could vouch for I had not invited him. We went to the top of Goatfell, where I left him in the company of two men who came from Loch Ranza and were going to Brodick. I went down to Corrie and met some friends, and we afterwards visited the hotel where we met several of the gentlemen who were camping out, and I left for Brodick about. ten. I could easily prove that what I say is true, but I decline to bring the names of my friends into this disgraceful affair. So will content myself by wishing them a last adieu.—Yours truly, John W. Laurie."

The second letter, which is addressed to the *Glasgow Herald*, is dated 27th August, 1889. It is as follows :—

invited him.   12/8/89
                                 JW

We went to the top of
Goatfell where I left him
in the company of two men
who came ~~to~~ *from* Loch Ranza
and were going to Brodick

I went down to Corrie
and met some friends and
we afterwards ~~went to~~ *visited* the
Hotel where we met several
of the gentlemen who were
camping out and I left
for Brodick about ten

I could easily prove that
what I say is true, but
I decline to bring the
names of my friends
into this disgraceful affair
so will content myself

Facsimile of Laurie's letter to the "North British Daily Mail."

I sincerely wish that I had learned to appreciate sooner as if I had I would have been in a very different position today.

As regards McZ Rose poor fellow, no one who knows me will beleive for one moment that I had any complicats in his death.

The morning I left for tran I was in the company of two friends on Rothesay tier, when Mr Rose came to me and said that he was going to spend a few days with me at tran

I was very much surprised at this as my friends could voutch for I had not

Evidence for Prosecution.

" Sir,—I expected that the letter which I so foolishly addressed to the *Mail* would have been my last, but I read so many absurd and mad things in the daily papers, that I feel it my duty to correct some of them. And the first of these is the assertion . . . that I am kept out of the way by friends. I have not come across a friend since I left Glasgow, nor have I been in communication with any one. I don't deny the fact that I would like to meet some of my friends again, but I am more careful than allow myself to be lured like the moth to the flame. Although I am entirely guiltless of the crime I am so much wanted for, yet I can recognise that I am a ruined man in any case, so it is far from my intention to give myself up. I first went to Glasgow in the spring of 1882, but being among strangers I became homesick, so was glad of the offer held out to me of something to do at Uddingston. Messrs. John Gray & Co. were at that time making a winding engine, also several steam cranes, for the underground railway, and during the months of June, July, and August I assisted Mr. John Swan to make the patterns. I remember Mr. Swan as being a very nice gentleman, but I have no recollection of a man the name of Alexander. I was not at Hamilton eight weeks ago, and I certainly did not smile to Alexander on the way there. If I had travelled in a train where I was known, don't you think it likely that I would have left at the first stoppage? The stories about me being seen are all imagination. I have not been seen by any one who knows me, and I have been travelling all the time in England and Ireland, and as I can see that this is no land for me I will be off again. It is true that I did take a room for a week at 10 Greek Street, Liverpool, which I paid in advance. I only stayed three days. I did not board with the lady of the house, and after destroying my papers I left my box, with no intention of ever calling for it again, as it was an encumbrance to me. The *Mail* takes credit to itself in this case, which does not belong to it at all, for it was a friend of mine who felt it his duty to inform the authorities that Mr. Rose left Rothesay with me, and when I saw from an evening paper that Mr. Rose had not returned to his lodgings,

John Watson Laurie.

Pannel's Letters

I began at once to arrange for my departure, for I had told so many about him. Seemingly there was a motive to do away with poor Rose; it was not to secure his valuables. Mr. Rose was to all appearance worse off than myself, indeed he assured me that he had spent so much on his tour, that he had barely sufficient to last till he got home. He wore an old Geneva watch with no gold albert attached, and I am sure that no one saw him wear a ring on his tour, and no one saw me wear one, and well —— knew that he was speaking a lie when he said that he saw me wear a ring at Rothesay. A nice picture this fellow made of me, purely out of ill-will, because I had fooled his precious brother. He says that when he saw me I was wearing a ring and had one of my hands gloved; this is a preposterous falsehood; indeed, his whole story from beginning to end was a lie. I met him one morning in Shamrock Street, not Cambridge Street, and I caught hold of his arm when he asked a boy to call a policeman, there was no striking on either side, but if there had been I leave those who know us to judge who would come off second best. . . . However, these are trivial matters uninteresting to all but those immediately concerned, and as I am not inclined to say any more I hope this will be the last the public will hear of me.—Yours truly, John W. Laurie."

JAMES GORDON, examined by Mr. GRAHAM MURRAY—I am a police constable of Rosebank, in the parish of Dalserf, Lanarkshire. On the afternoon of 3rd September last I apprehended the accused. I was told about him at Ferniegair Railway Station, and then I saw him on the Carlisle Road. I followed him. The accused turned the corner at the end of the dyke and got out of my sight. I ran after him and made ground on him for a considerable distance. When the accused saw that I was overtaking him he got very uneasy, looked several times round about him, and then went through a gate into a grass field, and ran across the railway on to the Lanark and Hamilton turnpike road. I saw some miners, and I got them to surround a wood into which he had gone. I walked down a clover field adjoining the wood, and a little boy said to me, "There is something

166

Evidence for Prosecution.

James Gordon

in that bush." I crossed the fence, walked to the bush, and saw lying under it the accused, with an open razor in his hand and his throat cut. I asked him why he had done that, and he said the only thing that he was sorry for was that he had not done it right. I was in uniform and arrested him, telling him that he was wanted on the charge of murder, and cautioning him that anything he said in regard to his own case might be used in evidence against him. He said, " I robbed the man, but I did not murder him." A man behind me took the razor.

Cross-examined by the DEAN OF FACULTY—These were all the words that passed between you?—Yes.

You swear to these particular words?—Yes.

You have told us all that was said?—Yes.

MICHAEL CROWN, examined by Mr. GRAHAM MURRAY—I am a miner and I reside at Buchanan's Buildings, Greenfield, Hamilton. On 3rd September last I joined in the chase after the accused. I was one of the miners who surrounded the wood, following the directions of the policeman. After the wood was surrounded, I went into the wood by the path, and I heard the policeman saying that it was Laurie. Before that, I had heard a little boy calling out about a person being in the wood. I then went up to the bush with the policeman and I saw the accused under it. I went forward and caught him by the arm, and I saw that his throat was cut, and that he had an open razor in his hand. I said, " You should not have done that." He said, " I wish I had done it right." He said he was not a murderer. That was all that passed, and then he was taken in charge by the policeman.

PRISONER'S DECLARATIONS.

The CLERK OF JUSTICIARY (Mr. C. Scott) then read the prisoner's declarations. The first of these, taken at Rothesay, on 4th September, 1889, before Sheriff-Substitute M'Kirdy, stated—

" Compeared a prisoner along with Mr. John M'Intyre, writer, Glasgow, as his agent, and a charge of murder against

John Watson Laurie.

him having been read over and explained to him, and he having been judicially admonished and examined thereanent, declares : ' My name is John Watson Laurie. I am twenty-five years of age. I was born in Kirkintilloch. I was last employed as a patternmaker, and my last place of residence was with Mrs. King, Number (I think) 26 North Frederick Street, Glasgow. I am not married. I have nothing to say to the charge in the meantime. All which is truth.

(Sgd.)   ' John W. Laurie.' "

The second declaration, dated 11th September, 1889, taken in presence of Sheriff-Substitute Orr, at Greenock, stated— " I adhere to my former declaration and have nothing to add. [Being shown a walking stick, a cap, a pocket knife, a pencil, two pieces of a waterproof coat, and a button.] I wish to say nothing about any of these articles.

(Sgd.)   " John W. Laurie."

Evidence for Defence.

Evidence for the Defence.

COSIMO LATONA, examined by the DEAN OF FACULTY—I reside at Corrie and I am an Italian by birth. For the last three years I have been acting as a guide at Brodick. As a guide I know the tracks tourists usually take for the purpose of reaching the points of view and seeing the scenery. I know the place where the deceased's cap was found and I know the road from the top of Goatfell to Glen Sannox by Corr-na-Fourin. That is not the ordinary track used by tourists. The Saddle route is the road people are in the habit of going by. I never heard of anybody coming down from Goatfell by Corr-na-Fourin till this occurrence took place. I have come down that way since. The route from the top of the ridge to where Rose's body was found is very dangerous; it is very rough ground from the ridge to the boulder. Most of the ground is granite stone, very steep in some places and usually very slippery. There are parts where a person might lose his footing and fall down. Sometimes you require to use your hands as well as your feet to get down.

Cross-examined by Mr. GRAHAM MURRAY—How long have you been in Arran?—About three years.

Are you a fisherman to trade?—Yes, a fisherman in the winter.

How many times have you guided people over the hills in Arran?—I did not guide any people until the body of Rose was found.

Had you ever been in Glen Sannox at all before Rose's body was found?—No.

But you went there the other day to help the constable and some gentlemen who were taking photographs?—Yes.

JEANIE PARK, examined by Mr. SCOTT DICKSON—I live with my mother at Kelburn, Baillieston. I have known the accused for several years. He was in the habit of visiting our house. He was of a quiet disposition, agreeable, and of pleasant temper. In July last I stayed for a fortnight in Rothesay

John Watson Laurie.

Jeanie Park

with my sister and my brother. I saw the accused there during that time. I remember that on the morning of Saturday, 13th July, he went away by the boat to Arran. My sister and I were at the pier when the boat started. He spoke to my sister, saying that he and another gentleman were going, and that he was coming back on Tuesday or Wednesday. He had a white tennis shirt on. I saw him again on the Tuesday evening when he called on us. He was in his usual spirits, quite chatty and agreeable. I saw him once or twice after that in Rothesay, and I did not notice any change in him in any way.

Cross-examined by Mr. GRAHAM MURRAY—Did he mention to you about having been up Goatfell?—Yes.

Did he tell you how long he had taken?—I asked him how long he had taken, but he did not say.

Did he seem to evade the question? He seemed disinclined to answer it, and did not answer it?—Yes.

Re-examined by Mr. SCOTT DICKSON—What do you mean by saying that he seemed to evade the question?—He did not seem to be willing to tell me. He told me, however, that the ascent was very slow because his friend was a slow climber.

ANN M'EACHERN, examined by Mr. SCOTT DICKSON—I am a domestic servant in the employment of the Rev. Mr. Brown, Kirkintilloch. Last July I stayed with my mother at Corrie. I made the acquaintance of Peterina M'Donald and David M'Kenzie, the shepherd. I remember being with them both near Glen Sannox burying-ground one night about nine o'clock. I do not remember the day of the month, but it was a Monday. I did not see any one else there.

Did M'Kenzie say anything to you about seeing a man, an apparent stranger, who he thought looked tired and "travelled"?—No.

Was anything of that kind said?—No.

Cross-examined by Mr. GRAHAM MURRAY—You were a stranger to the island and would not know, consequently, who were strangers and who were not?—Yes.

Could you say that M'Kenzie did not direct attention to a stranger of tired appearance?—I cannot say I heard him.

170

Evidence for Defence.

Might M'Kenzie have made such a remark without you hearing it?—Yes, he might.

Re-examined by Mr. SCOTT DICKSON—On the Saturday afterwards there was, of course, talk of Rose having gone amissing, and people began to search for him?—Yes.

When did you leave the island?—On the 31st of July.

Up to the time you left, were you seeing M'Kenzie fairly frequently?—Yes.

Did he ever at any time say anything to you about his having seen any one on the day Rose went amissing?—No.

PETERINA M'DONALD, examined by Mr. SCOTT DICKSON—I am a domestic servant and I was in Arran last July. I accompanied the witnesses M'Eachern and M'Kenzie on a walk to Glen Sannox burying-ground. I remember seeing that night a lady and two girls, but I never saw any man coming out of the glen, nor did M'Kenzie say anything to me about seeing a tired-looking man coming out.

Cross-examined by Mr. GRAHAM MURRAY—Is it quite possible that M'Kenzie might have made some remark about seeing the man without you hearing him?—It is possible.

Re-examined by Mr. SCOTT DICKSON—You would hear, of course, that Rose was missing?—Yes.

Was that ever the subject of talk between M'Kenzie and you?—No.

You met him, I think, several times afterwards, and he never suggested that he had seen the man on the evening in question?—That is correct.

Dr. PATRICK HERON WATSON, examined by the DEAN OF FACULTY—I am surgeon to the Queen in Scotland and consulting surgeon to Edinburgh Royal Infirmary. I have read the three medical reports which have formed part of the evidence in this case, and I was present yesterday during the whole time that the evidence as to the facts was being adduced. I think that, having regard to the facts described in the medical reports, and to what I heard stated orally yesterday, death was instantaneous at the time of the injury, because there seems to have been so little bleeding about the

171

John Watson Laurie.

Dr Patrick H. Watson

body and so little soiling of the deceased's clothes. I have not visited the ground, but I have heard the descriptions of it. I have heard it said that, on the left side, coming down the gully, nearly opposite to where the cap was found, there is a clear drop of 19 feet, and that somewhat farther down there is a drop of 32 feet, and I have heard the ground described as consisting of granite boulders and the like. If a person coming down that gully had fallen down either of these places and alighted on his head, I would expect him to receive a great smash on the upper part of the head and a commensurate fracture of the base of the skull.

Having regard to the whole of the facts, does it appear to you perfectly possible that the injuries you have heard described were caused by a fall?—It is extremely probable.

Give us, in a little more detail, the effect of such a fall upon the skull and its vertex?—If a body falls from a moderate height, and the force is not too great, there may be but a limited amount of fissure of the vertex, but that fissure tends to produce a continuation of it across one of the portions of the base of the skull.

Does such a fall sometimes affect the vertex by smashing it up into a number of small pieces and sometimes by making fractures along its surface?—According to the nature of the surface which it strikes. If it struck upon a pointed surface of no great elevation, it would probably fissure up in a star shape. If it struck upon a rough surface, a surface presenting various points of contact, there might be fissures and starrings in various directions.

From the description that you heard given yesterday, to which of these characters did the injuries belong?—The vertex appeared to me to have been driven in from an excessive height, so that one side of the skull was completely driven in, along with the frontal on both sides. In speaking of an excessive height I am speaking rather experimentally. If you let a corpse fall down the well of a stair, in order to discover the direction and appearance of the fractures which would be presented on the skull, and if you do so from a greater height than about 10 feet, you are apt to have such a smashing in of the head that you can hardly recognise the details that attend upon a less degree of injury.

172

Evidence for Defence.

Dr Patrick H. Watson

Would the injuries you heard described yesterday be quite consistent with a fall from such a height as 19 feet or 32 feet?—Quite consistent.

You heard the discussions in the report of the injuries at the base of the skull. Were these such as you would expect after such a fall?—I think these precisely corresponded to the driven-in portion of the skull, which was described as constituting the injury to the vertex. If he had received a blow upon the head such as might be inflicted with a weapon like a heavy hammer, implicating a comparatively limited surface, and a fracture of the base of the skull had occurred in connection with it, it would have occurred in connection with the fossa on the base of the skull which corresponded to the lesion of the fractures. If that occurred, there would be a fissure into that fossa, but after dissolution of the continuity of the vertex had once fairly taken place, repeated applications of the hammer, although they might produce fissures corresponding to the fractures at different points, would never give one continuous line of fissure from the front to the back in the way described in this case.

Might that be expressed otherwise by saying that the general or universal injury involving the whole of the fractures would be attended with a universal injury to the base of the skull, whereas a group of local injuries would be attended by a group of local injuries on the opposite side?—That is putting it generally.

By the COURT—One great injury would probably cause a corresponding injury at the base, but a number of smaller fractures combined would have produced the same effect at the base.

Examination continued—Having regard to what you have now said, does it appear to you that the injuries described were not only consistent with such a fall as I have mentioned, but were rather more consistent with that than with a series of blows?—To my mind they were much more so. The fact that the left side of the head had been completely broken in would be perfectly consistent with such a fall.

And if you were told that the dislocation and displacement downwards of the upper jaw-bone was not consistent with

John Watson Laurie.

Dr Patrick H. Watson

such a fall, what would you say?—I have seen such injury occur where fracture of the base of the skull has been produced by a fall.

Is the condition of the jaw which you have heard described, in your judgment and according to your experience, not only consistent with such a fall but just the result you would expect from it?—From the very fact that there was a smash up, I think it is quite consistent.

Does the absence of blood upon the clothing, so far as can be seen, in any way affect your opinion?—Either there must have been little bleeding in connection with the injury, or, if there was much, the head must have lain in a lower position than the body, so that the blood flowed away from the neck downwards, and did not stain the clothes.

Supposing the injury took place from such a fall as I have asked you to assume, what would have been the effect in the matter of bleeding?—A fall producing such extensive injury would, to my mind, render it not improbable that the first vertebra of the neck was broken, causing instantaneous death; and, therefore, the heart's action speedily ceasing, there would be very little bleeding at all.

Now, if you were asked on the contrary to assume that the mischief to the body had been brought about by a series of blows with some blunt instrument—a stone, it is said— would that have produced instantaneous death, and consequent absence of bleeding?—No, it would not. The fracture of the skull requires the application of very considerable force. I have on many occasions fractured skulls for purposes of demonstration, and to do so requires a considerable amount of violence, which it is not pleasant to use on a dead body, and is extremely unpleasant when used before a class. In these circumstances, therefore, I always make the fractures to skulls privately. No doubt if you took a small claw hammer you might product a fracture with a sharp stroke; but if you are to give a stroke that is to drive in any considerable portion of it, it requires very great force. It requires, in fact, a hammer like a sledge hammer, in order to enable you to do it; and the great difficulty is that, unless you have the head fitted into a corner, it is hardly possible

174

Evidence for Defence.

Dr Patrick H. Watson

to do it until you have gone on making blows for a consider-able length of time. The head is so moveable that it shifts away, the scalp becomes broken down and glides to one side, and you are very apt to find that you have not attained the object you have in view.

What would you say to a suggestion that such injuries were made with no more effective weapon than a rough stone in a man's hand?—I cannot conceive that it could be done in that way. A stone of any size and weight, with which you might give impulsive force to inflict injury, would very often fail, because you do not strike the head with a stone in the hand in the same way as you might sling a stone; so that I am quite at a loss to understand how it could be produced in that way. It seems to me unlikely, as com-pared with the other theory. A stone of any size and weight would of itself be a very awkward instrument with which to smash in a skull.

As between two men such as you have heard described, of comparatively similar age and under the circumstances you have heard?—Precisely.

Apart from probability, what would be the effect of such a series of assaults upon bleeding?—Unless the person was actually dead, there must have been copious bleeding from the jaw when it was torn from the base of the skull, and also from the injured parts themselves.

How would that blood have gone to the outside?—Through the nose, mouth, surface of the skull, and probably through the ear on the left side.

In conducting a post-mortem examination on such a ques-tion, would you have thought it proper to look inside the cavity of the ear, the pharynx, and certain internal organs? —Yes, looking to the probability of a local injury.

Is it your opinion that if death was brought about by a series of blows it would not be such as is suggested here, the first blow which would bring about the death, but after an interval of time?—My opinion is that such an extent of injury could not have been produced by any limited surface striking against the head unless it had been very frequently repeated.

John Watson Laurie.

Dr Patrick H. Watson

By the COURT—Might not one injury have caused the death and the others been added afterwards?—That is very difficult to say with certainty.

Examination continued—Assuming that several blows were struck, that the first blow was not fatal, would there be, even although the time measured by the clock was short, time for copious bleeding?—I think most copious bleeding would occur when the upper jaw was torn away from the base of the skull; the bleeding would occur from the nose.

If that final breaking up of the base of the skull had been due to a series of blows, would it have been while the series was well advanced?—No, the fracture to the base of the skull occurred almost instantly, I think. The pressure in the interior of the skull is almost the same as that of water contained in a closed cavity—the pressure is great in every direction, and as soon as the skull is broken in the base, it bursts, to allow of the escape of the brain.

You heard what was said in regard to the injury to the left shoulder? Does that affect your opinion as to the cause of death?—No; I think that injury occurred at the same time as the injury to the head.

Does there appear to you to be any difficulty in that view? —None. If, in descending, the deceased fell head-first down a height of either 19 feet or 32 feet, and came with the left side of his head in contact with a hard surface of stone, having an elevation or nodule against which the head came, the head would be smashed in and the flatter portion of it upon which the shoulder impinged would explain the injury to the shoulder and the detachment of the two ribs.

Supposing you are invited to assume that the fall had been from a clear drop, at the end of one or more smooth granite slopes, how do you think a person might very likely fall from such a place?—I think from what is said the probability is, that where the perpendicular fall occurred, it was not recognisable as such from a little way above. He may have been coming down carelessly, without anticipating the danger in front of him from these sloping portions of granite, and hurrying down he suddenly came to the brink and realised what his danger was. He then extended his right hand in

176

Evidence for Defence.

Dr Patrick H. Watson

which he had a stick in order to prevent his falling—to try to check himself. This produced no effect in stopping his onward progress, but gave a new direction to the axis in which his body had begun to turn round to the left; and then he went over the cliff headlong, leaning backwards towards the left.

Would such a fall produce exactly the phenomena as seen on this body?—It would.

Suppose it is suggested that a man falling would throw out his arms to save himself, and that there would be lesions on the arms?—A man falling forward is certain to throw out his arms, unless they are disabled; but, if falling backwards, they would not save him nor come in contact with any surface before he alighted. That suggestion introduces no new difficulty.

What do you say to the highest cervical vertebra having been found loose when the body was found under the stone?—I think it is extremely likely that it had been dislocated at the time of the injury. Such a fall upon the side and back of the head would double the head forward and give it a twist towards the right side, and in doing so it would be extremely likely to produce a dislocation of the atlas or the first vertebra.

Suppose death to have taken place on 15th July, and the body to have been discovered on 4th August, might such a setting free of the highest vertebra be due to decay, or would you attribute it to the other cause?—Probably both conditions.

It has been suggested that, if death had been due to such a fall as I have asked you to assume, the abdominal viscera or some of them would have been injuriously affected?—If the abdominal viscera had been struck by the body falling against something in the first instance, that is extremely likely. But in instances where a fall takes place from a high elevation, and laceration or rupture of the liver or spleen takes place, that is usually where the person falls upon his feet. In such circumstances the liver, which is attached to the under surface of the diaphragm and is a heavy substance, attempts to continue its descent in the

N   177

John Watson Laurie.

Dr Patrick H. Watson

abdomen, tears its ligamentous surroundings, and produces some degree of laceration of the liver. In the instance, however, of a man falling from a height and descending on his head, the impetus given to the liver is in the other direction—upwards—against the under surface of the diaphragm. The condition of the liver would be very much like that of a man falling from a trapeze into a net.

Does the fact that the liver was unruptured in this case modify or affect your opinion of the cause of death?—No, it does not. If it was urged as a reason, I should say it was less likely to occur with such an explanation than if the person had fallen in any other way.

It has been suggested that, in such a fall, the collar-bone would have been broken?—I should have expected it would have suffered at the same time as the tendon to which it is attached; but, if he fell on the shoulder blade, the collar-bone need not necessarily have been broken.

Do I understand you to say that, in your judgment, the clavicle would be more likely to be broken by a blow aimed at the head and partly missing it than by a pitch down?—Yes, taking it for granted that the assailant stood in front of the victim.

Do you attach any importance to the fact that the two uppermost ribs have been separated from the back-bone?—I think it probably indicates that the injury has been chiefly upon the back part of the shoulder.

In short, after the head and the parts of the shoulder you have described, would the two uppermost ribs be the next bones in the body to feel the impact?—They would.

And they were the next two things to give way?—Yes.

Looking at all the injuries, do they seem to afford to you a simple explanation?—Yes.

Do you think they would be brought about by assault with a stone or other blunt weapon?—No, it is very unlikely.

Much more unlikely than the explanation of a fall?—Yes.

Cross-examined by the SOLICITOR-GENERAL—Do you agree it is quite possible that the injuries may have been inflicted by a number of blows with a hard instrument?—I do not think it is very probable.

178

Evidence for Defence.

Dr Patrick H. Watson

Do you think that if a man were standing above another with a large stone, and aimed it downwards, it is possible that such a blow might account for the injuries on the top of the head?—Well, while I am quite ready to admit that anything is possible, I do not think is is probable. I think a blow would probably drive the head aside, and so would not cause such severe injuries to the skull. The head would require to be fixed into a corner to prevent yielding, before blows would cause such an effect.

But a heavy blow might have the effect of stunning?—I quite admit that.

Supposing that were so, the injuries are consistent with subsequent direct blows administered by a hard, blunt weapon?—Not to my mind consistent. To my mind, the whole injuries to the skull, the fractures above and below, were inflicted at one time and by one stroke.

Therefore you are of opinion that the two fractures—the fractures of the top and base of the skull—were the result of one blow? But you do not at all exclude the possibility of these two injuries being the result of two blows, insensibility having been produced by the first?—I again do not object to possibility; but, as far as the facts have been placed before me, I would certainly be in favour of a fall upon the vertex.

With regard to the injuries to the face, these also are quite consistent with the theory of blows—a number of blows delivered directly?—That is a possibility also.

There is nothing to prevent the first injury causing death and the other injuries being inflicted afterwards?—If death occurred from the first injury, there would have been no necessity for inflicting blows.

We are not talking of necessity. Is not that perfectly possible?—It is a possibility.

I am assuming that the first blow caused the injuries on the top of the head and that that produced death. There was nothing in the appearance of the body to exclude the opinion that the subsequent injuries were inflicted after death?—That, but not the other, may have been inflicted after death.

You agree that the upper jaw-bone is a very strong bone?—

179

John Watson Laurie.

Dr Patrick H. Watson

I do not think so; it is as thin as paper. In all its outlines, except where the teeth are inserted, it is a hollow cavity. It is often broken, both in young children and adults.

Is the upper jaw often broken except by direct impact?—I have seen it broken in the manner spoken of.

What were the circumstances?—All I remember is that the surface of the skull was smashed in and there was a fracture of the vertex and the base, and the jaw-bone broken.

Your view, then, is that death was caused by a fall from a height?—Yes.

Was it a fall from a very great height?—I should think not.

You are speaking at random?—No, I am speaking of what would have produced such an injury. I have inflicted similar injuries by dropping a corpse from a height of 20 feet.

Your view is that, if there was a fall, it would not have been a fall forward. If it was a fall backward, that would be accounted for by a push?—Not necessarily.

A man does not go over a precipice backwards?—I explained in my evidence what I thought was the probable way in which he fell.

Do you commit yourself to that view?—It is the only reasonable one to meet the circumstances.

If death occurred in the way you have mentioned, by slipping down, the slope must have been so steep and so smooth that a man would not have been able to check himself?—I believe he could not have checked himself.

You imagine a clear descent over this precipice?—I suppose a surface sloping towards the ground, not covered by bushes, but granite of a crumbling kind, so that if any one wished to stop himself he could not do so merely by sticking his stick into it.

Then you must imagine the turning over of the body?—I do suppose that.

It is necessary to your theory that he should have gone down head-foremost?—Yes.

At the same time, you must imagine that there was a nodule on the rock so placed as to catch his face and inflict

180

Evidence for Defence.

Dr Patrick H. Watson

the injuries there?—No, the injuries to the face were consequent on the fracture on the base of the skull.

Well, your pointed rock is necessary owing to the injury to the shoulder?—No, the pointed rock staved in the side of the head.

Then you think there were three surfaces upon which the man fell? You have the surface upon which the top of the head fell, the surface upon which the side of the head was smashed, and the projection which smashed the shoulder-blade?—No, the first two are the same. What I say is, that a nodule like this [indicating a small water carafe]—a nodule about the size of this water carafe—would account for the injuries on the head and face. In such granite masses we often have prominent places in which there has been water wearing.

What is the position of the rock which produced the injury on the shoulder-blade?—The flat surface of the rock did that.

Do you suppose the head and the shoulder came in contact with the rock at the same moment?—The difference is so minute in the fall of a body of, say, 8 stone from 19 feet or 32 feet, that you can hardly calculate it. But I think the shoulder struck first, and that the shock came into operation and almost simultaneously broke up the skull.

You suppose that the head and shoulder came upon that rock at the same moment?—I think so.

In the case of a fall backwards, down such a height as you have supposed, it would not be at all necessary that the body should alight on its head?—It might or it might not. From the evidence, there were no bruises anywhere else.

The back would be quite as likely a place for the body to alight on?—I think not. A person diving does not fall on his back, but on his hands and head.

By the COURT—Do not divers fall upon their stomachs?—I do not think so. I have never fallen in that manner.

Cross-examination continued—I suppose, as the body would not all at once be upside down, it would be quite natural that it should descend very much as it left the top?—In beginning to leave the top, and falling over, a body, having the height of the human body, begins to incline a little, and the force of gravity does all the rest.

181

John Watson Laurie.

Dr Patrick H. Watson

Let us take the case of a man being pushed backwards over a height of 19 feet. Would you not rather expect that he would fall on his back?—Not in the case of losing his footing and slipping.

Then, again, it is necessary for your theory that he must have, in slipping downwards, turned completely round before he reached the ledge in question?—No; I would say only about two-thirds.

I think you admit that it would have been, at all events, a very natural thing that in such a fall the body would not have alighted on its head, but upon its back?—Well, I would not like to say that. There are many instances in which, falling from some heights, bodies alight on the head, and there are others where they alight on the back.

You have not seen a case, in hospital or elsewhere, of fracture of the vertex having taken place accompanied with displacement of the facial bones and injury to the scapula? —With displacement of the facial bones, not with injury to the scapula.

The fact of the collar-bone not having been injured by the injury to the scapula indicates that the point of impact of the shoulder-blade on whatever it struck must have been very limited?—Not necessarily.

A blow delivered from behind might cause such an injury to the shoulder-blade?—Part of it.

A blow with great force?—Certainly.

And with a blunt instrument like a stone?—Yes.

The condition of the face was quite consistent with the theory of blows having been delivered after death?—Quite consistent.

By the Court—Is it possible for an ordinary man to take up a rigid dead body and put it over his shoulder?—I think he might. I have often seen men carrying bodies on their shoulders; they often carry them over the shoulder with the legs in front. I cannot say I have ever seen a man lift a body from the ground.

If he could not lift the body, he might possibly be able to drag it?—Yes, certainly.

By a Juryman—Are the radiations of one of the fractures
182

Evidence for Defence.

Dr Patrick H. Watson

in the skull, which were spoken to by Dr. Fullarton as being the result of a blow, consistent with injuries received from a fall?—Yes, quite consistent.

> [At the request of the jury, the witness pointed out on a skull the lines of fracture observed on the skull of the deceased.]

By the COURT—Can this continuous fracture which has been spoken of be accounted for without assuming several lesions?—No.

Dr. CHARLES WATSON MACGILLIVRAY, examined by the DEAN OF FACULTY—I am senior assistant surgeon at Edinburgh Royal Infirmary and lecturer on surgery in the Edinburgh Medical School. At the request of those in charge of the defence in this case I went to Arran on Monday last, along with Dr. Henry Alexis Thomson, with a view to examining the localities which are material in this inquiry, and forming an opinion as to the probable cause of death. I knew the island of Arran pretty well before, but not this particular place. Where the cap, knife, and pencil were found, there is a gully. If one were going down to Corrie from this point, one would go to the right, which would be the easiest route. From the point (x) on the plan there is nothing like a trodden or visible track on either side. There are shelving rocks about the point where the knife was said to be found, the spot being pointed out to me by Francis Logan. When I arrived at the top, I could see that one would be quite unaware of the nature of the ground below, or that there was such a fall as we had noticed from below when going up. There are three shelving rocks lying one above the other, the lowest one projecting over the gully and directly above the place where the articles were found. The character of the stone, of which the rocks consist, is rough granite. We measured the height coming down. We went up to the left-hand side of the gully to the place where the cap was found. We could not cross there, and had to make a detour in order to come down the right side. At this point I attached a stone to a measuring tape, and, sitting about 12 feet from the edge of the rocks, I threw the tape over.

183

John Watson Laurie.

Dr Charles W. Macgillivray

The stone was found by one of the men who accompanied me almost exactly in the place where the knife and button were found. I found the distance of the vertical drop to be 32 feet.

Had you gone as far down the slope as you could with safety?—Logan managed to crawl round on the second shelving below me. I warned him to take care.

Was that a place at which a person coming down, unaware of the danger, might readily find himself?—You could not possibly see that there was any such drop. A person might easily find himself there. From that point I went round about 20 feet to the right, from which a boulder was pushed over, it being smashed into fragments where the cap was found.

Coming down the left side, what would a person find?— That consisted of shelving granite rock of considerable slope.

The spot where the cap was found was pointed out to you? —Yes, when we went up the left side. Just at the point above where it was found, on the left side of the gully, there is a sheer drop of 19 feet.

Might a person coming down the left side, unaware of the danger, have found himself on that?—It is not on the absolutely direct route coming down, but if he had gone to the edge of the gully to see what it was like, he would then have found himself at this point. The nature of the rock at the 19-feet drop is rough granite, and any one falling from the top would have landed at or about where the cap was found. The 32-feet drop is rough, irregular masses of granite.

By the COURT—How far was the boulder from where the cap was found?—About 200 yards in a direct line.

Examination continued—The site of the 19-feet drop is somewhere about 40 yards higher up than the site of the 32-feet drop, and it would be proportionately nearer to the boulder.

You have read the medical reports in this case, and heard the evidence as to the condition of Rose's body. What do you think would be likely to cause such injuries?—Severe violence applied to the left side of the head, the cranium, and a part of the shoulder and neck.

Evidence for Defence.

Dr Charles W. Macgillivray

Supposing that Rose had fallen over either the 19-feet drop or the 32-feet drop and alighted on his head, would such a thing be sufficient to produce all the injuries you have heard described?—I think it would, certainly.

And would that be a natural explanation of those injuries? —I think it would.

You have also heard of the injury to the shoulder. Would such a fall, as I am asking you to assume, be competent to produce that at the same time as it produced the injuries to the head?—It would, if the body fell on the back of the shoulder.

If you were further told that, when the body was first discovered, the uppermost cervical vertebra was detached, would that have any influence on your opinion?—I should think that makes the theory of a fall more likely.

Supposing that this death occurred on 15th July, and that the body was found on 4th August, do you think it likely that, in such a short time as that, decomposition alone could have completely separated the uppermost cervical vertebra from the rest of the spinal column?—I do not.

If you were further told that the two uppermost ribs on the left side were dislocated, and that there were no other bones in the body broken except those of the head and shoulder, would that have any effect?—I should think it was probably caused by a fall, taking this with the other injuries.

Then it appears to you that all these injuries could quite well be produced by a fall such as I have asked you to assume?—I think they could.

Would the fact that you found such injuries confirm the theory of a fall, as against blows on the head?—It would.

Cross-examined by Mr. GRAHAM MURRAY—This gully was a dangerous place?—Yes.

Do you say that a person going down to Glen Sannox would naturally go down on to these three rocks?—I think he would. He would not see the 32-feet fall.

What would take him near to the danger?—Because the easiest way down is on the right side of the gully, and there is general danger associated with the gully to the left.

And on going on to these rocks he is always keeping to

John Watson Laurie.

Dr Charles W. Macgillivray

the left?—Not necessarily. He could not go to the right at that point without retracing his steps.

You spoke of Logan having ventured on to a shelf. Did his position appear to be dangerous?—Knowing, as I did, there was a 32-feet drop below . . .

Assuming you did not know that. A person would be exercising care, would he not? Supposing you take the left-hand side instead of the right, there you say you came to a possible drop of 19 feet above the place where you were told the cap was discovered. That, from your description, I would gather, rather differed from the 32-feet drop in this, that there seemed to be nothing to indicate the danger from above?—Nothing whatever.

So far as the injuries were concerned, were there any of them inconsistent with the idea of their having been caused by the direct application of a heavy body, such as a stone, wielded by a powerful man?—By a very heavy stone, with application of great power.

So far as the injuries to the head and scapula were concerned, they might have been caused by a stone wielded by a powerful man?—Yes, wielded with very great power.

Would the amount of power, which a man having a large stone in his hand could apply, be very much increased if the assailant was, at the moment of attack, on a higher level than the victim?—Yes.

The character of the ground here admits of two people being in such a position that one might be close behind the other and yet upon a rather higher level?—Yes.

What is the nature of the ground from the point where the cap was found to the boulder?—It is extremely rough.

How far is it?—Two hundred yards.

Do you think any one could carry a human body from the drop to the boulder?—I do not think so.

Could they throw it down?—They might be able to do that.

As to the detachment of the upper vertebra, the cords of attachment are ligaments which, like other tissues of that sort, are subject to decomposition?—Yes, but decomposition in their case takes longer.

Decomposition occurs more or less rapidly according as there is exposure to the air?—Yes.

186

Evidence for Defence.

Dr Charles W. Macgillivray

And it is also assisted if the tissues surrounding the parts have been battered in any way by violence?—Yes.

Of course, animal agencies have a great deal to do with decomposition?—Yes.

And, therefore, an animal agency, which has been set up in a tissue rendered very apt for the purpose by being battered, might then propagate itself to neighbouring tissues which had not been directly attacked?—There is a natural tendency to do so.

What is your objection to the theory that the injuries which you observed upon the head and shoulder were the effect of repeated blows?—My principal reason for rejecting that is because of the widespread nature of these injuries. I mean by that, that they were not limited to the head alone, but spread to the neck and shoulder. I think it is extremely improbable that a person battering in the head would also strike the back of the neck and the shoulder. I cannot see any object in battering on the shoulder and neck.

Supposing a blow was aimed at the top of the head and missed, would not that account for the breaking of the shoulder?—That would depend on the way it hit the shoulder.

Blows necessary to produce death would be of a violent nature. That would account for the widespread nature of the injuries?—Blows directed at the head would not also strike the shoulder.

Well, you agree that a blow aimed at the head, which missed, would account for the shoulder injury?—As I have said, that would depend on how it struck the shoulder.

Certainly I do not suppose he could break the shoulder without hitting it. Now, would not a blow directly given on the front of the face account for the destruction of the upper jaw-bone?—I think not. I think it was described as denuded of soft parts and displaced downwards, whereas a direct blow would smash it.

Can you say that it was displaced downwards? There is nothing about downward displacement in the report. May I take it that you have no doubt that a blow directly on the front of the face would break the upper jaw?—No doubt.

It being possible that these injuries are consistent with

187

John Watson Laurie.

Dr Charles W. Macgillivray

the idea of blows, can you give any reason why a succession of blows should not have been given by a person who wished to murder another, other than the reason that death would have followed one of the blows, and that therefore there was no use of striking further?—I think the skull would have been more injured on the opposite side if there had been a series of blows. I think it is improbable that the assailant would have aimed at the shoulder.

You have given it as your opinion that these injuries were effected by one impact, namely, a fall. Of course, there are injuries here where there could not have been a point of contact at the fall?—That is so.

Therefore, in this case, according to your view, there is a concomitant injury to the injury at the point of contact. Could you not have that injury at a point different from that where there was impact, if you suppose the force to be blows and not a fall?—That is so.

It is consistent with both explanations?—Yes; but, to me, more consistent with the idea of a fall.

Re-examined by the DEAN OF FACULTY—You do not think they are equally consistent, although they are both consistent?—I think not. From the facts, I think a fall is the more probable cause, though the injury below might have been caused by a blow. I believe the jaw was driven down by the same shock as fractured the vertex and the lower part of the skull.

If, as is suggested, the mischief had been produced by direct blows on the face, would not the jaw-bone have been shattered into pieces?—It would. The bone is of such a texture that a blow which would produce a fracture on the top of the head would shatter it; it is a weak bone.

Are the brain and heart soft tissues?—They are.

And are the ligaments attached to the vertebrae at the back-bone very strong?—Yes.

They are not so liable to be destroyed by maggots as the other tissues?—No. It is my opinion that the period of time stated would not have caused that tissue to decay unless there had been a lesion.

Evidence for Defence.

Dr Henry A. Thomson

Dr. HENRY ALEXIS THOMSON, examined by the DEAN OF
FACULTY—I am a Fellow of the Royal College of Surgeons
and I am surgical tutor at the Royal Infirmary, Edinburgh.
On Monday last I accompanied Dr. Macgillivray to Arran.
I was generally familiar with the Arran hills before that. I
was asked to visit this gully. I first went up the left side
of the gully to the top and then came down. I went from
the ridge to the boulder under which the deceased's body was
found. Although I know the Arran hills fairly well, I had
never been down this place before, but I had heard of it as
a difficult track. The ground from the top of the ridge
runs down on a slope of about 45 degrees. It consists of
blocks of granite interspersed with gravel, on which footing
is uncertain. I was shown by Francis Logan the place where
the cap was found. There was a point on the left of the
gully, to which reference has been made, from which one
might fall about 19 feet. It was a very steep slope, barely
off the perpendicular. A person falling down the cliff, whatever way he fell, would fall clear of the base. On the right
side, where the knife, pencil, and button were found, I
observed a place from which it is possible to have a higher
fall. That is the 32-feet drop. It was a place at the edge
of which a person might find himself before noticing his
danger. There were shelving slopes of granite, the end of
which one could not see. At the foot of this rock the ground
was hard granite, somewhat shelving, with lumps of various
forms and ragged surfaces. It is really similar to the ground
at the foot of the 19-feet drop. I have read the three medical
reports produced, and I heard the evidence as to the condition
of Rose's body.

Does it appear to you that it is quite possible that the
injuries described in the reports and by verbal testimony
might have been produced by falling from either of these
two high places which you have seen?—It is most probable.

More probable than the theory of blows?—Undoubtedly.

A person falling over and alighting on his head would
receive the injuries to the head which had been described in
the reports?—Yes.

And the shoulder?—The injury there may also have been
caused by the same means.

John Watson Laurie.

Dr Henry A. Thomson

As to the condition of the vertebræ, looking to the time which elapsed before the body was discovered, do you have any difficulty in understanding why the first vertebra alone was implicated?—Certainly. I cannot understand why the first vertebra should have been affected by decomposition in the manner described. I do not think that decomposition should have affected the ligaments of that part of the vertebræ and no other.

Having regard to the facts stated, do you think that decay alone would have produced this effect?—I cannot see how it could. There must have been dislocation of the vertebræ before death.

That would be a separate circumstance leading to the conclusion that the injuries were due to a fall?—Undoubtedly, in my opinion. I would not draw so definite a conclusion from the circumstances if the ribs were separated from the spinal column.

It is your opinion, then, that Rose's death occurred as the result of a fall?—Yes.

Cross-examined by the SOLICITOR-GENERAL—You do not mean to suggest that the descent by Corr-na-Fourin in broad daylight would be dangerous for an ordinary man?—I would not say it was dangerous for myself.

As you came down from the ridge, before you reached any of the points where the articles were found, the gully was quite obvious?—Yes.

As regards the drop of 19 feet, the top of the rock for a certain area is tolerably flat?—Yes.

Anybody coming down would see that the rocks are sheer? —That is difficult to appreciate. The gully looks like a white mark.

The most direct course is to keep as much to the right as the ground allows you?—Probably.

Any sensible man would prefer that?—It is the most direct course.

With regard to the injuries, you say that in your opinion they could be accounted for by a fall. You will also say that they could be accounted for by repeated blows?—It is within the limits of possibility.

190

Evidence for Defence.

Dr Henry A. Thomson

I suppose the theory of a fall would require you, in the first place, to imagine a sheer fall, and that the body goes down head-first?—Yes, head-first.

Re-examined by the DEAN OF FACULTY—Speaking as a medical man, whether do you think the theory of blows or the theory of a fall is the more probable?—I consider that the fall is the more probable explanation of the injuries described in the reports. The condition of the shoulder and the upper cervical vertebra corroborate that.

The DEAN OF FACULTY—My Lord, that concludes the evidence for the defence.

> [At this stage the jury were shown a large-scale map of the island of Arran, and the various localities mentioned in the course of the evidence were pointed out by counsel. The photographs of the *locus* were also shown to them.]

The Solicitor-General's Address to the Jury.

The SOLICITOR-GENERAL—Gentlemen of the jury, you have been investigating during these two days a tragedy the circumstances of which lie far out of the ordinary track of crime. The recent acquaintance of these two young men, Laurie and Rose, the holiday character of their expedition, the solitude and grandeur of the scene in which the crime took place, all incline to invest it with an interest altogether exceptional. Undoubtedly, if there was a murder, it was a murder of a peculiarly atrocious character. That a young man, a stranger, a visitor to our shores, in the midst of a summer holiday, with life and spirits at their highest, should be suddenly set upon and butchered, apparently through no motive of revenge or malice, but only for the sake of the murderer appropriating what means the victim possessed, is undoubtedly a combination of circumstances calculated to arouse the strongest feelings of reprobation. I should not be doing my duty as public prosecutor

John Watson Laurie.

The Solicitor-General

if I did not say to you that this very circumstance imposes upon you a double duty of a very delicate character. In the first place, you must not allow your natural indignation at all to obscure your judgment in answering the only question that is before you—whether or not the prisoner at the bar is guilty of murder. On the other hand, you must not shrink from doing your duty merely because the evidence, to a large extent, is circumstantial. That is necessarily so. The darker and more atrocious forms of crime are almost invariably done in secret; and the law would be feeble and impotent indeed if it were unable to reach the perpetrator of this species of crime, merely because no human eye witnessed its perpetration. No man can complain of being judged by the ordinary rules of human conduct, by ordinary standards being applied to it; and it will be in accordance with these, applied to the prisoner's own conduct, that I shall ask you to consider your verdict.

The salient facts of the case are these: Two young men went up a hill together and only one came down. The other was found, after an interval of weeks, with his body horribly mutilated, hidden away among the rocks of the hillside, and with all his portable property removed. The one who came down was seen within a few hours of the time when the death of his friend must have taken place. He returned from the excursion on which they both started, and gave no sign or hint that anything had happened to his friend, or that he had not returned with him. The next morning he left Arran, and resumed his ordinary occupation until the hue and cry began. Then, when it did begin, he took to flight; and, finally, when he was about to be arrested, he attempted to cut his throat.

These are the facts of the case, and I would be failing in my duty, if I did not assist as far as I can, by explaining them and giving my authority for them. Let us look first at the history of the accused's own proceedings in the matter. The first thing we know about him is that he arrived in Rothesay on 6th July under an assumed name. I do not wish to lay too much stress upon that, but it indicates a certain amount of mystery, which, I think, has not sufficiently

192

The Solicitor=General (Stormonth Darling).

Solicitor-General's Address to the Jury.

been accounted for. He took lodgings at Port Bannatyne with Mrs. Currie. On the 12th, by the merest accident, he made the acquaintance of Mr. Edwin Rose, and I think you will all be of the opinion that Rose was a young man of agreeable manners, ready to take up with any one he met, affable, cheerful, and—though his friends said, not robust— of a healthy frame and accustomed to take part in athletic exercises. This accidental acquaintance, formed on the steamer going to Arran, led to a plan for spending from Saturday till Tuesday or Wednesday at Brodick, which they did. They took up their residence at the lodgings of Mrs. Walker. When they arrived, Rose had with him a black bag and Laurie a brown one. Laurie was wearing a straw hat.

Now, I do not think you can have any reasonable doubt that the two ascended Goatfell on Monday, 15th July, and reached the top. This is a most important part of the case, and it is right that you should be fully satisfied regarding it. It rests, in the first place, on the evidence of Morrison and Purdon, who met them going up; also on the evidence of those who overtook them going up; and by various links we have a complete and satisfactory chain of evidence bringing them to the top of Goatfell. Apparently they left the summit before those who have given evidence— the brothers Francis and the Hind party—and I think you will not have very much doubt that they left the top of Goatfell together about six o'clock, to descend into Glen Sannox by way of the ridge. That was the last time that Rose was seen alive. But, leaving for a moment the narrative of what happened to Rose, we will follow the accused. He was next seen by the witness David M'Kenzie, the shepherd, who was perfectly confident that he had seen a stranger coming out of the glen and crossing the short cut to Corrie. M'Kenzie said that the man corresponded to the accused. His statement is not disproved by the negative evidence of the two witnesses for the defence; but the evidence as to the accused's movements does not rest alone on the testimony of M'Kenzie. Half an hour later—and I think you can have no doubt about this—the accused entered the Corrie

o   193

John Watson Laurie.

The Solicitor-General

Hotel and had a drink at the bar. You have heard the witness Wilson testify to that. After that we lose sight of him for two hours, but there is very little doubt, I think, about what he did. He pursued his journey from Corrie to Brodick along the shore; he spent the night in the room which he and Rose had there; and next morning left before any of the people of the house had seen him, without paying the bill. He emptied the basin and left the room in a condition to suggest that two people had occupied it.

The DEAN OF FACULTY—One basin, one bed—nothing to suggest two people having been there.

The SOLICITOR-GENERAL—I am not founding on that. Next morning, gentlemen, the accused left, obliterating every trace of Rose, leaving nothing except the tennis racket—which, as it bore the name of Rose, it would have been awkward for him to have carried away—a straw hat, a pair of slippers, and a mackintosh. Accordingly, he was seen that morning carrying a couple of bags, one black and the other brown, to the steamer for Ardrossan, which left at seven o'clock. He was again seen with the black bag, which it has been proved belonged to Rose, on the way to Glasgow. There we lose sight of the bag, but Laurie himself arrived in Glasgow, and that same afternoon returned to Rothesay, apparently for the purpose of fulfilling his holiday programme. He went back to Mrs. Currie's, bringing with him a paper parcel containing a chocolate-and-white striped tennis jacket, tennis shoes, and a peaked yachting cap, and he was wearing a grey felt hat. That grey felt hat, it has been proved, was the property of the deceased. Therefore, you have the fact that Laurie, who had left Mrs. Currie's wearing a straw hat, returned on the 16th of July wearing Rose's grey hat. I think you can also have very little doubt that the contents of the parcel which he carried were, to some extent at least, Rose's property. The tennis jacket has been spoken to by a sister of the deceased, and the proof of the identity of the tennis shoes is unusually complete. There is the evidence of the shoemaker himself that he had repaired them for the deceased. In order to account for the remainder of Rose's property, you will observe that, when Laurie went

194

Solicitor-General's Address to the Jury.

to Liverpool, he took with him a trunk, which he left at Mrs. Ennitt's. When that trunk was taken possession of by the police and opened, it was found to contain a number of toilet articles, every one of which, with the exception of a box containing a stamp, which belonged to Laurie, was clearly identified as having been the property of the deceased. After staying a few days at Rothesay, the accused, without paying his bill, returned to Glasgow, and to his work at Springburn. He left that work on 31st July. I think he had a very good reason for doing so, because the hue and cry had then been raised about the disappearance of Rose. It was on this day that he had that most remarkable conversation with Mr. Aitken; and it was the most natural thing in the world that Mr. Aitken, having seen the account of Rose's disappearance, should follow up his questions the more searchingly. Then the accused went to Liverpool, and you have heard narrated the circumstances leading up to his capture.

Now, let me direct particular attention to the fate of Rose. There can be no doubt that it was Rose's body that was found under the boulder. It is perfectly clear, further, that the deceased was placed there by the hand of man and that his pockets were rifled of their contents by the hand of man. We have not been able to recover anything he was carrying in his pockets; we do not know what amount of money he had on his person, but he must have had sufficient for his lodgings and enough to pay his way during the rest of his holidays. Accordingly, the question comes to be :—Whose hand was it that rifled the pockets and placed the body of the deceased under the boulder? I think you will have very little difficulty in dismissing the notion that the accused was not with the deceased down to the end. A suggestion may have been made in one of the accused's letters —it is at all events made dimly—that he had parted with Rose on the top of the hill and saw no more of him; but I think that is absolutely excluded by the facts of the case. Why, if he left him on the hill, did not the prisoner do what ninety-nine men out of a hundred would have done—come straight down to Brodick and give immediate information

John Watson Laurie.

of the loss and disappearance of his friend? But when, instead of that, the accused is found to be in possession of Rose's property, there is no difficulty whatever in coming to the conclusion that, at all events, the accused was with the deceased down to the period of his death and his burial beneath the boulder. If that were so, it was the accused's hand that rifled his pockets, and laid him in the position in which he was found.

Then the question arises: Was it at the accused's hands that he met his death? I suppose I must deal with the supposition that the deceased's death was the result of accident, and that the robbery and secretion of the body were the work of the accused. This case is so inherently—I had almost said, so wildly—improbable, that you will hesitate before you give it credence. You will hesitate upon the ordinary grounds of human conduct, apart altogether from questions of medical evidence. The supposition presented is that the accused's friend met with a sudden and fatal fall. Well, I think that would solemnise most people, and not only solemnise them, but would make them—I am speaking about men of sound mind and reasonable, ordinary disposition—go down at once and give the alarm. Another theory is that, after seeing his friend die before his eyes, he conceived the notion of robbing him and hiding the body away. Such an act would indicate a depravity of mind which is only a little removed from the depravity of mind of a murderer.

With regard to the theory of a fall, let us consider first the nature of the ground. I do not think it can be seriously maintained that this is a dangerous descent, in any ordinary or reasonable sense of the word, for two young men of active habits, in broad daylight in the month of July. The only witness who has said that it would be dangerous is the Italian fisherman, Latona, who is really not accustomed to mountain climbing, and has spent his life at sea. And when it was directly put to him, he stated candidly that it was not a descent of which he would be in the least afraid. Dr. Alexis Thomson, another witness for the defence, said that he would not be in the least afraid to take that road in daylight. It is not, it is true, the ordinary descent into Glen Sannox;

196

Solicitor-General's Address to the Jury.

but there is an explanation of that. If it was not the ordinary descent, then it was all the more suitable for the commission of the deed which is here charged against the accused.

With regard to the injuries, they were, in the first place, on the top of the head; in the second place, they were at the base of the skull; and, in the third place, the face was entirely smashed. There was also an injury to the shoulder. Just let us look at the number of conditions that must combine before one fall, such as is suggested, could cause all these injuries. There are many of them, according to Dr. Heron Watson. In the first place, it must have been a sheer fall; secondly, it must have been a fall backwards; thirdly, it must have occurred at the foot of a slope; and, in the fourth place, it must have been upon a rock so shaped that it would catch the top of the head and at the same time injure the shoulder. It is for you to consider, not so much what is possible, because all things are possible where you are dealing with medical testimony, but what probably happened. It is for you to say whether this is a reasonable supposition. To my mind, what is absolutely fatal to the theory of Dr. Heron Watson—and I do not mean in the medical sense, but in the common sense—is that at the place where the body was found there was no rock with a slope above it of the kind which he required. To reach the 32-feet rock Rose must have gone voluntarily out of his way to the edge of what he knew to be a precipice. It is reasonable to suppose that he stepped voluntarily aside from his course and went over that drop backwards? But what very definitely disposes of this is, that it was at a point 40 yards below that the cap of the deceased was found. I do not think that any one can doubt that the position of the cap had something to do with this—everything to do with it, in fact. It was put in the position in which it was found by a human hand, in a place where it was difficult to reach from below. Then as regards the other drop, the 19-feet one, which is certainly above where the cap was found, it so happens that at the upper edge of it there is a comparatively flat stone. It does not have a smooth sloping top, and thus it does not satisfy the essential condition of Dr. Heron Watson's theory.

197

John Watson Laurie.

The Solicitor-General

Therefore, gentlemen, I venture to think that, apart from the medical evidence altogether, you will be able by the application of plain common sense to come to the conclusion that there could have been no such accidental fall which could possibly account for Rose's death upon this hillside, and if it was not a fall, then we are brought to the theory that the death resulted from blows. Whether they were all struck before or after death I cannot tell you. We are groping in the dark as to the cause of death; but my theory—I want you to note that I do not offer it as a positive suggestion—is that there was first such a blow as would at all events stun the man, and that it was followed up by such others as were necessary to cause death. It is my view, also, that these severe injuries were inflicted for the sake of preventing recognition. You have heard that the evidence for the defence—I am speaking about the medical evidence—did not exclude that theory, although, of course, they preferred the theory of a fall. You will remember that Dr. Gilmour and Dr. Fullarton, both unconnected with each other and unconnected with the Crown, came to the conclusion, after seeing the place, that blows offered the preferable and more reasonable explanation. I do not profess to be able to give you much assistance as to the purely surgical conflict between the doctors, nor do I think it very material. You will always find medical men in a matter of this kind ready to differ from each other upon points of speculation. What I do say is, that the reasonable conclusion is that injuries so diverse and numerous over the head, which are, at the same time, coupled with an utter absence of injury to the other parts of the body, point clearly to direct and repeated violence applied by the hand of man. Again, I think that undoubtedly it is the prisoner's own conduct which affords us the readiest solution of this mystery. I ask you to consider that conduct, to consider it fairly, but still fearlessly, and apply to it the ordinary standard of human conduct, and to ask yourselves this question: Whether any man would have so conducted himself who was not the murderer of Rose? If the accused was the murderer, then all that occurred afterwards is amply explained.

It may be said that the motive was very inadequate for so

Solicitor-General's Address to the Jury.

The Solicitor-General

frightful and atrocious a crime, and no doubt it is; but we find in the annals of crime that it is often impossible to gauge the motives of a man who is in such a state of mind as to commit such a crime. There can be no adequate motive for murder, but we can usually find one which is, at least, fairly intelligible. I put it to you strongly that the accused was with Rose down to the last, that his was the hand that robbed him, and that his was the hand which laid him under the boulder. Any motive which explains the accused's conduct consistently with accidental death is more unintelligible than the motive of desire to plunder. If, again, you are to accept the theory that death having been purely accidental, the accused then robbed the body, there is a very obvious difficulty. If the property to be obtained by the murder was small—at all events, the accused did not know how much it would be—I say if, after Rose's death, he found that the property was small in value, I should have thought that his plain course was to avoid all suspicion by coming down and giving information to his friends. I cannot imagine that any man could have plundered that body without knowing that he was subjecting himself to the most fearful risk of being thought guilty of the crime of murder. It is inconceivable that any man could voluntarily take that risk merely because he had suddenly taken it into his head to rob the body, and particularly if he found that what he was getting was very small in value. If, on the other hand, he murdered him, then by that time the die was cast. Then, he had done it anticipating, no doubt, that what he would get might be more than it actually was; but he had done it, and he must go through with it. That, I submit, is what happened.

Gentlemen, if you come to the conclusion, as I have done, that Laurie's was the hand which inflicted the death blow, then all his subsequent conduct is explained. The character and nature of the ground and the other circumstances I have mentioned all point clearly and conclusively to the fact that Rose was killed by the accused. It is to that conclusion that I reluctantly and sorrowfully, yet distinctly and clearly, ask you to come. Gentlemen, it is beyond all reasonable doubt that the accused is guilty of this murder, and I ask for your verdict accordingly.

John Watson Laurie.

The Dean of Faculty's Address to the Jury.

The DEAN OF FACULTY—The Solicitor-General has made the remark that the present case lies out of the ordinary track of crime. Although I shall differ from the Solicitor-General in many things, I entirely agree with him in that. I shall go further and say that the murder, if murder there was, is one of a most atrocious and unprecedented kind. Since this case is without precedent, the onus of proof is, therefore, all the heavier on the Crown. If this was a murder, it is, as I have said, of a peculiarly atrocious character; and I hope that fact will have the effect of leading you to be very careful and very anxious in considering the evidence, before you affirm that so unprecedented and incredibly atrocious a murder could have been committed under the circumstances that have been disclosed in the charge of the Crown. If you view the matter in the light of antecedent probability, every probability—I think I may even say, every possibility—is against it. I hope, in the course of what I have to say, to show that not only is there no evidence to sustain the theory of murder, but that there is no evidence even making materially towards sustaining it. And in the discharge of such a sad and painful duty as you have to perform, nothing except evidence, absolutely clear to your minds, will either entitle you or call upon you to return a verdict of guilty. Even if you think a case of suspicion has been established, you must not forget that suspicion is not proof; and in this matter, where a mistake or error on your part will be irreparable and where the life of a fellow being is in question, you will be careful to give a dispassionate and unbiased judgment.

The matters involved in this case may be dealt with under two heads. Wherever you have a charge of murder, it involves two questions—first, whether the person who is said to have been murdered died by wilful violence, or whether he died by accident, misadventure, or natural causes. Unless and until you are satisfied that this was a wilful murder, it will be useless for you to consider the question of who perpetrated the murder. Even if you do come to be of opinion

200

Dean of Faculty's Address to the Jury.

that violent hands were laid upon the deceased during his life, you will then have, secondly, to consider whether there is sufficient evidence to show that the murder was committed by the accused. Before you can possibly arrive at a verdict of guilty, you will have to be clear in your minds not only upon one, but upon both of these points.

I think it will be most convenient if I follow the most logical order and examine the first question first, namely, whether it is proved that there was any murder at all. What are the facts bearing upon that question? Some things are certain : one is that the body was found, in the circumstances which have been described, on 4th August. There is no doubt about the condition of the body—the head was terribly smashed, the bone of the shoulder was also smashed, the highest joint of the back-bone was detached, and the two uppermost ribs were detached from the back-bone at their base at the back. There was no other injury upon the body. I might point out here that there was no trace or sign of any struggle, and it is admitted that there was no appearance of the body having been dragged. Now, what you have to consider in the first instance is : What is the conclusion to be drawn from the appearance of the body? If, upon a balance of the medical opinion, you come to be of the mind that that opinion is consistent with the theory of the Crown, but still more consistent with the theory that the death was by accident or misadventure, for the producing of which you have the means in the neighbourhood, your duty is clearly to find that the case for the Crown has not been made out.

With regard to the difference of expert opinion in the case, I shall certainly not say anything disrespectful about the medical gentlemen who gave evidence for the Crown, because no doubt they honestly, and according to their judgment and belief, told us what they thought. Perhaps it may be thought that Dr. Gilmour was a little too hasty in coming to the conclusion he did on the examination of the body on the first two occasions, particularly on the first occasion. If there is to be judgment upon theory, it must be based upon mature consideration, and not upon preconceived opinion. The theory of the Crown is that the injuries to the head and

John Watson Laurie.

the face were the result of a succession of blows. I can quite understand that there are many cases in which, when an injured body is found along with something that could bring about the injuries on the body, one would say that a murder had been committed. If, for example, you found a body with a pistol shot in it and a pistol lying in the neighbourhood, there would be no question. But—and you will observe this closely—there is no suggestion of any instrument of any sort having been found in the neighbourhood to which this murder could be attributed at all. As I understand the theory of the Crown, it is that some person took up a stone, and, by battering the head and face, killed this man. If there had been any stone used for such a purpose, one would have supposed at all events that it must have borne marks of blood. Now, although every inch of that ground has been beaten over, it is not suggested that any weapon likely to produce that result has been found. Then, what is the view of the doctors with regard to the opposing theory? As I understand it, although the medical witnesses examined for the Crown preferred the theory of direct violence, they virtually admitted in the end that it was possible that a fall might produce what was seen upon the body.

But before coming to that, I want to examine the conditions that must have existed in order to enable one man to attack another with a stone so as to bring about these results. It is a remarkable fact that the injuries were upon the left side. That, at the very outset, should exclude the theory of the men facing up to each other, and I do not think you will accept the theory that one man marched up to the other and, in his sight and vision, did this thing. The question has also been raised: " Would the man come up behind? " But if any one who was murderously inclined came up behind, one would rather expect that the injuries would have been on the right-hand side instead of on the left. No right-handed man would ever have assailed the deceased upon that side, and there is no suggestion that the accused is a left-handed man. I ask you whether it is possible that any man coming up behind would batter his victim in that way; he could, naturally, only strike him on the side that lay

Dean of Faculty's Address to the Jury.

next his hand. That, however, is a small matter. In my view, the injuries are far more consistent with the theory of accident than of murder. Such extensive injuries as were here caused involve the application of great violence to a large part of the head. That has been proved to be the case by the fact that, not only were there fractures across the top of the head, but also on account of there being corresponding fractures at the base of the skull. Now, if these injuries were caused by a stone, you would have a number of corresponding marks on the opposite side of the skull. But these were not present here; and the suggestion of the Crown that the character of the injuries indicate the application of violence to more than one part of the skull is of no avail, because that also is consistent with the theory of a fall, and I will show that the place where the fall took place supplies points sufficient to make these injuries.

Coming down to details, when you examine the evidence of the doctors on the character of the injuries and their probable cause, I think you will have little difficulty in concluding that there is a balance of medical opinion in favour of the view submitted by the defence. With regard to the injury to the left shoulder, I think it is absolutely ludicrous for the Crown to suggest, as they do, that that injury was caused by a blow aimed at the head and striking the shoulder. The fact that there is a hole in the waterproof coat, another in the clothing, and a corresponding one in the tissues, all at the place where the injury to the shoulder was situated, is more consistent with a fall than a blow. The severance of the highest joint of the back-bone when the body was turned over is also more consistent with accident than with blows; because, as the ligaments are hard, strong bands, it is impossible, according to skilled witnesses, that between 15th July and 4th August they could have been destroyed either by decay or by insects. Therefore, the conclusion is that the neck must have been broken at or about death. I have heard no suggestion from the Solicitor-General that there were blows struck which would break the neck. That is not the way blows by stones would operate. It is remarkable that this exactly fits and tallies in every particular with the con-

203

John Watson Laurie.

sequences of a pitch down, which would have the effect of fracturing the skull and the shoulder. But it does not end there, because we have the detachment of the two upper ribs from the back-bone. The suggestion made by the Crown witnesses was that that might perhaps have been due to decay. That was not accepted by the medical men examined for the defence; and I am justified in making this remark, that when you have combined together great injuries to the left side and dislocation of the neck, the next points which would meet the strain of the fall would be the shoulder and the ribs. You have all these elements here. All these separate injuries point to the theory of the defence as being the preferable one; and the combined effects, as existing in that body, strengthen the theory enormously, because it is not suggested that the dislocation of the neck and breaking of the ribs would be brought about by the blow of a stone.

The next point is whether there is any place in the neighbourhood capable of producing such injuries by a fall. I quite understand that, if a weapon had been found competent to inflict the injuries, and if you did not find a place in or about the neighbourhood where the body was recovered competent to produce such lesions, then the theory which I put forward might not have been sustainable or might have been more doubtful. While there is no instrument of violence such as is suggested by the Crown, you have ready to hand, not many yards from that spot, two declivities that would bring about such results as these. The higher of these is somewhere about 200 yards above the site of the boulder; the other is about 40 or 46 yards lower down. On the left side of the stream down which undoubtedly Rose was coming, whether alone or accompanied, there is a place with a clear drop of 19 feet upon granite boulders, rough and jagged, below. On the other side, a little lower down, there is a clear drop of 32 feet, again upon jagged boulders. If you accept the theory of Dr. Heron Watson and those who followed him, you have to your hand the cause that would bring about the result; you have to your hand means competent to produce such results, and much more probable to produce them than the means which the Solicitor-General has put

204

Dean of Faculty's Address to the Jury.

forward. With regard to the finding of the cap in the stream, it is difficult to see what the Crown theory is in this matter. They say there was a stone upon the cap, and that that stone was put there by the hand of man; but the spot, according to one of their own witnesses, was difficult to get at and dangerous. Other causes might easily account for the condition and position of the cap, and it cannot be suggested that the stone was put there to conceal the cap, because it did not conceal it at all.

On this whole matter here I make my first point against the case for the Crown. It is this: that they have failed to prove a murder; that the probability on the medical testimony is that the injuries were due to causes other than the wilful infliction of violence; and that those other causes are at hand, with belongings of the man said to have been murdered, close by. I do not know where the Crown say the murder was committed. If it was up at that place, I have made my remark upon it; if it was at the boulder, how came these things at the places where they were found? Concealment could not have been the object, because the things were there. If this had been a case of murder, in that not very large island it is perfectly certain that before very long there would be a search and these things would be found. They were lying perfectly open; and upon this matter the weight of the evidence is upon the side of the defence. It appears to me that the only difficulty on the part of the Crown witnesses in accepting the theory of the defence really, in the end, comes to be that the upper jaw had been detached in one piece; but Dr. Heron Watson and Dr. Macgillivray say that that is not surprising, but is even consistent with their theory. If you take the view I have submitted to you, the rest of your duty is easy.

You will have noticed that the Solicitor-General relies very much in support of this charge of murder upon what he calls the accused's conduct. I will not omit to notice that point; but I would prefer now to come to the question whether the accused perpetrated the murder, or whether the evidence upon this part of the case is so strong as to turn the balance and lead you to reject the theory of the defence. The extra-

John Watson Laurie.

The Dean of Faculty

ordinary character of the crime, and you will remember the Solicitor-General remarked upon it, makes it all the more necessary for the Crown to prove with absolute clearness that such an unprecedented thing as this was done; and that such an atrocious and almost incredible crime was committed. The more improbable, according to the experience of human action and conduct, anything is the more difficult will be your task in arriving at that conclusion. In proving murder, the burden is laid upon the Crown to overcome improbabilities, and to show that something, not only contrary to human experience, but contrary to human nature, was done in this particular case. I submit that what is said to have been done here is highly improbable. These two young men were out for a holiday. They were similar in age and position and had got upon friendly terms. Surely these were circumstances the least likely to lead to murder. Something has been said by the Solicitor-General of Laurie having gone down to the coast under the fictitious name of Annandale. It is true he called himself Annandale, but it is not very uncommon for young men through freak, or for some other cause, to assume another name. The principal point about this is, has it any connection with the case? Laurie went to Rothesay and called himself Annandale; but Laurie was known to many people there. Laurie, you will remember also, never knew that he was to meet Rose. He took his lodgings on the 5th, and did not see Rose until the 12th; so that a topic of that kind is absolutely immaterial for the purpose of a jury considering human motive and human conduct. The meeting was not brought about by Laurie or sought by Laurie. It was a meeting like that of many hundreds and thousands of young men on holiday. Rose was about the last man that could excite malice or ill-feeling in anybody, and certainly about the last man upon whom any one in his company could be supposed to lay murderous hands. The meeting was brought about upon the steamer going to Arran on the 12th by Rose coming up to Laurie, and mistaking him for some member of the company staying at Glenburn Hydropathic. The accused said he was not one of the Hydropathic party, and the deceased replied:

Dean of Faculty's Address to the Jury.

The Dean of Faculty

" Oh, I am glad to see you on the steamer all the same."
There were people on board that boat who knew the accused,
and Aitken introduced him as Laurie to the two Allens. I
therefore do not see the bearing of introducing that topic
of Laurie's fictitious name, and, if I may say so, I do not
think you will see the reason either.

Now, what was the errand upon which Laurie was pro-
ceeding that day? He certainly had no idea of joining the
society of Rose or anybody else, except people perhaps whom
he knew and might meet by chance upon his journey. He
was going down to take lodgings for himself, and accordingly
he took lodgings with Mrs. Walker, agreeing to pay her 17s.
a week for his room. At that season of the year there is a
demand for lodgings, and the deceased, having made the
acquaintance of Laurie, asked to be allowed to share his bed.
That was agreed to, and that is the beginning of it.
Apparently, at the first, the accused thought that Rose was
only going to stay one day, because he said so to Miss Park
on the pier. Then, having learned that Rose intended to
stay for a few days, he went back and told Miss Park that
also. I ask you, can you believe that, at that time, any
such design as has been imputed to Laurie could be in his
mind? These two young men came back on the 12th. Rose,
apparently, having taken a fancy to Laurie, asked him to
call at the Hydropathic in the evening; and, while he was
changing his clothes, he asked another of the party to show
Laurie through the house. That gentleman left Laurie in
the recreation room, and I suppose the rest of the evening
would be spent in the manner usual in such a place. The
point to notice is that you have nothing in the shape of
Laurie hunting Rose or anything like it. On the Saturday
they went down to Arran and took up their abode in that
small dwelling of Mrs. Walker's. Laurie got his meals in
the house while Rose got his at Wooley's. They passed the
Saturday and the Sunday going about among people, and in
company with two other young men had tea at the Gilmours',
Laurie being introduced as Rose's friend. There again the
initiative was taken by the deceased. Then came the
Monday, and it was passed in a similar way. Laurie seemed

207

John Watson Laurie.

to be suffering from toothache. Some witness has suggested that he was silent and that Rose was more talkative. I suppose that every one who has had the misfortune to be afflicted with toothache would rather sympathise with any one who was somewhat silent while suffering from it.

When I turn to the matter of what took place at Goatfell, the evidence shows that there were at least seven people on the hill that afternoon. If the accused had been capable of entertaining any nefarious design, every one of these persons would be certain to be witnesses in this inquiry. They lost sight of Rose and Laurie at the top of Goatfell, and from that point onwards, until Laurie turned up at Corrie in the evening, we have no evidence whatever, as to a large part of that time, of where either of them was; and as to the part which is said to have been passed by the accused going by the burying-ground, only the evidence—the very uncertain and quite unsatisfactory evidence—of M'Kenzie, the shepherd. At the top of the hill, then, they pass from sight. One of the letters, which is said to be Laurie's, speaks to their having parted there, and there is no evidence against that—nothing to show that they did not part there. The accused says that Rose met two people who intended to go back to Brodick, and that he saw no more of them. It is true Rose did not go back to Brodick, but, so far as the evidence goes, he may either have gone down that place alone or with other persons, for he appears to have been a man ready to take up with anybody. It is quite enough for me to point out to you that there is no evidence that the deceased and the accused were ever together again in this world from the time, about 6.25, when they were seen on the top of the hill. The Solicitor-General is quite mistaken in stating that the defence admits that the two were together. There is no evidence that they were together. It must be taken as a thing not proved that they were together. Whoever removed the body—I hope you will understand that you do not go to deliberate upon your verdict on the supposition that it is the theory or suggestion of the defence that the moving of the body was done by Laurie—nobody knows by whom it was done.

What is the next said to have been seen of Laurie?

The Dean of Faculty (Balfour).

Dean of Faculty's Address to the Jury.

The Dean of Faculty

M'Kenzie, the shepherd, said that a little after nine o'clock he saw a weary traveller coming out of Glen Sannox, and that it was Laurie; but he was entirely contradicted by the two servant girls who were with him. There is no doubt that Laurie was at Corrie Hotel at ten o'clock; and the theory of the Crown is that he went into that hotel a red-handed murderer. But were there any appearances or signs of that upon him? No; he was just like anybody else. This matter is important. There was no blood upon Rose's clothes, and that is consistent with the theory of the deceased having died suddenly as the result of a fall. If, as the Crown says, he was smashed to death by a series of blows, there would have been traces of blood; but there were none. There was no suggestion that, either at Corrie or next morning at Brodick, there was any mark or trace of blood upon Laurie.

I cannot be asked, nor can the accused be asked, to say how or by whom that body was put in that place, because, of course, that is a matter as to which there is no evidence whatever. The Solicitor-General asks you to take it, without any evidence, that Laurie did it. There were plenty of other people on the island besides Laurie. The Solicitor-General seems to think that we, for the defence, are admitting that Laurie robbed the body of Rose. We admit nothing of the kind. It may be that somebody did it. Very likely, at these Fair holidays, there would be plenty of people on the island who would do that. It is perfectly consistent with the evidence that the deceased having fallen over one of these precipices came to his death, whether there was somebody with him or nobody with him. If there was somebody with him, that person may have robbed him; but if there was nobody with him, somebody may have found his body and put it where it was, after robbing it. But on this question of robbery, I pray you to keep in mind that there has not been one article which Rose had with him on that day which has been traced to Laurie. He did have some other articles of his, and, absolutely careless, he carried these about with him. That points rather to this, that if he had done such a thing as is charged, he would not likely have carried these articles about with him.

John Watson Laurie.

The Dean of Faculty

There are some other facts in this case which rather seem to suggest that neither Laurie nor any one man could have performed that operation, because it is proved by the Crown witnesses that the body had not been dragged. It must have been lifted and taken to the place where it was found; and it is for you to consider whether a man of Laurie's size and strength could have carried a body, and put it where it was, without aid or assistance. One of the stones piled in front of the body was $1\frac{1}{2}$ cwt. in weight, and that is a kind of stone that would more likely require two men to lift than one. I am not going into the question of time in detail, because, if there was a murder, it must have taken a good deal of time. The accused left the top of the hill about six o'clock, and was seen at Corrie about ten. If walking all the time, he would have covered the distance. But the absolutely indefinite time needed to do all the things which the Crown says he did would not have been short. What I say to you is that, while there is no evidence whatever as to who moved the body, there are considerations which go rather to show that it must have been moved by more persons than one. Even if the accused had the diabolical mind to murder this man, the evidence is of such a nature that he could not have done it. If the theory of the Crown is that murder took place at the boulder, how about the cap, the knife, and the stick lying at different places up the gully? The position of these things is more consistent with the theory of the defence, namely, a pitch over, and the things flying in all directions.

I now wish to say a word on the question of motive. If this was a murder, it was a murder in the very coldest of cold blood. The idea of quarrel or revenge does not enter the case. The deceased was a man with whom no one would quarrel. The only suggestion which I have heard by the Solicitor-General upon this matter is, that the accused murdered his friend, who had been living and sleeping with him all these days, for the sake of what he had on him. Some of the things he had upon him were left in the burn, but there is no evidence to show what he had upon him other than the things which were strewn along the burn. It has

210

Dean of Faculty's Address to the Jury.

The Dean of Faculty

been said that the accused was seen with a watch. There is no evidence to show what money was upon the deceased, but, he being only a clerk near the end of his holidays, it could not have been much; and therefore the suggestion of pecuniary motive for murder disappears. The hazards run by any one in committing a murder there are enormous. And this is alleged to have been a murder in broad daylight, and the place is within the vision of people who may have been on the hill. I ask you, in considering the question of motive and of the probability of detection in the act, whether you are prepared, not only upon imperfect evidence but without evidence, to affirm that the deed was done by the accused.

The point upon which the Solicitor-General chiefly relies is what he calls the subsequent conduct of Laurie. Before we can draw any conclusion from conduct, we must be certain that that conduct is consistent with guilt. What was the accused's conduct? He went away, it is true, next morning, the 15th, by the early boat. It has been proved that he took away several of the deceased's things with him. There is no doubt about that. He apparently made no secret of it, because he wore the cap at Rothesay, among the very people who knew them both. That is not very like concealment. He had a tennis jacket, also belonging to Rose. In fact, he took his bag. I am not going to justify that action. Whether Laurie thought that, because the deceased had not turned up, he might take his things, I am not going to inquire, because I deal with the case upon the assumption that he improperly took away such property belonging to Rose as he found in the lodging. What conclusion does that lead to? If you had been trying a case of comparatively petty theft, it might have been deserving of very serious consideration. But what connection has that with the murder of Rose? That is what I want to know. What did the accused do with the things he took? Did he get rid of them, or conceal them? Not at all. He was perfectly open with them. He stamped his name on a couple of the shirts. The value of them can be measured by shillings. But contrast the things belonging to Rose which he improperly took with the things which I deny that

John Watson Laurie.

The Dean of Faculty

he took. Not one article which was upon the person of Rose when he went up Goatfell that afternoon has ever been traced to the accused. I should have thought that, if a man committed a murder, the last thing we should expect would be that he would be found with any one of the other man's things, because they would bring him under suspicion. In point of fact, that is the very first thing which happened in this case, because the witness Aitken put a question to Laurie about a cap which he had worn on the 31st of July. Going about in that open manner is not the way of a murderer, but it may well be the way of a person who improperly took away things from a friend's lodgings. Laurie certainly did not act as if the avenger of blood was on his track. The first thing he did was to go straight among his own friends. He went back to Rothesay with people who knew him. He travelled with Gilmour in the train to Glasgow, and in Bute he met with the very people who had seen him and Rose go away together. Is it conceivable that he would thus walk back into the lion's mouth? If he had been a criminal, would he have gone among the very people whom he had been living with in Rothesay about the time of his crime? It was just the way to invite suspicion, if there had been ground for it. He went back to his lodgings and to his work, and he was down for one day, the 27th, at Rothesay again. What is the first sign of that conduct which the Solicitor-General said was characteristic of the guilty conscience of the murderer? I understand that the suggestion is that it began on the 31st, when Aitken accosted him in the street. Aitken told us that when he saw him he said, "What about the Arran mystery? What about that cap? If that was Rose you were with, you had better go to the authorities and tell them all you know." Then he said that Laurie looked a little embarrassed, and said something about Rose having gone to Leeds, which, of course, was not true. And from that time he very soon disappeared. It is suggested that that is characteristic of guilt; but that is not a just conclusion to draw from it. I submit that his conduct was due to this: that having gone first among his friends and then to his work, with no sign of a guilty conscience upon

212

Dean of Faculty's Address to the Jury.

him from the time that he left on the morning of the 16th until then, when there was a suggestion made, first in the papers and afterwards by Aitken, that he might know something about it, Laurie reviewed his position; and in reviewing his position he would feel that there were such circumstances which, however absolutely innocent he might be of the crime, would be proof against him that he had committed it. In the first place, he would say to himself: "It is true that I was seen with Rose on Goatfell. Plenty of people saw me, and therefore that is a circumstance which will be relied upon against me," or, again, he might say: "When I left that morning I took some of his things, which I should not have done; that, again, will be relied upon against me." In short, there are circumstances which, if he once came to be suspected, would place him in jeopardy. It is not the first time that a man in these circumstances, feeling that he was in an equivocal situation, apparently of his own making, though he might be perfectly innocent of the crime, may have told untruths to put off a questioner and may have fled away, thinking: "What have I to say against it?" What I ask you to consider is, whether such conduct is indicative of guilt, or whether it does not rather show that up to that point he had no fear of a charge being made against him? If he had expected the charge or had consciousness of guilt, he would have disappeared on the 16th of July; he would not have been seen again. But he only disappeared when these suspicious circumstances arose, and then he went away to Liverpool. I ask you, as men of the world, whether you cannot recall to mind instances of which you have read or known where people in compromising or embarrassing situations acted similarly.

If you review his conduct as a whole, you will not omit to remember that for a fortnight immediately after the alleged crime the conduct of the accused was inconsistent with the idea of his having done such a deed. Upon what followed that, I make the same remark. He went into hiding, and when about to be captured he attempted to cut his throat. The fact that he had gone away he felt would be another element that was compromising. One of the witnesses has

213

John Watson Laurie.

said that, at the time of his apprehension, he said he wished he had done it right, meaning the cutting of his own throat, and that "I robbed the man, but did not murder him." What is the meaning of that expression? The Solicitor-General seems to think that is a confession that he robbed the body on the hill. It is nothing of the kind. What Laurie meant was this: "True it is I took these things in going away, but I was never a murderer;" so that, when he was not afraid to die by his own hand, he said he was not a murderer.

The Crown suggests that that deed must have been done by Laurie going down the hill behind Rose, and smashing a big stone upon his head; but you will remember that that is not the relative position in which these two men walked up the hill, because every witness for the Crown said that the accused generally kept leading, and one of them said that Rose made the remark, probably jocularly, that the accused was his guide. I venture to suggest that if these two men came down the hill together Laurie would be first and Rose second.

As the result of the whole case I submit to you that the Crown has absolutely and totally failed to make out either of the two propositions, both of which they must make out before the jury can be asked to return a verdict—first, that there was a murder, and, secondly, if there was a murder, that the murderer was the accused. On both points the evidence is not such as would warrant a conviction even in a much smaller matter than an issue of life and death. If you find that such an atrocious and unprecedented crime has been committed, it must be on evidence upon which there can be no reasonable doubt. I leave the matter in your hands with this observation in conclusion: I ask you to return a verdict which will acquit the prisoner at the bar from this most terrible, this most appalling charge.

Lord Justice-Clerk's Charge to the Jury.

The Lord Justice-Clerk's Charge to the Jury.

The LORD JUSTICE-CLERK—Gentlemen of the jury, it is now my duty to give you such aid as I can to assist you in your consideration of the facts of this case. It is a case of a most extraordinary nature, and it therefore will require your most serious consideration. There is a large body of evidence of a very important character. Two theories have been presented to you. Both of these theories present points almost inconceivable to the ordinary mind. It is certainly one of the most remarkable cases that have ever come before a Court of Justice.

I would point out at the outset that it is a case purely of circumstantial evidence, except in one or two very minor details. Circumstantial evidence is evidence which, if it be clear and conclusive, is about the best evidence in the world, because if a case is soundly based on circumstantial evidence, we are removed altogether from considerations of human frailty—which leads men to tell untruths, one against another—and there will be no ground whatever for doubt. But, of course, circumstantial evidence, on the other hand, requires the very greatest care and caution, because circumstances may be represented in two aspects, and it requires great consideration and care to determine the conclusion that is to be accepted. As this is a case of circumstantial evidence, I think that probably my best course will be, in the first place, to go over with you the facts about which there is no doubt. I may say in passing that we may congratulate ourselves upon having had the case presented to us from both sides of the bar with distinguished ability and great lucidity, and—of greater value—with sound moderation; and we must also congratulate ourselves that the accused has had the able assistance of the head of the Scottish Bar in laying his case before us.

Let us consider the facts about which there is no doubt. Up to a day about the second week in July the late Mr. Rose and the accused had no acquaintance whatever. It appears that while on board the steamer the deceased seems to have

John Watson Laurie.

The Lord Justice-Clerk

mistaken the accused for a gentleman whom he met at Glenburn Hydropathic. He made up to him and spoke to him. He explained then that he had made a mistake, and then he said, in his agreeable fashion, " Well, it does not matter, I am very glad to meet you all the same." They struck up a travelling acquaintance that day. But we have this to start with, that in making this acquaintance with Mr. Rose, the accused was, from what reason or motive we cannot tell, passing under an assumed name, and was using a card with that assumed name upon it in applying for lodgings. A circumstance comes in here to which I must warn you not to give too much weight, but it is part of the string of circumstances, and I am bound to bring it out. One of the friends of the deceased seems to have been struck with something about the accused — the man " Annandale " — and warned Rose not to associate with him as he had been doing. That, however, is based on matters which impressed the gentleman who gave evidence, but into which we cannot go.

Well, these two men, having become travelling acquaintances, went to Arran together. The deceased could not find lodgings there, and the accused took him into a place which he had engaged for himself, and they stayed there while in Arran. The next thing we find is that the two were seen together crossing the grounds of the Castle above Brodick on their way to Goatfell. There is a witness who gives distinct evidence of the fact that he saw the deceased's watch chain on his waistcoat. We know also that, at that time, he possessed in his pocket-book a return ticket for taking him back to London at the conclusion of his holidays. These two people ascended the hill together. They passed and were passed by and got mixed up with another party, the accused always being in front; the deceased, with his characteristic good nature, entered into conversation with the others. When they got near to the top, Rose and Laurie separated from the other party, and they were seen by the gentlemen below standing in such a manner as to suggest that they were talking about the road they would take. Their backs were turned to Ailsa Craig, and they were pointing down below, as if suggesting their route for descending the hill. From that time forward they were never seen together again. It

Lord Justice-Clerk's Charge to the Jury.

is quite certain that neither of them descended by the same route which they took on going up the hill. They took a route which, at some little distance from the top, is certainly more difficult than the ordinary one, but it is a route which the evidence shows people can take with reasonable safety. The path may present some danger, but it is not so dangerous that it cannot be taken by an ordinary person exercising reasonable care. Now, most undoubtedly, somewhere near the gully or in the gully which runs down that route the deceased met his death. His head was so smashed in that, when the body was found, some eight or nine pieces of skull had fallen into the cavity; his shoulder was broken; the front of his face was practically forced off, and the bony part of the nose was entirely broken. He undoubtedly met his death from violence of some kind. After death his body was hidden away carefully under a large boulder and covered with stones by some one, and his jacket was turned up over the head before the stones were placed on the body.

Passing over at present the question of where he met his death, it is undoubted that, if he met his death by falling over one of the cliffs, it must have been a work of great labour and difficulty to bring his body down to that boulder and hide it there. In addition to the body, things belonging to the deceased man were found there. His cap was found folded up in four, with a sufficiently heavy stone placed on it to hold it down; his stick was found at one place, and his waterproof, cut into two pieces, was found rolled up in the burn in the gully. His pockets were rifled, and one of them was turned inside out. No watch, no money, nor any other property was found upon his person—watch, money, and return ticket were gone. These are facts about which there is no doubt.

All this must have happened within a very few hours on a summer evening. A witness, who identified the accused, said that about nine o'clock he saw him passing the churchyard at Glen Sannox, and undoubtedly the accused did arrive at the inn at Corrie too late to obtain refreshment, the hour of closing under the new statute being ten o'clock. The Dean of Faculty has pointed out most properly that the two

217

John Watson Laurie.

young women, who were with the witness who stated that
he saw Laurie at nine, denied that he said to them what he
stated in evidence he did say, namely, that a man passed
him who looked tired and weary, as if he had had a hard
day's travelling on the hills. It is only fair, however, to
point out that the women said that the remark might have
been made without their noticing it. I do not think we
need attach much importance to whether this incident
occurred or not, in view of the fact that most undoubtedly
the accused passed in that direction to the inn at Corrie,
where he arrived, as I have said, after ten o'clock. By the
aid of a gentleman he did get a refreshment, and he took
some drink with him. He went on to Brodick that night.

Next morning, without any intimation to those in whose
house he had been living, he disappeared from the house,
taking with him his own bag and the bag of the deceased,
and leaving behind him two or three articles, one of which
was Mr. Rose's tennis racket. He was seen with those two
bags on his way to the steamer. He was seen with a black
bag by a friend on board the steamer, and that man saw
him again with the bag on the train going to Glasgow. On
that morning he was wearing the grey felt hat which the
deceased had been seen wearing during the time he was in
Arran: The accused, as you have heard, went back to Rothesay,
and he was seen wearing a chocolate-and-white striped jacket.
Mr. Rose had such a jacket with him, which he wore while
playing tennis, when he left London. He was also in possession of a white linen yachting cap similar to that which
was worn by Rose.

Having returned to Glasgow with the black bag, Laurie
went back to his lodgings in Frederick Street, returning to
work. A few days later he came across Mr. Aitken, whom
he knew. Mr. Aitken was standing at the door of his office
and he hailed the accused, entering into conversation with
him. Mr. Aitken asked him what the mystery in Arran
was, and the accused " hummed and hawed " and hesitated.
Aitken said : " Have you not been reading the papers and
seen that a man is missing in Arran? " The accused again
hesitated. Then Aitken said to him : " What is yon cap

218

Lord Justice-Clerk's Charge to the Jury.

you were wearing the other day?" and he got no reply, except that the accused said: "What! You do not mean to say that I am ——," and Aitken is not sure whether the word "thief" was added or not. Aitken advised him to go and tell the authorities, saying that, if he did not, he himself would feel it was his duty to do so. The accused then said that some one was coming up the street, and that he must be off.

In the middle of that week he got his wages for the few days from Saturday, when he had been paid, and said that he was going to work at Ramage & Ferguson's in Leith. He told his mate that he had a return ticket to London and that he thought of going there. To the man who gave him his wages he said he was going to Leith to be a traveller in the grain trade. He then sold his tools, left his lodgings, and apparently left Glasgow. In short, I do not think it is going too far to say that, at that time, he absconded. The next that was heard of him was that he was in Liverpool, and he took a lodging there from which he also disappeared, leaving behind him a box in which there were several articles which have been already proved to have belonged to Mr. Rose. The next information about him is that he wrote two letters to the *Glasgow Herald* and the *Daily Mail*. Very properly, these were handed over to the police. In these letters the accused said there could be no motive for his murdering Rose, because his watch was an old Geneva one and the chain was of little value. Laurie was then seen at a railway station in September, and he was chased. Getting into a wood, he was afterwards found under a bush with his throat cut. On being apprehended and cautioned not to say anything, he said he robbed the man, but did not murder him.

About these facts, gentlemen, there is no doubt whatever. The Crown say that all these facts point in the direction of the accused having committed the crime with which he is charged. The defence is, as I understand it, that the death of the deceased did not take place in the presence of the accused at all, that though they had gone to the top of Goatfell together they did not descend together, although the one met his death on the road which leads down by Glen

John Watson Laurie.

The Lord Justice-Clerk

Sannox to Corrie, and the other reached Corrie by the road to Glen Sannox. It is suggested—and this is for you to consider—that before anything happened to the deceased by accident or by malice he and the accused had parted company. But, then, of course, arriving at his lodgings in Brodick in the night, Laurie must surely have been surprised at the non-arrival of Rose; and the effect which that non-arrival had upon him was that, without saying a word to any one, he went off with his own and Mr. Rose's luggage. The suggestion of the Crown is that if Laurie had anything to do with the death of Rose it was of very great importance that it should appear, as soon as possible, that Rose had gone away from where he was staying with his things. That is the suggestion the Crown make. The defence say that it was a mean and not very nice action to take away Rose's things, but that it does not in any way indicate that Laurie knew Rose was dead. Upon the view which you will take of this matter a very great deal will depend. You will consider which suggestion commends itself to your minds; and I emphasise that a great deal will depend on this, in arriving at your decision.

In order to carry out what is pleaded in defence of the accused, it is suggested that the death of Mr. Rose, and his being placed under the boulder, must have been done by somebody else; because, according to the theory of the defence, Rose fell from one of the cliffs at a considerable distance from the boulder, and it would not have been possible, they say, for one man to have brought the body over ground, which is very rough and stony, down to the place at which it was found. I am afraid that there are two views about that theory. You will have to consider them both. There is the view that, because of the great difficulty in moving the body if Rose fell over the cliff, one man could not have done it. There is the other view, suggested by the Crown, that Mr. Rose did not meet his death by falling over the cliff, but from a series of blows which were delivered with stones, close to the boulder. In dealing with these views you will have to deal with the probabilities of the case as they present themselves to men of conscience and ordinary mind and not

Lord Justice-Clerk's Charge to the Jury.

with abstract possibilities. You will have to deal with reasonable probabilities. The Dean of Faculty, in his able argument, has suggested that, if the injury to the deceased took place near the boulder, how was it to be accounted for that the stick, the knife, and the cap were found farther up the gully? Here, again, I am very much afraid that, if Rose did meet his death near that boulder, it is not at all an extravagant assumption that the person who put him to death near the boulder should leave such things away from it, so that if the body should ever be found it might appear as if he had fallen over a precipice. I think a great deal will turn on the impression which you form as to whether these articles, or any of them, accidentally fell at the places where they were found, or whether they were put there afterwards by a human hand. As regards two of the articles, the circumstances are very remarkable. The cap was folded up into four and a stone of some weight placed upon it; and it is quite certain that the waterproof, which was cut, was not cut by the deceased. It must have been cut off his body after death, and that could only have been done by a human hand after his death. It is said by the defence that, if this happened, it happened in broad daylight, and that people were on the hill who might see it. Nobody doubts that the deceased met his death there that night, and it is for you, gentlemen, to say whether there is anything that commends itself to you in the suggestion that Rose, having gone down there alone, fell over the cliff by accident, his body afterwards being found by persons—more than one— who, for the sake of his old watch, railway ticket, and what money he had, took the dreadful risk of burying the body under the boulder where it was found.

The case for the defence is that the men were never seen together after they left the top of the hill, and you are asked by the defence to believe that they were not together at the time at which Rose met his death. But there is one circumstance, which is a very remarkable one, and that is, that it was not until ten o'clock in the evening that Laurie reached the Corrie Inn, while the other people who left the top of the hill at the same time reached Brodick in time to catch the

John Watson Laurie.

steamer at half-past eight. There was a remark made by the Dean of Faculty, to which I think I ought to call attention. The Dean of Faculty said, with great truth, that the evidence showed that, in ascending the hill, the accused was always in front of the party, and from that he deduced the conclusion that it was quite impossible that Laurie could have struck Rose with a boulder from behind. What comes to me at once when this suggestion is made is that, if there existed the intention to do the act which the Crown say the accused did do, the accused need not have continued in front in descending the hill.

That is all I have to say regarding the mere facts up to the time Rose disappeared. You will consider these facts and consider whether you can reconcile them in your minds with the idea that Laurie was not present at the time Mr. Rose met his death. If you believe that he was present, I do not think there is any escape from the conclusion that his was the hand which placed the body below the boulder and cut the waterproof off it; his was the hand which put the waterproof where it was found and which folded up the cap—if you believe that the cap was folded up. If that is the conclusion to which you come, the next question for you to consider is whether these things could possibly—I mean possibly in a reasonable sense—be done by a man who had witnessed a terrible death. Upon the answer to that question a very great deal of the case will depend, and in answering that question all Laurie's subsequent conduct requires to be taken into consideration—his leaving Brodick and taking possession of Rose's things without informing anybody, thus necessarily producing the impression on the minds of everybody around that Mr. Rose had levanted.

Then I come to the circumstance of Laurie's possession of the return ticket to London which was on the person of Mr. Rose when he died.

The DEAN OF FACULTY—I think there was no evidence whatever that when Rose went up Goatfell that day he had the return ticket with him.

The LORD JUSTICE-CLERK—I think one of the witnesses said that he had seen the ticket in his pocket-book; but, of course, it

Lord Justice-Clerk's Charge to the Jury.

is quite possible that he may have left his pocket-book in his lodgings when he went up Goatfell. There are three possibilities about the ticket : one is, that Rose had lost it ; another, that he had it on his person ; and the third, that he left it at the lodgings. You will consider the possibility of his having lost it. If Rose had the ticket on his person, and if Laurie was the man who buried the body, then he took the ticket. If the ticket was left at the lodgings, Laurie took it away along with the other things belonging to the deceased, which he also took.

It has been said, with truth, and in some respects with much force, that to a great extent, after leaving the lodgings, Laurie's conduct was of an open character—that he broadly and openly wore the chocolate-coloured coat and Rose's cap —and it is suggested that no person anxious to conceal such a crime would possibly have done that. You will consider that ; but I should be failing in my duty if I did not point out that very often it is the follies of those who have committed some crime that form the very threads of the web of justice. If criminals were always able successfully to get rid of all evidence, the ends of justice would fail altogether ; if they did not boldly do things which might afterwards be held as evidence against them, a vast number of cases in the Criminal Courts would fail. But it is worthy of consideration that, not only when going away from Arran, but in Rothesay, and on the return from Rothesay to Glasgow, Laurie exhibited about his person, without any concealment whatever, property which belonged to the deceased. It may be just one of these little points where rashness leads to detection.

I would now say a word upon the general character of the question of possibilities. It is always easy in cases to suggest possibilities. You may take a case and suggest possibilities from beginning to end. Taking the first point in it, you may suggest a possibility which could account for that point. Then, having laid that aside, you may take up a second point and suggest another possibility, which would enable you to set it aside ; and so on with the other points to the very last point. But that is not the way in which it

John Watson Laurie.

is your duty to form your opinions, nor, I take it, is it your practice in your own affairs so to form your opinions. You must take the evidence as a whole, rejecting, of course, every point which you are not satisfied is fairly and fully proved— you must take the whole of the rest of the case together, and say whether it justifies a conclusion which you think is reason- able and just.

This leads me to the medical evidence because, in medical evidence—which is to a great extent theoretical—there is naturally much reference to possibilities. On both sides of this case the witnesses have almost all been prepared to say that there was nothing suggested against the opinion they expressed which was not quite possible. This frankness is very satisfactory, and it shows at least that the witnesses are not prepared to deny possibilities which may, as possibilities, tell against their case. It is always an observation that those who saw the things they had to speak to in all their details, and examined them, are necessarily in a somewhat better position to give their evidence and opinions than those who merely form their opinions from evidence which they have heard. That is an observation which is always made in cases of this kind, but it is one to which you should not give too much weight. You must also consider evidence based on a careful reading of the reports and of the evidence given on the other side. It is not your province to decide upon medical opinions, given however candidly, what was on the whole the most probable cause of death. Your duty is to dis- cover what was the most probable cause of death, taking the whole incidents and facts of the case into view—not only the facts of the injuries but the whole facts of the case—along with the medical evidence. The suggestion on the part of counsel for the defence—the suggestion goes all through the evidence for the defence—is that the injuries were caused by a fall over a cliff. There has been a great deal of dis- cussion on the part of counsel as to whether a person could fall head downwards without any injury to the rest of the body. You will judge of the value of the argument on the one side or the other; but you will keep it firmly before you that you must form your opinion as to what happened in this case, both as regards the actual breaking of the man's

224

Lord Justice-Clerk's Charge to the Jury.

The Lord Justice-Clerk

skull and the injury to the shoulder, along with all the other evidence in the case. If you come to the conclusion that death was as the result of a fall, I am afraid that that does not conclude the question in this case; because, if the fall was occasioned by violence, that would be just the same as if, instead of being thrown down on the rock, he had been struck by a piece of rock. If you come to the conclusion that Laurie was the man who was there, and that he was the man who put the body under the boulder—put the body under the boulder and rolled the stones in front of it—if you are driven to that conclusion as reasonable men, it tends very much against the theory that death was caused by a fall over the cliff; because it is part of the theory of the defence itself that, if the man had fallen over the cliff, he could not have dropped where he was buried; it is against the theory of the defence that, after the man was dead, Laurie took the body and placed it where it was found. Therefore, if you come to the conclusion that Laurie buried the body, you will have to consider if, when the man fell over the cliff and after he was dead, Laurie took the body down to that place of burial. If you come to the conclusion that Laurie was there, then no motive has been suggested why, if Rose fell over the cliff and was killed, Laurie should afterwards have taken all that trouble to bury the body.

I ask you most earnestly, after listening to all that I have felt it my duty to say in the case, to dismiss from your minds anything which I may have said which does not commend itself to you as being fair guidance for your consideration. It is my bounden duty, and I cannot escape from it, to give you such guidance and help as I can effectually, to lead you to the salient points in the case; to tell you how to consider the evidence, and to point out the really salient points of that evidence. It is not, however, my province to exercise my mind for yours and to give you a decision. There is no law involved in the case which I would be bound to lay down to you, and which you would be bound to accept because it was given by me. The case is one purely of fact, and the responsibility and duty of, coming to a conclusion on fact lies with you. Anything I may have said which does

Q

John Watson Laurie.

not meet with your entire approval you are not only entitled, but absolutely bound to set aside. It is, of course, your bounden duty in such a case, if you have any reasonable doubt in your minds as to the case being made out, to give a verdict in favour of the accused. But I must say to you, in reference to that, that it must not be a doubt raised in your minds by sympathy, nor a doubt based upon an abstract possibility. It must be the doubt of reasonable men, not going on abstract possibilities, but judging of the matter in the same way as they would consider weighty matters in the ordinary affairs of life. You must be guided by your opinions as reasonable and experienced men, knowing the things of the world, and you must not shelter yourselves under any doubt which is a mere abstract possibility. On the other hand, as I have said, you must not refuse to give effect to any doubt which weighs upon your minds as a reasonable doubt. Lastly, let your verdict be given without regard, in one sense, to the consequences of what the verdict must be. As to those consequences, the State has given you no responsibility at all. What must follow if you convict the prisoner is the law of the land, for which you are not personally responsible. On the other hand, it is, of course, perfectly clear that in a case of such grave importance, and a case in which the consequences may be such as you know they may be, you must consider the case with the more earnestness and the more carefulness, giving your verdict manfully the one way or the other. You must remember that you are the masters of the evidence, and whatever decision you may come to, let it be the decision which commends itself to your consciences as a matter of fact, being assured that if you give such a verdict your consciences will always approve of that verdict afterwards.

The jury then retired. On returning at twenty-five minutes past ten, after an absence of three-quarters of an hour,

The CLERK OF JUSTICIARY—What is your verdict, gentlemen?

The FOREMAN OF THE JURY—The verdict is guilty by a majority.

226

Lord Justice-Clerk's Charge to the Jury.

The CLERK OF JUSTICIARY—Is this your verdict, gentlemen, " The jury, by a majority, find the prisoner guilty of the crime of murder "?

The FOREMAN OF THE JURY—Yes.

The verdict having been recorded and read over to the jury,

Mr. GRAHAM MURRAY—My Lord, I move for sentence to be passed.

The LORD JUSTICE-CLERK—John Watson Laurie, you have been convicted by the jury of one of the most terrible crimes that our country has ever known. You must be well aware that that conviction can only be followed by one sentence, which it is now my duty to pronounce. I beseech you to turn your thoughts away from this world to the next. Justice for the crime you have committed will end here, if you will repent of your crime and turn to the God whom you have offended. Turn to him, I beseech you. It is not too late for you to turn and secure that forgiveness which is freely offered to you. Our sad duty here is to carry out the law of the land, and, therefore, without further words, I must ask you to listen to the sentence of the Court. The sentence of the Court upon you is that you be removed to the prison of Edinburgh, and thence transferred to the prison of Greenock, in the precincts of which prison you will be hanged by the neck between the hours of eight and ten in the forenoon of 30th November. This I pronounce for doom, and may the Lord have mercy on your soul.

The ACCUSED [turning round in the dock, and addressing the crowded benches]—Ladies and gentlemen, I am innocent of this charge.

The LORD JUSTICE-CLERK—You cannot be allowed to address the Court.

The prisoner was then removed, and the Court rose.

APPENDICES.

APPENDIX I.

PETITION FOR REPRIEVE.

Unto the Most Honourable the Marquis of Lothian, Knight of the Thistle, Her Majesty's Secretary of State for Scotland, the Petition of the undersigned:

HUMBLY SHEWETH,

That your petitioners are desirous of submitting the following reasons why the sentence of death passed against JOHN WATSON LAURIE, presently in the prison of Greenock, for the murder of Edwin Rose, at Coir-na-fourin, Glen Sannox, Island of Arran, on 15th July last, should not be carried into effect, viz. :—

That the evidence did not sufficiently establish the guilt of the accused.

That the medical evidence was not conclusive.

That the other evidence for the Crown was purely circumstantial.

That the verdict of the jury was arrived at by a majority of one only, eight having voted for guilty and seven for not proven.

It is alleged by many persons to whom the prisoner and his relatives are well known that there has been, and is, insanity in the prisoner's family and the prisoner himself has shown from infancy decided symptoms of mental aberration, which accounts for the extraordinary and eccentric character of his conduct subsequent to the 15th July.

> May it therefore please the Most Noble the Secretary of State for Scotland to take the premises into his most favourable consideration, and thereafter advise Her Most Gracious Majesty to exercise Her Royal clemency to the effect of commuting the death sentence passed upon the prisoner, or of giving him such other relief in the premises as may seem just.
>
> And your petitioners will ever pray.

John Watson Laurie.

CONDITIONAL PARDON IN FAVOUR OF JOHN WATSON LAURIE.

OUR SOVEREIGN LADY ordains a letter of remission to be passed and expede under the Seal appointed by the Treaty of Union to be kept and made use of in Scotland in place of the Great Seal thereof, making mention, that whereas John Watson Laurie was at the High Court of Justiciary holden at Edinburgh on the ninth day of November, 1889, convicted of murder and sentenced to death.

Her Majesty in consideration of some circumstances humbly represented unto her, and of Her Majesty's Prerogative Royal, Proper Motion, Royal Clemency, and Good Pleasure has remitted, indemnified and pardoned, and by these presents remits, indemnifies, and pardons the said John Watson Laurie of the said crime of murder and of the said sentence of death passed upon him for the same, upon condition of his being kept in penal servitude for the term of his natural life.

And Her Majesty ordains the said letter to be extended with all clauses needful, and to pass the Seal aforementioned per saltum without passing any other seal or register. For doing whereof these presents shall be to the Director of Her Majesty's Chancellary for writing the same, and to the Lord Keeper of the said Seal for causing the same to be appended thereto a sufficient warrant.

Given at Her Majesty's Court at St. James's the 28th day of November, 1889, in the fifty-third year of Her Majesty's reign.

By Her Majesty's Command.

May it Please Your Majesty,
These contain Your Majesty's warrant for a letter of remission to be passed and expede under the Seal appointed by the Treaty of Union to be kept and made use of in Scotland in place of the Great Seal thereof remitting, indemnifying, and pardoning John Watson Laurie of the crime of murder and of the sentence of death passed upon him for the same; upon condition of his being kept in penal servitude for the term of his natural life.

Appendix III.

APPENDIX III.

Dr. Campbell Black's Pamphlet.

THE LAURIE CASE:
The Medical Evidence Dissected.
By Dr. Campbell Black.

Dedicated (without permission) to "Medical Experts."

"Blessed are the merciful; for they shall obtain mercy."—*The New Testament.*

"No heart is pure that is not passionate; no virtue is safe that is not enthusiastic."—*Ecce Homo.*

"Except that the victim was an Englishman, while the prisoner is a Scotchman, we can suggest no reason why Laurie should not be hanged."—*Saturday Review (Reviler?).*

Price Twopence.

Glasgow:
Hugh Hopkins, 85 Renfield Street.
William Love, 226 Argyle Street.

1889.

The Laurie Case.

Gentlemen of the Medical Profession,

I am most unwilling to introduce into this discussion matters of a personal nature, but I claim your indulgence in asking you to allow me but a sentence or two on this head. I have been seriously told that I have no right to interfere with "the finding of a Court of Justice." I do not assent to this proposition; and I have yet to learn that when, and where, I believe that a miscarriage of justice through insufficient or misleading evidence has occurred, that I exceed the perfect right of every member of the community, and especially in such a case as this, of every member of my own profession, in defending to the extent of my ability what I believe to be the cause of humanity, and the interests of justice and truth. The law is not superior to the makers of the law. It is the people that make the law, and the people have a right to expect and to demand its just administration. As there is a period at which submission to tyranny ceases to be a virtue, so there is a stage at which acquiescence in the faulty administration of justice or law merits neither sympathy nor commendation. Have the people who clamour for blood in this case seriously considered its eminently painful nature, and the attitude

233

John Watson Laurie.

that becomes them as a boasted and boastful Christian community? I can afford to smile at the criticisms of my opinions, on my own subject, of men whose business in life, however honourable in itself, has been to retail tea and sugar. I have been a student of my profession for over thirty years, and I hope I am not arrogating to myself too much in holding neither an idle nor an unobservant one. I have had the honour of occupying positions which afforded me a varied field of observation; and if I criticise one or two of my professional brethren in this case, I do so with pain, in the higher interests of that profession of which I am proud, and that justice and truth to which I owe a submissive and willing allegiance. " It may be hard to condemn a brother practitioner, but it will be still harder to ignore the public interest and condemn ourselves and our profession by concealing that which we know to be true, or by suppressing what we honestly believe. There is no etiquette in the profession which demands such a sacrifice of principle as this conduct involves."—Taylor's *Medical Jurisprudence.*

In the discussion of this painful subject, then, I beg it to be distinctly understood that I criticise the medical evidence alone, and in doing so I advisedly assert with the fullest sense of responsibility that the medical evidence for the prosecution was a mass of contradictions, and altogether of such a nature that it is abhorrent to me to conceive that on the strength of it a human being should be committed to the scaffold, and an indelible stain thus attached to people of an irreproachable character. I proceed now to justify these strong assertions.

Once more let us clear the ground. Here is a body which has been dead for over three weeks. It is decomposed beyond recognition, the last scavengers have made havoc with the citadels of life; the contents of the skull (the seat, we are told, of reason. Is this demonstrable in all persons?), and of the thoracic cavity have disappeared. Extensive injuries are found on the head. The body is found under *circumstances where such might have resulted from an accidental fall;* and the awful responsibility is taken, by men of undoubted integrity and ability, to fix a horrid and atrocious crime on a young and friendless outcast. *Had the body been found in an open field,* and the concomitant conditions, such as are well known in this case, *the circumstances would have been totally different.* As I have already remarked, it is not sufficient to discover *a* cause of death; it is *the* cause of death that is desiderated. If A wishes to hang a man on possibilities, B has a better right to defend him and attempt to save his life with the same weapons.

I shall now deal with the medical evidence of Mr. Gilmour. In a certificate dated 6th August, 1889, Mr. Gilmour of Linlithgow certifies " the body in some parts *was a little decomposed* (italics mine; and the accuracy of the newspaper report assumed). Almost in the same breath Mr. Gilmour says : " The bones on the left side of the top of the head were all fractured, and portions of them lying inside the skull or brain cavity, which was empty of brain

234

Appendix III.

matter. *All it contained was a heap of maggots* and pieces of fractured skull-bone, &c." . . . " The face was almost denuded of flesh. The greater part of the *left* side of the head was completely denuded of the integuments, muscles, and flesh. Towards the right region of the vertex of the skull there was a rugged edge of the scalp with dark hair adhering to it." *Question*—And the eyes were gone? *Answer*—Completely gone. " Nothing but a skeleton." . . . " On the left side it was also completely denuded of any portion of flesh. There was a large regular cavity, with pieces of bones showing a series of fractures[1] *radiating in every direction.* . . . *The whole of the brain matter had been destroyed by maggots,* and the bones were mixed up with maggots. . . . The decomposition had attacked these portions that had been broken at the time of death." *Question* by the Dean of Faculty—" You have described to us the condition of the face. *Was it plain that from decomposition the soft tissues gradually disappeared?* " *Answer*— " The greater part of them practically disappeared, &c." " Were the soft parts of the neck much decomposed? "—" Yes." Now, *all this* is what Mr. Gilmour characterises as " the body in some parts *was a little decomposed* ! " So much then for Mr. Gilmour's accuracy and authority on decomposition.

Let us see if he is stronger in anatomy. *Question* by Solicitor-General—" In addition to the bones of the face, including the upper jaw, the nasal-bone, the cheek-bone, and others were broken? " *Answer*—" They were detached from the adhesions. The upper jaw-bone *is one of the strongest* bones in the body." What says Dr. Heron Watson, one of the most distinguished and experienced surgeons in the kingdom? Examined by the Solicitor-General—" You agree that the upper jaw is a very strong bone? " *Answer*—" I do not think so; it is as thin as paper." I prefer to err with Watson and the anatomists.

Now, as to Mr. Gilmour's surgical views, I shall assume that the fractures are accurately described. Examined by the Dean of Faculty —" The whole of that part of the face comprising the upper jaw was detached in one piece. Will you explain that? What was the *one* piece in which the whole was detached? " *Answer*—" The upper jaw was detached from the cheek-bone. It was quite loose and could be removed (*sic*) by the hand." This is, *mirabile dictu,* what Mr. Gilmour calls " the whole of the upper part of the face being detached ! " I put it to any anatomist if the attachment of the maxillary process of the malar bone with the jaw-bone is a very strong one, and whether if this attachment were severed, it is accurate language to say, seeing that the upper jaw articulates beside the frontal, the ethmoid, the nasal, the lachrymal, the inferior turbinated, the palate, the vomer bone, and its fellow of the opposite side, that if not fractured, " the whole of the face comprising the upper jaw " could be " detached in one piece." I grieve to say I consider the statement preposterous.

---

[1] " Localised injury."

John Watson Laurie.

" Did you find the thoracic cavity empty? " *Answer—" I did not examine it!* I don't know whether they (the contained organs) were more decayed than the brain." " The whole of the brain matter had been destroyed by maggots "! " I thought it was useless after *tracing the distinct cause of death* (sic), to enter into secondary matters." Now, as I have already pointed out, this is where Mr. Gilmour, *especially in such a momentous case as this,* was, I submit with all deference, utterly and indefensibly wrong. It was not *a* cause of death that he was investigating, but *the* cause of death, and further examination might reveal to him that what he is pleased jauntily to term " secondary matters " might turn out *primary matters.* Did it occur to him that the life of a young man was in jeopardy? Or that the life of some one might be? Why did he assume that there was no disease of the heart, lungs, or great blood vessels? Mr. Gilmour is evidently not fresh on " Taylor," who says : " *All* causes which operate to produce death suddenly, as by syncope, asphyxia, or coma, *especially* demand the attention of a medical jurist. . . ." " What are the circumstances which lead you to suppose that death was *not* caused by natural disease ? " I ask Mr. Gilmour (and the people of Scotland will expect him to answer, in the words of Taylor)—" What are the circumstances which lead you to suppose that death was *not* caused by natural disease in the case of Rose? What led you to suppose that there was no disease in the thoracic or brain cavity? " Will he deign to answer these questions? He must not brush them aside. His own reputation and that of the profession of medicine are involved.

Let us now assume, gravely of course (for unfortunately this is no laughing matter), that the unfortunate Rose stood with the more than adamantine solidity of the Saxon, and allowed Laurie to batter in his head and shoulder with a " large boulder between his thumb and fingers "! and critically examine the surgical details on which this nightmare is based. By Mr. Graham Murray : " This portion in the last reading of your report was left out, ' the left shoulder-blade near the top where it forms the upper and outer boundary of the shoulder joint was broken off, *probably by a blow aimed at the head,* striking it in a slanting direction ' (dangerous and wicked assumption !), and then, just at the end, ' I have no hesitation in certifying that these fractures were *not produced* (confident language) by a fall down a cliff or steep incline ; but by a number of blows (*Horresco referens*)[2] inflicted by a blunt instrument, *such as a large*

---

[2] " I have no hesitation in certifying that these injuries were not produced by a fall down a cliff or steep incline, but by a number of blows inflicted by a hard, blunt instrument, *such as a large boulder !* "—(*Mr. Gilmour's* " *Medical Report.*") Methinks he protests too much. " Just confirm what I have said already as to the introduction of matter not proper to a medical report."—(Lord Deas in *M'Lachlan* case, 1862.) See context *statim*. I submit it was for the jury to determine this ; Mr. Gilmour was not counsel for the prosecution. " Stick to the facts, gentlemen. You have no right to draw narrow inferences in a medical report."—(Good old Harry Rainy.)

Referring to a remarkable trial (*Rex v. Donellan,* Warwick Lent Assizes, 1781), Taylor remarks : " Medical men were then, as now, apt to confound what is mere matter of *belief* with proof. In a Court of law, however, the difference is soon made apparent." I doubt it.—D. C. B.

Appendix III.

boulder (he evidently can't get clear of the boulder); that these blows produced the fracture of the skull and injury to the brain matter, which, in my opinion, was the cause of death.' " *Audi alteram partem,* and *not* a meaner authority than Mr. Gilmour of Linlithgow, Middeldorpf (beiträge Zur Lehre von den Knockenbrüchen, Breslau, 1853) relates " a case of fracture of the upper jaw and malar bone together with fracture of the vomer and ethmoid, accompanying fracture of the lower jaw, *from a fall.*" What do Mr. Gilmour and his friends say to that? Was this not a more complicated fracturing of the face than in the case of Rose? and here was a fracture of the lower jaw, and not as in the case of Rose a mere dislocation!

Question—" With reference to the injuries to the head and face there again your opinion is in favour of a blow or blows as against a fall? " *Answer*—" Yes." " Tell us in your own way what that is founded on," and then Mr. Gilmour proceeds indisputably in " his own way " : " It is founded on the *whole* (?) *of the injuries being confined to the left side of the head.* Had the man fallen, there would have been *other* parts of the head injured besides the left side. A fall could *not* have produced such *severe extended fractures* as were on the head." Well; so *there were* other parts of the head injured. Was there *not* a fracture of the base of the skull? Can the base of the skull in any anatomical phraseology, but Mr. Gilmour's, be said to be on the left side of the head? " If a blow be caused by a blunt object, or by *a fall on the head*, it will most likely result in a *widely extended* fissure, running perhaps across the vault or *base* of the skull, and tearing arteries, sinuses, or nerves on its way. Fracture of the base, for example, *is common when the patient falls on his head from a height*, so that the weight of the whole body *tells upon the base of the skull* through the spinal column " (Druitt's *Surgeon's Vade-Mecum*, p. 338). Who is right, Druitt or Gilmour? Let me ask any medical man of experience whether the starring, if a fracture of the vertex of the skull arising from a fall upon it, is more uniform than the starring on a sheet of plate glass by the projection of a pebble against it? A man falls into the hold of a ship (within a year on South Side, seen by Dr. Shaw of Govan), and his skull is found to be a bundle of broken bones. A child falls from a flight of two stairs in Westminster Terrace (seen by Dr. T. D. Buchanan), and the condition of the skull was graphically described " like a dried bladder full of oyster shells."

Question by Solicitor-General—" Did you observe on the occasion of the finding of the body what the condition of the back-bone was? Was there any detachment of the highest vertebra from what was above it? " *Answer*—" It was lying alone." " That is, the uppermost joint of the backbone was lying alone? "—" Yes. That was the condition before I turned the body round." And here Mr. Gilmour enters into a philological disquisition for the instruction of counsel, in which, it is gratifying to say, he shows to better advantage than

237

John Watson Laurie.

as a medical expert. " I took out the atlas bone and examined it."
" The parts of the body which had been protected by the skin from
the atmosphere were in a better state of preservation." " In this
case (he is referring to the atlas) decay must have set in and destroyed
the ligaments which hold the small bones connecting the principal
part of the spinal column to the brain-box." I ask any boy in the
dissecting room to reflect on the position and structure of the occipito-
altoid ligaments, and answer me whether decay must have set in
them before it appeared on, or in, the abdomen.

Let it be noted that I do not want to strain one single iota of the
evidence for or against, and I consequently do not assume that there
was fracture of the atlas, as Dr. Watson does, for Mr. Gilmour
remarks : " I took out the atlas bone and examined it, and could
find no trace of anything." Rather funny, seeing that he had the
by no means insignificant atlas in his hand, but which I take, dealing
with Mr. Gilmour's characteristically loose phraseology, to mean that
there was no fracture, " no trace of violence." But is there fracture
of these vertebræ in instantaneous death from hanging ? Dr. Littlejohn says that " injury to the spine was pointed out to him by Dr.
Fullarton." Of such is the medical evidence for the prosecution in
this sad case of Mr. Andrew Gilmour of Linlithgow, licentiate of the
Royal College of Physicians in Edinburgh, licentiate of the Faculty
of Physicians and Surgeons in Glasgow, and surgeon-major in the
Auxiliary Forces, from whose tender mercies and forensic skill " Good
Lord deliver us ! " Hazy on decomposition, doubtful in surgery,
illogical in argument, strong in assumption, consistent alone in the
theory of the defence. Thus : *Question* by Solicitor-General—" Is it
possible that all these injuries could have been caused by the impact
of the body upon anything ? "—" *Impossible.*" In the same breath :
" There *is* a possibility that if a body had fallen from a considerable height injuries *very similar* might have been inflicted." How
different, then, if " *very similar.*" By the Dean of Faculty—
" Suppose a person pitched on his head down from a great height,
the vertex of the head would strike first, and the head being full,
relief must be got somewhere else, and might cause a fracture at the
point opposite where the injury took place ? " *Answer*—" *It is
possible that would happen.*" " So that if a fall were of such a
nature as to involve a large part of the upper head you would expect
a correspondingly large part of the base to be involved ? " *Answer*—
" There is no doubt of that." " And all these features were present
here ? "—" Yes." Now, seriously and solemnly, is it on such
" medical evidence " as this that a charge of murder is not only
based but established.

Let us see how Dr. Fullerton of Lamlash stands; how a little
blanket-tossing will affect him. Firstly, then, I note : " There was
a fissure extending from the line of fracture down to the middle
of the temporal forehead. This, so far as I saw, was the only injury
to the right side of the head." Good! But what becomes, in the
face of this statement, of the inference of his colleague, Mr. Gilmour :

238

Appendix III.

" Had the man fallen there would have been *other parts of the head injured* besides the left side." Well, here we have Dr. Fullerton telling us that *there was* a fracture on "*the right* side of the head, and there was a fracture of the base of the skull." Where is the door of escape here? Which of the two *savants* is to be relied upon? Both cannot be right. What is the value of these inferences?

" My opinion, as expressed in the report signed by Dr. Gilmour and myself, is that the injuries to the head were the result of *repeated* blows inflicted by some heavy blunt instrument." A boulder held between the finger and thumb! eh? *Question*—" What led you to that opinion? " *Answer*—" The severity and the extent of the fractures, as well as the general outline of them." I suppose Dr. Fullerton never heard of Middeldorpf (the name hasn't a Gaelic sound), or his case, already referred to, or to thousands of similar cases. It is not to his discredit in the least that he has not seen much cerebral surgery. I know a gentleman who is a distinguished authority on the subject; and he takes my view. *Question*—" Was there anything in the nature of the injuries themselves which led you to the opinion that they could not have resulted from the impact of the head upon any hard substance? " And then follows an answer which cannot be characterised otherwise than as the sheerest non-sense : " The curvature, as described on the outside of the skull by the fracture, leads me to the opinion that it was the result of repeated blows." Would Dr. Fullerton kindly explain to benighted practitioners in a large city how or why " the position in the fracture of the shoulder seemed to indicate it was not caused by a fall, unless in an unconscious person? " " Any conscious person falling would have had *his hands before him*." But how could a *conscious* person falling backwards, and alighting on the vertex of his head, " have his hands before him," except in a Hibernian sense? By the Solicitor-General—" If the body, in falling, were to roll or bound from one point to another that would increase the likelihood of there being injuries to other parts of the person? " *Answer*—" It would; the injury to the shoulder might have been inflicted in that way." Very well; this accounts for the neck injury, and also for the shoulder injury. By the Dean of Faculty—" I think the first reason you gave for the opinion that these injuries resulted from repeated blows was the severity and the extent of the line of frac-ture? " *Answer*—" Severity of the fracture and extent." *Question*—(*Middeldorpf's case again*) " Would there be, apart from direction, a kind of proportion between the severity of the blow and the extent of the resulting injuries? Could you imagine anything more likely to shatter a man's head than a fall down a cliff of 19 feet? " And the *savant* answers : " I could not "; and *risum teneatis amice!* (hold your sides, my friend) "*that is the reason why I think it was a blow!*" " The injury was localised."[3]   Dr. Fullerton's idea of " localised injury " is this : the left side of the head fractured to a

---

[3] "*Injuries so diversified over the head.*"—Solicitor-General.   Who *is* to be believed?

239

John Watson Laurie.

pulp, the right side fractured extensively, a fracture of the base of the skull, fracture of the scapula, fracture of two ribs, and fracture or dislocation of the upper (cervical) portion of the spinal column! Verily, the " Heathen Chinee " is not in it with the medical expert! Is it really necessary to deal further with Dr. Fullerton?

Henry D. Littlejohn,[4] medical officer of health, Edinburgh, surgeon of police for Edinburgh, an accomplished medical man, and, unfortunately, an expert; a gentleman of whose expertness a distinguished criminal judge not long ago testified : " I have never known my friend Dr. Littlejohn express a doubt. He is certain even as to prophecy ! " And Dr. Littlejohn shows us that, at least in this case, he continues to merit the high encomiums of Lord Fraser, for he tells us : " We examined more particularly the *contents of the greater cavities* of the body "; while, according to his own showing, *two* of the *three* great cavities *had not contents at all!* Shade of the Wizard of the North ! " The brain was totally destroyed. . . . The cavity of the chest was empty, and no portion of the heart or great vessels or lungs could be discovered." For what reason, then, did he proceed to examine the " contents " of the skull and thorax? To study the natural history of our last and closest friend, the maggot ! " You have heard the evidence given, and the report given by the other doctors. Judging from these, and your own examination of the body, what is your opinion as to the cause of death? " *Answer*—" The condition of the cranium, as I saw it in the coffin, was at once suggestive of direct violence, *such as blows.*" Now, this is hardly a straight answer. *I* say, too, that the condition was suggestive of " direct violence," but that the direct violence *probably* resulted from falling backwards, on boulders and pointed stones, on the vertex of the skull, from a height of from 19 to 32 feet, and *not likely* from blows " What do you say as to the explanation of a fall? " *Answer*—" A fall, in my opinion, would not have inflicted such *localised violence*[5] as I saw in the head and face of the deceased without producing severe injuries to the extremities and to the internal organs of the abdomen." " Localised violence " again ! If a man fell on the vertex of his skull backwards from a height of from 19 to 32 feet, why, in the name of wonder, should, or how could, the extremities be injured. On this point let us hear Dr. Heron Watson. Examined by Mr. Balfour—" Suppose it suggested that a man falling would throw out his arms to save himself and that there would be lesions on the arms? " *Answer*—" A man falling forward is certain to throw out his arms, unless they are disabled, *or he is falling backwards.*" Are there three members of the medical profession in Scotland, but Drs. Littlejohn, Gilmour, and Fullerton, who can conceive that a man falling *backwards* can throw his arms *forwards?* I certainly give it up. As to the thoracic organs, as

---

[4] Dr. Littlejohn examined the body *over two months* after death !

[5] Solicitor-General—"*Injuries so diversified!*" How is it that Drs. Fullerton and Littlejohn are dead on for "*localised injuries,*" which it is quite apparent the injuries *were not?*

Appendix III.

already stated, Dr. Littlejohn says : " I saw no vestige of these organs." Supposing Dr. Littlejohn to be examining a body for the police authorities in Edinburgh finds a wound on the head, would he consider it unnecessary to examine the thorax in order to be certain as to the cause of death? I do not think so meanly of Dr. Littlejohn that he would. I am sure you wouldn't, doctor! Do tell us? We are " duffers " in the west. We know nothing of the " contents " of two empty cavities! Then how does Dr. Littlejohn know that the unfortunate Rose was not the subject of extensive and unsuspected disease in the chest?

Question—" Did the absence of fractures or injuries of any kind to the other parts of the body seem to you to be an important element? " *Answer*—" I was struck by the *absence of injury to the spine* and to the extremities. I should have suspected in a fall that injuries would have been found in these parts of the body." Do my eyes deceive me, Dr. Littlejohn, or are our friends the maggots where they hardly yet ought to be? Have you not said that there *was* " injury in the upper vertebra, which was pointed out to me by Dr. Fullerton? " Is this of no consequence in determining how this unfortunate man met with his death?

" You spoke of the abdominal viscera and particularly the liver. Do you mean that the liver was sometimes ruptured by a heavy fall? " *Answer*—" Always." I have already taken exception to this extraordinary statement; and I am hopeful that Dr. Littlejohn is not correctly reported. What says Dr. Heron Watson? " It has been suggested that if death had been due to a fall, as I have asked you to assume, that the abdominal viscera or some of them would have been injured by it? " *Answer*—" Well, if the abdominal viscera had been struck against by the body falling against something in the first instance, then it is extremely likely," but mark the addendum of the careful scientific witness : " In instances where a fall takes place *from a height,* and laceration of the liver or spleen takes place, the injury is *usually in cases* where *the person falls upon his feet.* In such circumstances the liver, which is attached to the under surface of the diaphragm, and is a heavy substance, attempts to continue its descent in the abdomen, tears its ligamentous surroundings, and produces some degree of laceration of the liver. But in the instance of a man falling upon his head, the impetus given to the liver is in the opposite direction—upwards against the under surface of the diaphragm, which forms a natural netting to the impact of the liver," and I would take leave to add, against an elastic buffer, the lung, of from 8 to 10 inches in depth. So that the liver being unruptured in Rose's case points *to his having fallen on the head.* I say nothing regarding the psychological argument touched on in my letter of the 12th (*and my suspicion has since been confirmed on the best authority*); and as for the medical evidence I homologate *every word* of it. Drs. Heron Watson and M'Gillivray require no commendation from me. It would be an impertinence to

John Watson Laurie.

offer it. My theory is the theory of the medical defence. It meets all the requirements of a perfect one. It almost amounts to a demonstration. All the admitted facts *can be explained by it*, and by *no other*. It shows—

1st.—That it has *not* been proved that Rose was murdered at all.

2nd.—That death was instantaneous, thus accounting for the absence of much or any hæmorrhage.

3rd.—That Rose fell on the vertex of the skull, falling backwards, and that all the fractures thereof occurred then and thereby.

4th.—That the injury to the spinal column was probably the cause of instant death, and that it *could only* be produced in this manner.

The Crown appoints three professors of medical jurisprudence to three Universities in Scotland. Will one, or the whole three, of them justify its trust in them by traversing this my argument? If not, will they not raise a finger to save a human life? I ask them before the tribunal of the healing art. Come one; come all.

Will Drs. Littlejohn, Gilmour, and Fullerton vindicate their claim to being considered reliable medical experts by overturning the positions advanced above, as they are honourable and respected members of the medical profession? Personally I pay them all the deference which is justly due to them. For their opinions in this case I have no respect.

Sons of toil! This is a momentous question. The blood-bought liberties of Scotland are assailed. Do you forget Docherty? I am ashamed by the country I love so well and humiliated by at least some of the followers of "the meek and lowly Jesus," when I think of that boy's *judicial murder*, and the consequent death of a brokenhearted father. Death could not divide them. They moulder in the earth, the common mother of us all, to whose bosom you and I are fast tending. But in the solitude of the night and the contemplation of the day, a still small voice reaches us from another world : "How long, O Lord! how long? How long will capital punishment continue to be a blot on our civilisation and a satire upon two thousand years' preaching of the Gospel of Peace?" Another life trembles in the balance. The bloodhounds of the law are about to be unleashed. The rack and the pinion go merrily on. The black familiars of the Inquisition are hovering about. The work of Hell is imminent!

Citizens of Glasgow, brethren of the medical profession in Scotland, of the noblest of all guilds, *our* honour is at stake! Will *you* allow this unfortunate young outcast—this wayward, misguided, and possibly very wicked, if not morally irresponsible, young man—to go to the scaffold under these circumstances (feebly, no doubt, but honestly and unselfishly brought thus under your notice) without murmur or protest?

I am,

Your obedient Servant,

D. CAMPBELL BLACK.

Appendix III.

" To my mind nothing could be better put than the statements your letter contains (Dr. Campbell Black's letter in *Herald* of the 12th inst.) on the facts and fictions of the case."—Patrick Heron Watson, Surgeon in Ordinary to the Queen in Scotland [*vide infra*].

APPENDIX IV.

LEADING ARTICLES AND CORRESPONDENCE RELATING TO THE CASE PUBLISHED IN THE CONTEMPORARY NEWSPAPER PRESS.

---

(1) THE ARRAN MURDER.

North British Daily Mail, Tuesday, 6th August, 1889.

We are now in possession of information which appears to show conclusively that the death of the unfortunate tourist, whose remains were buried yesterday in the old graveyard at Sannox, was not the result of an accident. The medical gentlemen who examined the body found that no limbs had been broken, as would inevitably have been the case if Mr. Rose had fallen down the rugged and precipitous hillside where his remains were discovered. An examination of the skull showed also that the injuries were such as could not have been caused by a fall. The skull had been not merely fractured as by the weight of the body bringing it into contact with the rocks, but had been shattered into such fragments that its condition could only be accounted for by repeated blows from some heavy instrument. No other conclusion seemed to be possible from the appearance it presented than that Mr. Rose had been brutally hammered on the head with a weighty stone furiously wielded by strong hands. It is clear that he was murdered. The crime having been committed, the body appears to have been dragged to the spot where it was concealed. Thrusting it into the hole beneath the boulder, the murderer had gathered stones and built them up against the mouth of the cavity to hide the remains of his victim and the evidence of his guilt. It is thought that the murder was committed on the top of the ridge. One theory is that Mr. Rose was first pushed over the precipice, and then followed and killed where he lay disabled; but this supposition does not agree with the fact that the limbs were found to be free from injury. A more likely theory is that Mr. Rose, while resting on the hilltop after the exhausting climb over the Saddle from Goatfell, was attacked from behind, his assailant using a heavy stone and beating in the crown of the head; and that when the horrible work was completed the body was dragged down the hillside by the murderer, for the purpose of concealment. Still,

243

on the other hand, there is the important fact that the murdered man's waterproof overcoat and walking-stick were found not at the top, but on the side of the hill. They might, of course, have fallen down if there had been a struggle at the top; but the smashing of the skull without injury to other parts of the body seems to indicate that Mr. Rose was taken by surprise and struck at once on the head without having the opportunity of defending himself. There is a third theory which removes the difficulty suggested by the position of the overcoat and walking-stick, and it is that Mr. Rose had partly descended the hillside when he was struck on the back of the head by a person who was following in his footsteps. If this was so, it was very easy to overcome him, and then to drag the body a little lower down to the nearest hole in which it could be hidden. Considering the care and deliberation with which the hiding was done, it is surprising that the murderer did not go back for the overcoat and walking-stick, and conceal them along with the body, so that nothing belonging to his victim might be visible to attract the attention of any chance explorer to the spot. It being evident that a murder was committed, what was the motive? That also has been made clear. An examination of the dead man's clothes has shown that his pockets were rifled, and his watch and purse and other articles taken. Mr. Rose was robbed as well as murdered, and the only possible conclusion is that he was murdered in order that he might be robbed. As the state of the skull puts accident out of the question, so the state of the pockets shuts out the idea of the murder having been the unpremeditated consequence of a quarrel. The robbery, begun on the mountainside near the head of Glen Sannox, was completed in the cottage at Invercloy, Mr. Rose's travelling-bag and other property having been carried off the following morning; and everything points to the belief that what was begun at the one place was completed at the other by the same hand. Now, although it is not a matter of actual knowledge who it was who commenced the work, it is positively known who it was who finished it. When Mr. Rose went from Brodick to ascend Goatfell he left his tennis suit at his lodgings, and that suit was worn two days afterwards and the two following days at Port Bannatyne by the man who passed under the name of John Annandale. The movements of this man are easily traced up to a certain point—and beyond that point we look to the police to follow them. On Saturday, the 6th of July, Annandale engaged apartments for a fortnight at Port Bannatyne. There he made the acquaintance of Mr. Rose, who had come from London to spend his holidays, and was staying at one of the hydropathic establishments. On Friday, the 12th, he told his landlady that he was going to Arran and would not return till the following Tuesday. He did go to Arran on the Friday, and took a room at Invercloy for a week. Then he went away and came back next day with Mr. Rose, who in the course of conversation with a gentleman in Brodick the following day, Sunday, remarked that he had got among a " drinking set " and had been induced to take up his

Appendix IV.

quarters there by a stranger whom he had met—the statement being made as if he felt uncomfortable about his position. On the afternoon of the next day, Monday, the 15th, Mr. Rose and Annandale ascended Goatfell together, and were seen at the top at ten minutes past six. At about a couple of hours' walk over the Saddle from that point, Mr. Rose was murdered and robbed and his body concealed. About midnight a face, supposed to be that of Annandale, was seen looking out of the wood which surrounds Brodick Castle. Next morning a person answering the description of Annandale left Brodick by the steamer for Ardrossan. On the room which Mr. Rose and he had occupied being entered, it was found that all their property had been removed, excepting an old topcoat, a tennis racquet, and a pair of slippers, belonging to Annandale. On the evening of the same day Annandale returned to Port Bannatyne—as he had told his landlady there he would do. He stayed at Port Bannatyne till Saturday, the 20th, and then disappeared, leaving his bill for board and lodging unpaid, as he had done at Brodick. The story appears to be that of a man without money reduced to desperate straits, seeking the acquaintance of a gentleman who seemed to be well off, inducing him to go in his company to a distant and lonely place, and there deliberately and of set purpose murdering him for his money. If there be any other explanation it is for Annandale to appear and give it. The tragedy is horrible in its circumstances of brutality, and still more horrible in its apparent premeditation— for never was a crime, to all appearance, more coolly and callously planned. For the fate of the deceased there must be the deepest sorrow, and for his mourning relatives the deepest sympathy. As for the murderer, for him there must be the hangman's rope. The public look to the police to bring him to justice, and there is reason to hope that if the man calling himself Annandale be the criminal he will be in prison before the day is over.

---

(2) JOHN LAURIE'S ESCAPE.

North British Daily Mail, Friday, 9th August, 1889.

The strange story comes to us from Mossend that yesterday afternoon a man employed at the ironworks found on the wall around the top of an old pit shaft a paper bearing the words : " I'm the murderer," that near by there lay some bread and tinned meat tied up in a pocket-handkerchief, and that wood appeared to have been recently removed from the wall as if a person had been trying to climb over. Whether this has any connection with John Laurie, the man who is suspected of having committed the Arran murder, it will be for the police to discover. We had hoped that by this time Laurie would have been in their hands. Short of going about the streets shouting " I am 'John Annandale,' " Laurie did pretty nearly all that was possible to put the police upon his track. What

John Watson Laurie.

strikes one most strongly about his conduct since the night of the tragedy is its sheer stupidity. He acted with the utmost recklessness, apparently on the extraordinary assumption that no inquiry would be made regarding the missing gentleman by his relatives, or at least that the murder would remain unknown and that the body would never be discovered. On the morning after the crime was committed, Laurie travelled direct from Brodick to Glasgow, went to his lodgings wearing Mr. Rose's tennis suit and carrying Mr. Rose's travelling-bag in his hand, and told his fellow-lodger that he had just returned from Arran and was going down to Rothesay. Three days later—on Friday, 19th July—still wearing the tennis suit—he spoke at Rothesay to a young man who knew him, and showed the tourist ticket which is believed to have belonged to Mr. Rose, saying that he intended to go to London before the end of the year. The following day—which was the day " Annandale " left Rothesay, leaving his Port Bannatyne landlady unpaid—Laurie was on the steamer " Caledonia " when she ran down a small boat as she was coming out of Rothesay Bay, and he volunteered to give evidence regarding the accident, if required, and gave his card bearing his name and address. Laurie afterwards related to his fellow-lodger in Glasgow how he had been on board and had witnessed the accident. After resuming work in Glasgow on Monday, the 22nd, he told his fellow-workmen that he had been at Rothesay and in Arran, and had ascended Goatfell. He afterwards said to an apprentice lad that he had obtained the return half of a tourist ticket to London, and that he intended to use it at the New Year holidays. This he repeated to several of the workmen, at the same time showing the ticket. Laurie betrayed considerable anxiety to see the morning papers, buying them at the gate of the works, when it was reported that efforts were being made to discover Mr. Rose's body; and on the morning of Wednesday, 31st July, on learning from the *Mail* that a large search party was being organised to go over the whole of the ground, he suddenly left his work. An hour or two afterwards he left his lodgings, telling his fellow-lodger that he had a return ticket for London, and would be going there. On Friday, 2nd August, his landlady received from him a letter, posted at Hamilton, asking her not to answer any questions about him, as some persons were trying to get him into serious trouble. Laurie left at his lodgings the vest and knickerbockers which he had worn at Rothesay and Brodick. On Saturday, 3rd August, he took a trip from Glasgow to Tillietudlem with a young lady, and saw her to her home in Coatbridge; and he spoke moodily and mysteriously of having to leave Glasgow, and of that being the last time he would see her— giving no reason, though pressed to explain. Early on Monday he telephoned to her from Glasgow making an evening appointment, which he did not keep. Laurie fled that day, when the *Mail* announced that Mr. Rose's body had been found. The chain of circumstances which we have followed link by link completely establishes the identity of " Annandale " and Laurie. The police have

246

Appendix IV.

not yet laid their hands upon the fugitive, but if there be nothing in the theory of suicide they should very soon be able to apprehend him, and have him brought to trial for the Arran murder.

---

(3) LAURIE'S CAPTURE.

North British Daily Mail, Wednesday, 4th September, 1889.

John Watson Laurie, *alias* John Annandale, the man who is suspected of having murdered Mr. Edwin R. Rose, near the head of Glen Sannox, on the night of the 15th of July, was captured yesterday afternoon in the quarry or bog wood, about a mile from Larkhall. Laurie was hanging about outside Ferniegair Railway Station, and on the approach of a policeman he moved off along the road. The policeman started in pursuit, and was joined by a number of miners. Laurie crossed some fields to the wood, which the men quickly surrounded, and one of them then went in and caught the fugitive in the act of attempting to cut his throat with a razor. It will be a satisfaction to the public to know that this man, who had dodged the police for a month, has at length been captured. When he first disappeared from Glasgow, it was thought that the police would very soon lay their hands upon him, but as time went by, and he was heard of every now and then, roving about the country with impunity—visiting Liverpool, suddenly turning up at Aberdeen, boldly returning to Glasgow, taking train to Uddingston, and walking to Coatbridge—people began to fear that, after all, he might escape, the detectives being always too late in getting on his track. It is not pleasant to think that a criminal may laugh at the machinery for the detection and punishment of crime. The public mind will be relieved by the knowledge that Laurie is safe in prison. But his capture does not involve his conviction, and even now it must not be assumed that it was he who murdered Mr. Rose. Laurie may be guilty, but his guilt has yet to be proved. Meanwhile—though no one else can be suspected, and though the chain of evidence against him is almost complete—he must receive the benefit of such doubt as there may be, and not have his case prejudged before he is brought to trial. No one saw him commit the crime. The evidence is purely circumstantial. It starts with the admitted fact that Mr. Rose and he left Brodick and ascended Goatfell together on the afternoon of Monday, the 15th of July. Three gentlemen saw them together at or near the top about ten minutes to six. Mr. Rose was not again seen alive. Laurie turned up, alone, at the Corrie Hotel shortly before ten o'clock. In the course of the night the room which Mr. Rose and he had occupied at Invercloy, Brodick, was entered, and all their property taken away, except an old coat, hat, and pair of slippers belonging to Laurie. The latter left Brodick by the steamer on Tuesday morning for Ardrossan, and travelled thence by rail to Glasgow, where he went to his lodgings, wearing Mr. Rose's

John Watson Laurie.

tennis suit, and carrying Mr. Rose's travelling-bag in his hand. On the afternoon of the same day he went to Port Bannatyne, and there wore till the end of the week Mr. Rose's tennis jacket, cap, and shoes. On Saturday, 20th July, he returned to Glasgow, without paying for his lodgings, leaving behind him Mr. Rose's tennis suit. Laurie resumed work at Springburn on Monday, the 22nd. He showed to several of his fellow-workmen, and to his fellow-lodger in Glasgow, the half of a tourist ticket for London, which is believed to have been Mr. Rose's ticket. It was observed that Laurie showed great anxiety to get a newspaper every morning at the gate of the works, and to glance through it as soon as possible. On the morning of Wednesday, 31st July, on learning from the *Mail* that a large party was being organised to search for the body of Mr. Rose, Laurie suddenly left his work, returned to his lodgings, and then disappeared. On Friday, 2nd August, his landlady received a letter from him, bearing the Hamilton postmark, asking her not to answer any questions regarding him. Laurie was seen in Glasgow on Monday, 4th August, the day the *Mail* announced the finding of Mr. Rose's body, and the same day he fled, beginning the month's dodging of the police which has ended with his capture. The chain of evidence is exceedingly strong. Still, it does not prove that Laurie committed the murder, though it proves that he stole Mr. Rose's property. When the body was discovered it was found that the murdered man's pockets had been rifled. It has yet to be shown that Laurie had in his possession anything which Mr. Rose had carried about his person. The evidence seems to be uncertain as to Laurie having had Mr. Rose's watch, purse, or ring, after the murder; and the tourist ticket might have been in the travelling-bag or a pocket of the tennis suit. But the strongest point for the defence seems to be the time at which Laurie reached Corrie on the night of the tragedy. Mr. Rose and he did not arrive at the summit of Goatfell till after six. The body was found below the Saddle in Glen Sannox, and those who know the place say that it would take two hours to walk there from Goatfell, as there is some very stiff climbing down to and across the ridge connecting Goatfell with Am Bennein, and then over the western extremity of the latter hill to the Saddle dividing Glen Sannox and Glen Rosa. The murderer must have occupied not far short of an hour in hiding the body—gathering upwards of 40 large stones, and building them up in a wall against the opening under the boulder. Then he would have a walk of about an hour and a half—perhaps more, seeing that darkness was setting in— down the glen to Sannox, and it would take him at least twenty minutes to get along the road from there to Corrie. Now, if these calculations be correct, the murderer could not have reached Corrie much before eleven, whereas it is the fact that Laurie was there before ten. No doubt, those who defend him will make the most of this—as they are entitled to do; and they will probably endeavour also to make something out of his statement that he left Mr. Rose at the top of Goatfell with two men who came from Lochranza, and

248

Appendix IV.

said they were going to Brodick. Nothing can be done to clear Laurie of robbery; whether he can be cleared of the murder remains to be seen. But it may be said, without fear of contradiction, that he has acted all along as if he were guilty.

---

(4) THE LAURIE TRIAL.

Scotsman, Monday, 11th November, 1889.

On Saturday evening, after a long and patient trial, John Watson Laurie was convicted of the murder of Edwin Rose in Arran, in July last. Few crimes of the kind have ever excited a keener interest in Scotland and through the kingdom generally than has this. The strangeness of the disappearance of the murdered man; the strangeness of the subsequent conduct of the man who was supposed to be his murderer; the long hunt after that man; and, finally, his capture and attempted suicide—all tended to impress the public with a keen sense of interest in the terrible drama. The whole facts of the case have only now been made public. Generally it was known that Laurie and the murdered man Rose had gone up Goatfell together, and that only one had returned. Then it was known that, after long and careful search, the body of the other man, Rose, had been found hidden on the hillside; but all the details that tended to show how Rose met with his death, and what was the subsequent conduct of Laurie, could only become known when the evidence for the Crown was given in Court. The story is one that, if it were made the plot of a novel, would be regarded as highly sensational, if it was not also regarded as in the last degree improbable.

Edwin Rose was clerk to a builder in London named Goodman. He was a highly intelligent young fellow, careful, honest, thoroughly trusted. Mr. Goodman had a brother, a clergyman, who had come to Rothesay to spend his holiday. It was at his suggestion that Rose determined to go up to Rothesay for his holiday. He left London in the first week of July, and went to the Glenburn Hydropathic establishment. John Watson Laurie was a patternmaker employed at the Springburn Works in Glasgow. He had a reputation for being fond of dress, and of aping men in a higher position in life than that in which he was placed. On the 6th of July he had gone on a holiday to Bute, and on that day, calling himself Annandale, he took lodgings with a Mrs. Currie at Port Bannatyne. On the 12th of July a party of friends from the Glenburn Hydropathic went for a day's excursion to Arran. Rose was one of the party. Laurie, calling himself Annandale, was also on board the steamer. In the course of the day's trip they struck up a sort of acquaintanceship, and, on the return of the steamer to Rothesay, Rose took Annandale to the hydropathic establishment and introduced him to persons staying there as his friend. There is some evidence that one or two of the friends of Rose cautioned him against Laurie, whose manners did not impress them.

249

John Watson Laurie.

These cautions, however, had no effect, and the two seem to have planned that they would go the next day for a short stay in Arran. Accordingly, on the 13th of July, a Saturday, they travelled together to Arran, and took lodgings in the house of Mrs. Walker at Brodick. They occupied the same room, and in all respects acted as if in close friendship. They strolled about the island on the Saturday evening and throughout the Sunday, but made it known that they had resolved to ascend Goatfell on the Monday. That Monday was the 15th of July. They started in the afternoon for their walk up. They were met by people who knew them, and they were accompanied part of the way by others, with whom they entered into conversation. The summit of Goatfell was reached, and shortly after six o'clock they were seen standing on a boulder, Laurie pointing in a particular direction, as if to indicate a return path. This direction was not that of the ordinary ascent and descent. From that moment Rose was never again seen alive. One witness swears that he saw Laurie coming out of Glen Sannox about half-past nine in the evening— more than three hours after he and Rose had been seen on the summit; and a policeman who had walked the distance between the summit and the place where Laurie was seen stated that he did so in an hour and forty minutes. Subsequently, Laurie went into a hotel at Corrie, and there got drink at the bar. The next that was seen of him, so far as the evidence shows, was the following morning when he went on board a steamer, carrying with him two bags, and wearing a hat which undoubtedly had belonged to Rose. How he became possessed of these things was clear enough. After Mrs. Walker had gone to bed, neither of her lodgers having come home, Laurie must have entered the house and taken away not only what belonged to himself, but almost everything that belonged to Rose. It is not denied that he did this. He went to Glasgow, returned to Rothesay again, spent the rest of his holiday there, then went to Glasgow on the 22nd of July, returned to work at Springburn, remained there till the 30th of July, and on the 31st of that month left his employment and began a series of wanderings which took him to Liverpool and other places, and ended in his capture as the suspected murderer of Rose.

Meantime, Mrs. Walker had made known the fact that her lodgers had disappeared. Apparently, however, this disappearance of summer lodgers in Arran is not so uncommon as to create interest or anxiety. It simply means that some honest person has not received the rent that was her due. Thus it was that in Arran no particular anxiety seems to have been felt; but in London, Rose's friends, not hearing from him, became extremely anxious, and made inquiries in various directions. His brother came up to Bute and on to Arran, and there learned not only that Edwin Rose had never been known to return from his ascent of Goatfell, but that the man called Annandale, who had accompanied him in his ascent, had been seen afterwards. A search was instituted, and for a week all the glens and corries of Goatfell were scoured for traces of the missing man. At

Appendix IV.

last, on the 4th of August, his body was found by Francis Logan. It was practically hidden away under a huge boulder, and heavy stones had been heaped upon it and in front of it. The pockets of the dead man were turned inside out. The head had been beaten to a jelly, corruption had set in to a frightful extent, and identification would have been all but impossible except for the clothes that were worn. A cap which had belonged to Rose was found in a stream close by with a stone placed over it. There were no traces of blood in the neighbourhood, and nothing to indicate any struggle. Those who found the body came at once to the conclusion, a most natural one in the circumstances, that a murder had been committed, and suspicion fell upon Annandale. It will be seen that the evidence against him, so far, was of a strong presumptive character. He was the last man seen with Rose before the latter's death. He was twice as long getting from the summit of Goatfell to the Corrie Hotel as he would have been if he had come straight down. He went to the lodgings he and Rose had occupied, and he carried off Rose's belongings. Subsequently, when he had learned that a search was being made for the body of Rose, he left his employment in Glasgow and went away, evading the search that soon began to be made for him.

In all this it will be obvious that the connection between Annandale or Laurie and Rose is completely proved. They were seen together on the summit of the hill; they were never seen together afterwards. Rose was found dead. Laurie behaved in a most suspicious manner. No one could doubt that Rose's death had been caused by violence. The theory of the Crown was that he had been knocked down by a blow with a heavy stone, and that his head had then been battered into a jelly; after which his pockets had been rifled, and the body had been placed where it was subsequently found. The Crown insisted that this had all been done by Laurie. The theory of the defence was that the two men parted at the top of Goatfell; that Rose had fallen over a precipice; that his body had been found by some one, who had robbed him of all he had, and had then put the body where it was found. The medical evidence on the side of the Crown was that such injuries as had been received could not have been caused by a fall over a precipice. The medical evidence for the defence, based upon the statements of the condition of the body, was that the injuries could have been caused by a fall. In effect this was the point the jury had to decide. Laurie might be a scoundrel. He might have robbed his companion. He might have told innumerable falsehoods, but all these things would be compatible with his innocence of murder. Nay, there was another possibility that might have been taken into account, though it does not seem to have been urged by counsel for the defence. Rose might have slipped and fallen, being stunned or perhaps killed in the fall; and then Laurie, horrified at this accident, might have yielded to the temptation to rob him. If this theory were the correct one, it would be impossible for the jury to find Laurie guilty of murder. Not only was this defence not urged; but it was insisted by the

John Watson Laurie.

Dean of Faculty that it would have been impossible for Laurie to have placed the body where it was found, and that it must have been so placed by at least two people, passers-by. The Lord Justice-Clerk, in summing up, cautioned the jury as to the medical evidence, pointing out the difference that must exist between evidence given after actual inspection of the body and what may be called theoretical evidence, given on the reports of those who had seen the body. No doubt the jury gave full effect to this advice. They found the theory for the defence too hard for belief. In the first place, if Laurie had parted from Rose on the summit of Goatfell, and had not seen him afterwards, how did it happen that he took first of all a much longer time than was necessary to descend the mountain, and that afterwards he went to the lodgings he and Rose had occupied, and carried off Rose's belongings? He could not get away from the island until the next morning. If, then, he was innocent of all knowledge of Rose's death, he would never have thought of taking away Rose's belongings from the lodgings, because he would have expected him to return some time during the night. If his action in entering Mrs. Walker's house surreptitiously and leaving it surreptitiously with the things belonging to Rose does not prove his guilt, it throws the strongest possible suspicion upon him. All his subsequent actions might be accounted for by a fear of being misjudged, but the one action that could not be so interpreted was his robbery of Rose's luggage at Mrs. Walker's. No ordinary mind will doubt that when he took Rose's bag away he knew that Rose was dead, and, if he knew that this was the case, the theory of the defence is thoroughly broken down. It was said that none of the articles known to be in the possession of Rose when he ascended Goatfell had been found or seen in the possession of Laurie. This is literally true; but things were found in Laurie's possession that there is reason to believe Rose would be carrying in his pockets on that fatal day. This, however, is a matter of small importance. The whole case practically turns upon very narrow points. Was Rose murdered? The jury have believed that he was, and no one who reads the evidence can doubt that, though he might have been injured previously by a fall, he was maltreated afterwards, and this maltreatment would have been sufficient to cause death. Who, then, murdered him? The actions of Laurie point to him as the culprit. If he had known nothing of Rose's death, he could not have done what he did that night. It is difficult, then, to see how the jury could rightly have returned any other verdict. Short of direct evidence of the crime, such as that of a witness who saw it committed, there could not be a stronger case than is made out against the wretched prisoner by the strong circumstantial evidence that has been adduced.

Appendix IV.

(5) Letters to the Editor of the *Glasgow Herald*.

Glasgow, 11th November, 1889.

Sir,—One of the most painful cases occurring during the past years in the range of criminal jurisprudence, and almost amid unparalleled public excitement in the west of Scotland, terminated late on Saturday; and as I consider that the conclusions arrived at by the jury were not warranted, by the medical evidence at least, I shall feel obliged, by your permission, briefly to state, through your columns, the grounds on which this opinion is based.

1st. It has not been proved that Rose was murdered by Laurie, or indeed that Rose was murdered by any person. A body is found three weeks after death in a state of advanced decomposition, two of the most important cavities, so far as concerns medical investigation, are found empty—viz., the skull and the thoracic cavity—there are extensive injuries on the head, and it is at once concluded not only that these injuries have been the cause of death, but that they were inflicted with murderous intent by a given individual. Neither conclusion seems to me to follow. It is a principle in medical jurisprudence that in arriving at any conclusion as to the cause of death it is not sufficient to discover a possible cause of death, but every other possible cause of death must be eliminated. The reason for this will be obvious to the meanest intelligence. The question to be solved is, to which of many causes, to what group of causes, is death most justly and most probably to be ascribed? I shall illustrate this position. A year or two ago I was suddenly summoned to see a gentleman who had been a patient of mine for years previously. I attended him for trifling ailments, chiefly dyspeptic, from time to time. I had occasion to examine his chest and abdominal organs, and I never had reason to suspect serious disease in either cavity. After a hard day's work, he returned home in the evening feeling slightly fatigued. He sat down to dinner with his family, conversed as usual, showing no signs of illness, when, in the act of putting a spoonful of soup to his mouth, he was seen to fall sideways from his chair and never moved or spoke. He was dead. The only explanation of death which a medical friend and I could give was that it was due to embolism. An unsuspected and undiscoverable fragment of organised material, probably situate on one of the valves of the heart, became detached, found its way into the circulation, plugged up an artery in the brain, and death was instantaneous. Supposing this gentleman had so died at the top of a cliff, had then fallen over, and in the descent received on the head such injuries as the medical witnesses for the prosecution admit Rose might possibly have received in this manner, is it necessary to ask any one whether it would not have been fallacious to conclude in such a case that the injuries received after death were the cause of the death, and not the latent disease of the heart or brain? Would it not have been still more difficult to prove—would it not have been impossible to prove—that death was not due to disease of the heart or brain when

John Watson Laurie.

there was no vestige of these organs to be found? Was any attempt made to show that the unfortunate tourist in this case had neither disease of the heart, lungs, great blood vessels, or brain. Could it be proved that he had not? Had he no valvular disease of the heart, no aneurism of the aorta? Could death not have been due to embolism or apoplexy? Is it not possible that death was so occasioned, and that after death Rose fell over a precipice from 20 to 30 feet in height, and then and thereby received these terrible injuries to the head described by the medical witnesses. If these contingencies are possible, then I have not the slightest hesitation in asserting my fullest conviction that it had never been proved at the trial that Rose's death was at all due to the injuries in question, and that all the conclusions based on this unwarrantable assumption are valueless.

2nd. After a lapse of any such period as three weeks, and the occurrence of such advanced decomposition as was found in the body of Rose, I hold that it would be impossible to pronounce whether the injuries to the head were caused before or after death; or whether some of them might not have been received during the fall, and cause death; and others of them had been caused after death, or to distinguish between the two kinds.

3rd. If Dr. Littlejohn is correctly reported as having stated that rupture of the liver is " always associated " with a fall, the answer must be pronounced as too absolute and misleading. That rupture of the liver may so occur is well known to all medical jurists, but that it is an invariable concomitant is what few would care to assert. " Ruptures of the liver may occur from falls or blows " (Taylor's *Medical Jurisprudence*, 1865, p. 549). If the jury considered this point, as they were entitled to do, as the opinion of such an experienced medical jurist as Dr. Littlejohn, what inference would they be likely to draw? If, as Dr. Littlejohn says, all falls are attended with rupture of the liver, and there was no rupture of the liver here, then Rose did not fall from a height, they would probably argue. But the premises I hold to be wrong and the conclusion would be necessarily vicious. But if all falls do not present this feature, could Dr. Littlejohn state the height necessary invariably to produce it?

The value of the medical evidence (unfortunately conflicting, as usual) was put in a nutshell by the learned judge. " Possibilities entered largely into such theories of the cause of death as the jury had heard, but it was noticeable that neither side would absolutely exclude from its theory the possibilities raised by the other side." In other words, the medical witnesses for the prosecution admitted that, while it was more probable that the injuries to the head (assuming them to have been the cause of death, which was, however, never proved) were caused by repeated blows, it was quite possible that they might have been caused by a fall; while the medical witnesses for the defence maintained the exactly contrary position, that while it was more probable that the injuries to the head were caused by a

Appendix IV.

fall, it was quite possible that they might have been caused by repeated blows. Putting the value of the medical testimony as equal —which is surely not arrogating too much—the medical evidence may be said to annihilate itself. For my part I entirely agree with the medical evidence for the defence.

There is just one other consideration on which I should like to say a word. *Nemo repente fuit turpissimus.* Is Laurie, as you remark, not a psychological puzzle? Is he a man of average mental soundness? I should hesitate to answer in the affirmative. Supposing Rose to have fallen over a rock, and to have thereby received fatal injuries, or to have immediately died in consequence, and Laurie finds himself in the presence of very compromising circumstances, was he a man, judged by his subsequent conduct, likely to have acted as an innocent man of a well-balanced mind? Supposing that for reasons that seemed on the spur of the moment good to his enfeebled intellect and perverted understanding, he proceeded to mutilate the body past recognition, as he possibly might hope, or to provide against its discovery, might the *post-mortem* injuries not have been such as were described by the witnesses? At all events this raises a point having as much probability in its favour as the theory of his guilt. Surely if ever there was a case where a verdict of "not proven" was justifiable this was one. Circumstantial evidence has doomed innocent men to penal servitude and to the scaffold before now. Better that a hundred guilty men should escape the vengeance of the law than that one innocent man should die the death of a felon.—I am, &c.,

D. CAMPBELL BLACK.

14th November, 1889.

Sir,—In the name of common sense, what is coming over us all that this hysterical howl for a reprieve is raised every time a person is convicted of murder nowadays? Are the people of England and Scotland losing all power of weighing evidence? Are my countrymen losing all the calm judgment, the fairsightedness, and shrewd good sense with which they have been generally credited? Truly it looks like it now. If ever circumstantial evidence is to convict, surely it has rightly done so in this case. If ever a foul and brutal murder was brought home to the murderer, step by step, with fatal certainty, by the silent evidence of circumstance after circumstance, this murder of a helpless traveller has been brought home to the man Laurie so clearly, so convincingly, that unless we are to wait to convict till the murderer selects an audience before whom to do the deed, I fail to see how murder is to be detected. The howl raised at present and that raised lately in behalf of a still more " interesting " criminal show two phases of public feeling unpleasant to contemplate now, and boding ill for the future—a certain secret sympathy with, or at least tolerance for, crime, and a certain defiance of and resistance to law—in fact, a placing of " trial by mob opinion " above that of " trial by jury decision." It is high time

John Watson Laurie.

for persons who are content to abide by the law, and who feel confidence in those who administer it, to raise their voices with no uncertain sound and try to stem this tide of maudlin sentimentality and secret lawlessness which is making its way among us. It will be monstrous if we allow this brutal murderer to escape *pour encourager les autres*, and so make our lovely and lonely Highland glens as dangerous to the solitary traveller as the passes of the Appennines or the mountains of Greece. Hoping that all who have the courage of their opinions will strive against the rising tide of sickly and dangerous sentimentality and allow the law to take its course upon this wretched man, who has cast such a deep shadow over a happy home, and such a reproach over his countrymen.—I am, &c.,

A SCOTCHWOMAN.

---

(6) Letters to the Editor of the *Evening Citizen*.

Sir,—If circumstantial evidence is to go for anything, there could scarcely be a clearer case of guilt than Laurie's. Yet I am surprised to observe certain well-meaning philanthropists are trying to work a reprieve for this man, who murdered his victim under the guise of friendship. I cannot believe they will succeed in getting a decent number of signatures to enable them to persevere with any chance of success; but in case they should, and to stifle this mawkish sentimentality in the bud, I propose that petitions be prepared to the effect that the law be allowed to take its course. If Laurie were to escape the death penalty, the hope of conviction by circumstantial evidence might as well be abandoned once and for ever.—I am, &c.,

JUSTITIA.

New Club, Glasgow, 18th November, 1889.

Sir,—Your correspondent, "Humanitarian," seems to be sadly exercised that we, as professing Christians, can stand and see the hangman making ready the dread preliminaries for butchering a fellow-creature. Now I, as a thinking, reasonable person, am of the opinion that I show more Christianity and humanity by acquiescing in his just fate than by adhibiting my name to a petition to have him reprieved. What guarantee have the public that Laurie when released from prison—as he ultimately will be if reprieved, if, as your correspondent argues, he is homicidally insane—that he will not straightway go and commit another crime of the same description? Would your correspondent sign a petition for his reprieve a second time? I am afraid that if he is a sensible person he would not, and therefore why do it the first time any more than the second? My firm belief is, however, that Laurie is not insane, and I cannot find any reasons or arguments in "Humanitarian's" letter to make me change that opinion. He says that "who but a maniac could commit such a deed?" Any person whom the love of finery and money, combined with a brutal, vain, and selfish disposi-

256

Appendix IV.

tion, had led away could do it, as this case has proved. As for his second argument, that none but a maniac could have evaded the law so long, Laurie may thank his parents for that. Had it not been that his father held such a respectable position, that he had been so well brought up, you may take my word for it that he would have been in prison long before the time that he was caught, for innumerable were the instances in which he was seen and recognised before his arrest, but no one would hand him over to the police simply because of his parents; and many people who are now signing the petition are doing so more for sympathy with them than with him. In conclusion, I can only say that I hope the Home Secretary will not accede to public clamour, but will deal out justice without fear or favour.—I am, &c.,

JUSTICE.

18th November, 1889.

———

(7) Letters to the Editor of the *Glasgow Herald*, continued.

112 Cambridge Street, 18th November.

Sir,—There is an anecdote of one of our old Scotch judges (Braxfield, I think) who interrupted the protesting pleadings of "an innocent victim of circumstances" by saying, "A weel, it may be a' just as you say, but in my opinion you'll no' be the waur o' a bit hangin'." It has been made abundantly evident that, whatever the manner of poor Rose's death, Laurie must have witnessed it, or was immediately cognisant; that he admittedly rifled the body of his comrade of but a few minutes back; that he stole his companion's portmanteau; that he immediately thereafter absconded; and from that time till the present moment has not emitted one word in explanation of his conduct, or that would enlighten the mystery of the mutilated body, and of its carefully devised and laboriously constructed place of concealment. It is therefore only natural that much concurrence should be expressed as to the sentence, notwithstanding that the verdict was the result of only a casting vote in an almost equally divided jury of fifteen. And it is still more natural that the larger jury of the general public should now express astonishment and disappointment that the doubt so notoriously felt by the jury has not found expression in the recommendation that usually follows that doubt. It is natural that this verdict should be freely canvassed, more especially as the facts bearing upon the actual manner of poor Rose's death are not shown to have been the action of Laurie or any person. It has only been by inference that Laurie has been implicated. And the inference is on several grounds reasonable, as well on account of his immediate associations with the deceased as on account of Laurie's habits and disposition. Laurie is without doubt a selfish, sensuous, self-sufficient, shallow-minded youth, resenting his position in society, and striving seemingly to get out of it by equivocal actions, such as masquerading under false

John Watson Laurie.

names and going clothed in deceptive garments. It is easy to conceive, in view of his selfish nature, that, however shocked at witnessing the sudden death of his companion—which I cannot doubt he did witness—his impulse would be to snatch at the chance of profit through the unknown contents of his companion's pocket and portmanteau. The absence, so far as we have evidence, of creditable moral impulse, conjoined with his very transparent self-sufficiency and weak-mindedness, bordering on incapacity, would make him inconsiderate of ordinary humane or generous sense of duty to the "near and dear ones" of his whilom comrade, or to the inevitable consequences of his shabby theft and want of common-sense recognition of the inferences unavoidably deducible from his flight.

But setting aside these very apparent considerations, and setting aside his fate, or judicial disposal, there are considerations attached to the bald verdict of "guilty" which will certainly affect judgment in future cases where death from evident violence has been unwitnessed. From a careful study of the entire evidence, and from no slight special experience, I am myself clearly satisfied that Rose's death was instantaneous—the result of a fall headlong from a height —and that very obviously there was no need, even assuming the disposition, for any subsequent battering and pounding of the corpse as alleged by the prosecution. Further, I am satisfied that no battering or pounding of the body could produce the injuries that have been described.

The principal facts, as I recognise them, clearly demonstrated are, that one side of the skull was shattered to the base, that the upper bone of the spine on which the skull rests was also fractured, that the two first ribs on the same side were fractured close to the spinal column, and that the projecting end, or epaulette, of the shoulder-blade of same side was broken and forced through the coat sleeve.

In valuing the import of these facts, I prefer giving reference to authoritative conclusions recorded by one who is not only beyond challenge, but beyond question, the most eminent expert in Europe —Dr. Casper, official referee to the Courts of Justiciary of Berlin (and in that connection to the entire kingdom of Prussia)—in his classical work on forensic medicine, translated into English by the Sydenham Society, translated into French, Italian, Dutch, &c., records in more or less detail 221 judicial cases investigated by himself personally during life, and 400 cases investigated after death, irrespective of details and summaries of "innumerable experimenta" made on the dead body, all illustrated by subsidiary references, during the twenty years of his medico-legal official term of office, and up to the date of publication of his great work. With reference to the experimental production of injuries upon dead bodies, "which have not previously been made anywhere on so great a scale, and which I still continue to repeat every academical session," he states (vol. 1, p. 245), in treating of fractures of the skull : "In making these experiments we have usually employed the wooden

Appendix IV.

mallet used to prop up the skull and spinal canal during the process of dissection. In other cases we have employed hammers and similar weapons. The most powerful blows struck downwards upon the body laid horizontally were usually without result, and only after repeated violent blows were we enabled to produce perhaps one or a few fissures in the occipital or parietal bones, or in the temporal bone (*i.e.*, the back part and side of skull). We were unable to produce more considerable effects, such as complete smashing of the skull, or fissures of its base, even in one single instance." Dr. Casper narrates instances, however, where the base was reached by pickaxe or cleaver. But of the various cases of death from fractures of the skull there is not one recorded where there was fracture of the atlas, or cervical bone, on which the skull rests. Similar and corroborative evidence from Taylor's book on *Medical Jurisprudence*, which is the English work of reference; from Chevers's large *Manual of Medical Jurisprudence for India*, and from many others, might be cited *ad nauseam*; but meanwhile I state that I have found nowhere recorded an instance that controverts Casper's extraordinary personal experience and unique evidence. Chevers (p. 433) states that the "not infrequent mode of homicide in the North-west, and specially in the Saugor and Nerbudda territories, is pounding the face with a heavy stone," and illustrates by detailing various cases where "the bones of the head and face were shattered to pieces," but no case of fracture of the base of the skull is cited or of the bone on which it rests. In quoting Casper's experience, as referred to, he adds : "There is no reason to believe that the dead skull is proof against comminution by blows from such instruments as a crowbar, or pickaxe, or the back of a billhook." To this I would say : *Cela va sans dire* whether the violence is applied to skull, vertebræ, or ribs. But the piercing and splintering caused by such sharp-pointed, angular implements are easily distinguishable from the pounding with a heavy stone, which is the theory of the prosecution in Laurie's case, and there was no suggestion, moreover, made to pickaxes or crowbars having been available or used.

With reference to fracture of ribs from crushing, stamping upon, kneeling, battering, &c., it is a remarkable fact that it is from the second or third rib downwards that these lesions occur. From their mode of attachment to breastbone and backbone, their shortness, and their being so shielded by the shoulder and shoulder-blade, these two upper ribs seem always to escape from under violence that fractures all the others. Chevers details above 25 cases in illustration of the fact that "murder is frequently perpetrated in India by pressing or trampling upon the chest." In almost all such cases the soft organs within the chest, such as the heart and lungs, are torn or ruptured, and the ribs fractured several inches from the back or breastbones. In Rose's body these organs were uninjured, and the two first ribs fractured close to the spine. Unless in cases where the body has been passed under a roller or subjected to pressure of an analogous kind, as by being forced

John Watson Laurie.

against a wall by a boiler or heavy piece of machinery or by a direct piercing indent, I am not aware of the first rib having been fractured by external violence.

Much stress was laid by the prosecution upon the fact that the liver was uninjured. This organ is soft and heavy, weighing about 4 lbs., and it hangs suspended from the under surface of the diaphragm, a fleshy partition dividing the chest from the abdomen. In a leap or fall from a height upon the feet it is liable to be jerked and torn from its slight suspending fold of membrane, and it is very liable to be crushed and lacerated by body blows inflicted either standing or lying, or when the body is being knelt upon. But when the body is inverted, as in a headlong fall, the liver then rests upon a soft fleshy carpet—equivalent in its action to the net used by acrobats to break a chance fall—and that carpet, so to speak, is supported by about 10 inches deep of a springy elastic cushion formed by the lungs—a cushion that may be likened to some 10 inches deep or thick of a moist sponge. Assuming a head-long fall, I am unable to conceive the possibility of the liver being ruptured. There are cases recorded "plenty as blackberries" of the liver being torn from its supports, bruised, or ruptured in consequence of falls upon the feet or from being thrown sideways to the ground, or from direct body blows, but there seems no case on record of rupture of the liver where the fall was head downwards. Of course a fall may occur from a height that will pulverise and smash to a pulp the entire body. But no such conditions were approached in the case of Rose's body.

I fear to become prolix and tedious, and my wish is merely to indicate something of what could be urged in support of my view that Rose's death was—as I have already assumed—instantaneous, and the result of a fall headlong from a height. And in venturing so to express my opinion, I may state that when some fifty years back I was demonstrator with Knox, the celebrated anatomist, I assisted in experiments on the dead body, which included those of Casper, as referred to. These experiments were conducted during autumn recess, by such men as Skae, lecturer on medical jurisprudence; Sir William (then plain William) Fergusson, John Reid of St. Andrews, Henry Lonsdale, and other well-known names, all now belonging to the majority. There had at that time, and for some years previous, been much attention given by the teachers of the Edinburgh Medical School to the discrimination of injuries inflicted on the body before, or after, death, whether by burning, bruising, or fracturing. And the practice of these experiments was initiated by the late Sir R. Christison and his colleagues, who gave evidence in connection with the trial of the infamous murderers, Burke and Hare. My old masters and teachers, Knox, Fergusson, and Reid, were among those who were assailed by ignorant popular clamour, and for some considerable time the experiments I refer to were not infrequent in the privacy of the practical anatomy rooms, of which I had charge. Several of my medical friends in Glasgow

Appendix IV.

who knew something of my antecedents and early associations have therefore appealed to me, privately, to express my opinion on the verdict in this present *cause célèbre*. I will now only add that my after experience, while surgeon to collieries, public factories, at a date before the present system of Government inspection and legislative precaution against accidents, together with my frequent engagements in criminal evidence, gave me abundant observation of mechanical injuries inflicted, as well on dead as on living bodies. That practical experience entirely corroborates the special experiments and experience of others as referred to in the foregoing.

Whether Laurie assisted in that fatal fall, which I have an unwavering conviction was the cause of death—whether Rose toppled over because of some breakdown in his eternal economy, as suggested by Dr. Black, are possibilities regarding which we are unlikely ever to have assurance. The latter possibility has been in my mind a probability from the first, having in common with my confrères of mature age had frequent experience of the thin partition which separates all of us from death while in the fullest flush of our mental and bodily functions. I have had die literally within my arms, and with not a moment of warning, one of the brightest intellects with which I have ever associated. Another equally eminent in another sphere of active energy bowed his head and ceased to be while waiting my expectant footfall, and for my promised visit and provisional sanction to enter upon renewed action immediately after my visit. Within the last few days I shook hands with a city merchant who at the moment was seemingly in fullest vigour of mind and body, and within ten minutes I was summoned to find him speechless and motionless, as he had dropped from his office chair, to die within a few hours. No more likely cause for testing a weak point in the human machine than the ascent and descent of Goatfell; and the death of the late member for Dundee is an apposite illustration.

Laurie's motives for his subsequent movements, after witnessing poor Rose's death, I will not discuss. Our great Poet-Analyst of the passions says—

> "One motive still is mainly dark,
> The kennin' why they do it."

But in view of the weakness of Laurie's character, so evident in his entire history as made known, and in view of the fact that his previous record does not include any criminal act, I conclude with the sentiment—

> "Who made the heart, 'tis He alone
> Decidedly can try us.
> He knows each chord, its various tone;
> Each spring, its various bias."

I am, &c.,

JAMES ADAMS, M.D.

261

John Watson Laurie.

Sir,—The present position of this case is a psychological puzzle. The majority of the jury decided on circumstantial evidence that Laurie murdered Rose, and without further question the convict is sentenced to death. But there exists a feeling that though the jury may have taken the common-sense view of the facts presented to them, yet there remains something to be explained in connection with the motive for the murder, and Laurie's whole conduct. The assigned motive—viz., the desire to possess a watch, some money, and a few articles of clothing—is not, taken alone, an adequate explanation either of the murder or of Laurie's subsequent conduct. We feel that a man in receipt of good wages who could do such a deed from such a motive is not as other men. But no other motive can be suggested, and therefore the question arises : Could a motive of so weak a nature under the circumstances of this case have operated with such determined power in other than a diseased mind? I believe not. Allow me briefly to state further my grounds for believing Laurie to be suffering from a subtle, though well-recognised, form of insanity. Certain facts regarding Laurie's antecedent history are now public property. These are mainly that from boyhood he has been restless and unsettled in disposition, not amenable to ordinary discipline, and in particular that he was inordinately vain. I take this vanity to be the chief known indication of his mental alienation, and around it gather all the other evidences of his mental defect. Let us not confound vanity with ambition, which aims high and plays for large stakes, and may therefore impel a man of sound mind to the perpetration of a great crime. Vanity is a vice of weak natures, and finds its full satisfaction in the mere toys of life. In order to obtain the satisfaction of this, which in Laurie seems to have amounted to an insane passion, he was pretentious in his language, lying and thieving in disposition, and when a great temptation came his way to possess himself of a little money, a watch, and some clothes, his judgment forsook him, the fear of detection and punishment failed him, and he yielded to the impulse to kill. I have not said that his right feelings of humanity forsook him, for I believe that owing to mental aberration he has none. It is the chief characteristic of the form of insanity from which I believe Laurie suffers that the moral sense is lost. We say in common language that a certain man is lost to all right feeling. In such cases as I am not alluding to it would be correct to say that all right feeling is lost to them. Dr. Maudsley in his work on *Responsibility in Mental Disease* thus describes such persons (p. 171) : " The affective life of the individual is profoundly deranged, and his derangement shows itself in what he feels, desires, and does. He has no capacity for true moral feeling; all his impulses and desires, to which he yields without check, are egoistic; his conduct appears to be governed by immoral motives, which are cherished and obeyed without any evident desire to resist them. There is an amazing moral insensibility. The intelligence is often acute enough, being not affected

Appendix IV.

otherwise than in being tainted by the morbid feelings under the influence of which the persons think and act; indeed, they often display an extraordinary ingenuity in explaining, excusing, or justifying their behaviour, exaggerating this, ignoring that, and so colouring the whole as to make themselves appear the victims of misrepresentation and persecution."

Laurie's conduct both before and after the deed confirms this view of his case. He wears the dead man's clothes, regardless alike of feeling and risk of detection. When arrested, he feels himself quite a hero, and regrets he didn't go to see his figure in a certain waxwork. After the dreadful ordeal of his trial and sentence, he declares his innocence in quite a dramatic fashion, and appears to be the least concerned man in Court. On his way to Greenock he wants to make a speech from the railway carriage! And now, nearing his doom, he sleeps and eats well, and dresses with his usual care. Surely this is the conduct of a person of unsound mind. In reply it might be said that a very wicked person might exhibit all this composure, and that surely we have not come to this, that wickedness is insanity. This would be a valid objection if it could be shown that Laurie was a very wicked person, apart from his insane passion. But if there is one thing more certain than another in his case it is this, that every act for which he has ever been called in question, including the dreadful crime of which he has been found guilty, has been in connection with his morbid vanity; it has been to him a veritable delusion, and all his actions have been the outcome of this one insane affection. I submit that this explanation gives us a coherent account of Laurie's mental history, and explains the crime of which he has been adjudged guilty. Without some such explanation as I have endeavoured to advance Laurie's crime and conduct are, as I have said, a psychological puzzle. What then, is to be done? Is Laurie to be held irresponsible? That some action must be taken is, I hold, incumbent upon the authorities. To execute the death sentence would outrage the moral sense of those who have given serious thought to the question of Laurie's state of mind. In regard to the question of responsibility in such cases, let me again quote from Dr. Maudsley's work (p. 181). He says: " Perhaps in any case the truest justice would be the admission of a modified responsibility, the degree thereof, where it existed, being determined by the particular circumstances of each case." That the question of responsibility and consequent punishment presents difficulties is no reason why it should not be faced.

No general rule regarding the degree of responsibility can be laid down with respect to these cases. Each must be dealt with on its own merits; and in this instance I do not think the question is a very difficult one. The commutation of the sentence into one of penal servitude for life would, it appears to me, meet the circumstances of the case, for it would place him under restraint and observation; it would be salutary in its influence upon his mind;

John Watson Laurie.

and it would accord both with the only reasonable explanation of the case and the finding of the jury.—I am, &c.,

J. CARSWELL,
Certifying Physician in Lunacy.

---

(8) THE REPRIEVE.

Scottish Leader, Tuesday, 19th November, 1889.

The movement to obtain a reprieve for the Arran murderer has very quickly acquired great force. In this there is much significance, because Laurie's case makes no adventitious calls upon sympathy such as was noticeable in the Maybrick trial. On the contrary, the whole circumstances of the Arran tragedy are of an especially forbidding type, the work, so far as we may venture to judge, of a peculiarly callous nature on which sympathy would be wasted. It may therefore be taken that in regard to Laurie there are special features which drive out of mind the unalloyed repulsiveness of the murder and impel men to ask mercy for him. In these columns protest against capital punishment has always been made on the broad ground of principle. We have argued that the practice of hanging has no real deterrent effect. Those whose low moral instincts permit them to take life have not the wit to be in dread of the hangman. What society has to do, then, is to deal with the dwarfed human types in a spirit, not of revenge, but of pity, and to take care that they are rendered powerless for further evil. What society unhappily does as a rule is to take upon itself the responsibility for the public executioner, and the burden of the acts of a functionary who, despite the social service he is supposed to be rendering, is regarded as rather worse than an outcast, fitted only to break the necks of fellow-creatures in its name. On no ground of reason or morals can this be defended, and the practice is persisted in simply because the ideas and sentiments relating to it are not analysed. We are barbarous indeed with the words of civilisation on our lips.

But in addition to the general reasons for asking clemency for Laurie there are very special reasons more or less apparent to all who consider the circumstances. In the first place, there is the uncertainty dwelling in men's minds as to whether an act literally to be described as murder was actually perpetrated; the dubiety arising from the absence of intelligent motive. There was no passion in the case; the association of the two men was accidental and unsought by Laurie; and all the hope of wealth that was held out cannot be conceived as tempting any one but an insane creature to an act so atrocious. If murder were done, then within Laurie's nature there is enclosed a psychological enigma which the general human experience is powerless to explain.

264

Appendix IV.

In the second place, those who are bestirring themselves in the interests of the prisoner are entitled to plead that the trial was unduly hurried. It was, doubtless, with the best of motives that Lord Kingsburgh announced his determination to finish the case at all hazards within two days; but when men are solemnly contemplating the extinction of life this determination to rush matters has an ugly look. Men are asking what the practical effect of it could have been on the minds of the jury. Fifteen citizens were in durance for two days. They were on their own showing but indifferently supplied with food and refreshment. Late on Saturday night, when called upon to give the verdict, they must have been worn out with the strain, excitement, and long confinement in bad air. In short, the whole conditions were such as to prevent men from bringing their faculties into full and vital activity on the evidence regarding which they had to form so grave a judgment. Without at this moment questioning their verdict in the least, we have no hesitation in saying that the 15 jurymen were men of jaded minds, and it is not to men in such a condition that the issue of life or death should be entrusted.

In the third place, there is a powerful reason for staying the hand of the executioner in the fact that the verdict was only obtained by a majority of one vote. The recourse to the ballot, as it happens, was an irregularity which the jury would probably not have fallen into had there been no pressure upon them to close the case. It has been so far profitable, however, as to show us by what proportion of the jury Laurie's life has been declared forfeit. The division of opinion revealed makes the infliction of the capital sentence a matter of deeper solemnity. It may be a defect in the law that no verdict was possible save that which either condemned or liberated Laurie; but it is horrible beyond expression to think that for this man the difference between absolute freedom and a criminal's death was determined by the vote of a single fagged-out juryman. Surely in a case so surrounded with difficulties, and when the deliberations of the jury so nearly came to the point of breaking down, the right, the reasonable, and the humane course is to take the side of leniency.

There are too many people in society, unfortunately, who can divest themselves of all responsibility for the law, thinking that when the matter has been taken out of their hands it moves along by some perfect machinery which it is presumptuous to question; but the great majority of citizens, we feel sure, will breathe all the more freely when they know that legalised murder is not to be done in their name on grounds so dubious.

John Watson Laurie.

(9) Letters to the Editor of the *Glasgow Herald*, continued.

Greenock, 20th November, 1889.

Sir,—I think your correspondent, "Reason," should be put along-side of Laurie for daring to put forward a plea of insanity for the crime committed. Laurie is not insane, and "Reason" cannot prove he is. If Laurie ever get reprieved, which I do not expect, "Reason" should see about getting him confined in an asylum. I may say Laurie should be hanged, for the crime he committed was one of the most brutal murders which ever took place in Scotland. —Yours respectfully,   JUSTICE.

Glasgow, 20th November, 1889.

Sir,—The petition at present being signed in Glasgow and else-where in favour of a reprieve for the condemned man Laurie seems to be drawing a great many names, but are all the signatures genuine? I for one can state that they are not. I can prove that I saw a friend's name on one of the sheets, with his address attached, and, knowing him to be strictly against a reprieve, I put the question to him as to signing the petition, and he denied that such was the case. Now, I would like to know how many more could say the same.

I would also like to know how many have signed it more than once. I can believe there have been a good few, especially boys, who are getting leave to sign it irrespective of age.—I am, &c.,

A. WALLACE.

Edinburgh, 20th November, 1889.

Sir,—Dr. Campbell Black is so overweighted with his desire to swear to Laurie's innocence, before the Lord High Chancellor if necessary, that he can see no sense in anything anybody else says.

My reference to the necessity of guilt being assumed before the plea of insanity can be urged must be quite plain to every thinking person, whether "educated" or not. It is sought to get Laurie a reprieve because he is innocent and, on the other hand, it is sought to get a reprieve because he is insane. But if he be innocent he is entitled to acquittal, whether insane or not—hence the plea of insanity is surplusage, unless he is guilty. And in no way can both innocence and insanity be effectually pleaded—the one destroys the other.—I am, &c.,   T. A. C.

20 Leven Street,
Pollokshields, 21st November, 1889.

Sir,—The varied opinions that have been ventilated through your columns regarding the unfortunate man Laurie may be said to be a reflex of public opinion. The exhaustive letter of Dr. Adams of yesterday is certainly of considerable significance. That a medical

266

Appendix IV.

gentleman should give in such a clear and forcible manner his positive assurance that all the injuries as detailed in evidence could and might be produced by accidental falling surely ought to cause further inquiry by the Home Secretary. That such an accident might take place the following will place beyond dispute :—A number of years ago I was investigating the character of the Arran granite, and went by the Campbeltown steamer to Lochranza in order to get a transverse examination of the island from Lochranza to Brodick. When approaching the north end of the island, a gentleman from Glasgow asked me if I knew the road to Brodick. I gave him the necessary information, and told him that I was going to Brodick through the range of mountains. He insisted to be allowed to accompany me. I made him aware of the dangerous path I was going by. He came with me. We got to the summit of the Suidhe-Fergus range, on the north side of Glen Sannox, opposite to where Mr. Rose's body was found. We got the setting sun from that altitude. The sight was grand beyond description. Whether it was the grandeur of the sight, or the altitude, or physical inability, I do not know; but during the few minutes we were there I accidentally turned round to pass a remark to my friend, and found him swooning, and about to fall over a deep precipice, and had I not been able to save him he would have fallen over a cliff of great depth, and certainly would have met his death. I was the only person he was seen with during the greater part of the day. The shepherd met us on our way up the mountain, consequently had an accident occurred it might have been asserted that he had met his death by foul means. I had no one to exonerate me from blame, and might have been put to no end of trouble. Now, sir, regarding Laurie's movements I have nothing to say. It would be satisfactory if he would make some statement. But from the above it will be inferred that it is within the range of probability that an accident did take place. The gentleman that I saved is still living, and no doubt this letter will recall to him the circumstance above related.— I am, &c., JAMES THOMSON.

Greenock, 21st November, 1889.

Sir,—I have read with some interest and not a little curiosity the letter in your issue yesterday, signed " Argumentum ad Judicium," on the above very momentous subject. The writer of that letter says : " Allow me space to say a few words condemnatory of the agitation in favour of a reprieve for the murderer, Laurie." I have often heard it said that " it would be a bad thing for society if all men were of one mind," and the truth of that statement is very apparent by the sentiments expressed by your correspondent : " Far from such a movement being creditable to society, it is disgraceful in the extreme, as it not only shows a weak, maudlin, vicious sentimentality—almost an abetting of the murderous spirit—but it shows disloyalty to the law of the land."—I am, &c., X.

John Watson Laurie.

Sir,—The views of various sections of our citizens have been given publicity to, and it may not be held amiss to consider in this Bible-reading city what the Pentateuch says on murder. I for one think direct proof is wanting of Laurie having been guilty of murder. It is not even proved he robbed the body of this hapless victim of either accident, or of some monster in human form. Still, one must not be too sure when we remember the case of Lipski, who confessed at the last. On the other hand, one must remember the Durham case, where a man was proved innocent after having suffered several years' penal servitude. If the law will admit of keeping Laurie in prison for being possessed of some of the murdered man's effects till the suspicions surrounding the case are cleared up, then I say, better let Laurie and 50 guilty men escape capital punishment than hang one innocent of blood guilt. Leave him to the vengeance of the Lord God, who holds the key of all secrets, and you punish more severely in this way than by hanging him. In Exodus, chapter 21, verses 12, 13, and 14, we find that "When a man lies not in wait to kill, I will appoint thee a place whither he shall flee; but if he come presumptuously and slay him with guile, then shalt thou take him from mine altar that he may die." In Leviticus, chapter 24, verse 17, " He that killeth a man shall surely be put to death." In Numbers, chapter 35, verses 16 and 17, and especially 22 : " But if he thrust him suddenly, without laying of wait." Verse 25 : " Then shall he be delivered out of the hand of the avenger of blood." I think most of your readers will admit that if Laurie did this murder there couldn't have been any " laying of wait." Therefore let us, 3300 years after this law of mercy was given to the world through Israel, not be any less merciful in these days of boasted civilisation. Let the convict, to whom doubtless strong suspicion clings, be allowed to flee to one of our modern cities of refuge, viz., to Dartmoor, and keep Mrs. Maybrick company, about whom suspicion is much stronger. Time works wonders, and after a few years the guilt or innocence of both may come out clearer. In the meantime let us exercise the noble prerogative of mercy.— I am, &c.,   A Son of Israel.

Blairbeth, Rutherglen, 21st November, 1889.

Sir,—I have been greatly exercised in my mind in considering all the points and theories that have been advanced, both probable and improbable, as a means to an end, viz., acquitting or condemning John Watson Laurie, the unfortunate young man now lying under sentence of death as the supposed murderer of Edwin Rose. From the very outset I have held to a strong unaccountable conviction that Laurie never committed any murder—that death to Rose was the result of an accident, and in no way attributable to Laurie. I have never changed my mind. I said then, and now I know it to be true, that Laurie is not altogether of sound mind or judgment, or one likely to act in any dilemma like the common race

Appendix IV.

of mankind. I believe Rose to have fallen from the top; and when Laurie discovered that he was really dead, he then and there conceived the insane idea of hiding him up or building him in out of sight once and for ever, in foolish fear lest he should be blamed, and simply took Rose's possessions, not for their intrinsic value, but to blot out any trace, and thus prevent identity should the body ever be found. Insane, inordinate vanity enabled him to wear the clothes afterwards, but he never, certainly in my opinion, murdered Rose to possess them.

On reading Dr. Adams's letter in the *Herald*, I was very much struck by his remarks regarding Rose, which bear a strong likeness to an incident that came under my own notice. And, however much I would shrink from publicity, nevertheless, if what I shall herein state as corroborative proof of his statement should in any way save Laurie from the scaffold, I shall not have written in vain.

In May, 1875, three young men made the ascent of Goatfell. They were students, two divinity and one medical. The day was intensely cold, and the Fell was ever and anon enveloped in white mist. When half-way up they considered much whether, on account of their unfortunate choice of a day, it would not be advisable to descend. But, as it had been a long-planned expedition, they all agreed to go up to the very top. On reaching the summit, and while standing at a very narrow pass, they were again enshrouded in the white mist, when suddenly and most unexpectedly one of the three cried out as if he were going to fall over, his nose commenced to bleed profusely, his brain swam with an indescribable cold, numb, and reeling or giving-way sensation, coupled with a dread horror of falling over.

I was married to that same young man in September, 1876, the year after, and when passing through Brodick a few days after our marriage I made the observation, on viewing Goatfell, " that it would be rather strange if we did not make it a visit." He asked if I very much desired to make the ascent. I replied, " Well, yes, I think so." Something in his tone struck me vaguely, and I looked up and said : " I rather think you don't fancy going," and with a look of dread, which I often recall, he said : " I can never think of standing up there on that summit but with a great sense of horror, like what I felt that day." My husband died two years afterwards—20th September, 1878—very suddenly, and apparently without cause, his heart being sound and his general health good.

Had it not been for my reading Dr. Adams's letter in your paper, I had not the most remote knowledge that I possessed any information likely to throw light on this subject, and would deem it a sin to withhold anything that may free the poor erring youth. And doubtless as he was then, so is he still, afraid to tell the simple truth, believing it would only be regarded as an idle tale, or a pure fabrication. Although no sane person could approve or imitate

John Watson Laurie.

Laurie's course of procedure, nevertheless, as he is, it is cruel and unjust to judge him by other men, and if my solution of the matter be correct, it exonerates him (being as he is) from all blame.—I am, &c.,   L. M. DUNBAR.

15 Argyle Street,
Glasgow, 21st November, 1889.

Sir,—In your issue of to-day I observe a complaint from an anonymous correspondent, who signs himself " Corriegenda," to the effect that many under age sign the petition in favour of Laurie's reprieve. It is clear your correspondent is in favour of the extreme sentence being carried out, but hides his identity behind a *nom-de-plume*. I have, since those sheets were placed in my hands, secured in my place of business here over 9000 signatures, not one of these being obtained from any person so far as I could discern, under sixteen years of age. I have often been requested by parties to be allowed to affix a friend or brother's name, but this request I invariably refused, and in no case has the same party signed twice with me. The printed rule on this point is plain and conspicuously placed where all may see it. I may mention that 90 out of every 100 with whom I come in contact express their firm conviction that poor Rose was not murdered at all. All are satisfied that the dead has been despoiled, but that death is too extreme a penalty for such a crime. " Blessed are the merciful."—Yours, &c.,

JAMES WALLACE THOM.

Corstorphine, 22nd November, 1889.

Sir,—The temperate and merciful views of your correspondent, " A Son of Israel," are very welcome. Still, they are defective in so far as they are directed chiefly towards the question of capital punishment and the Biblical grounds on which it rests. The question of capital punishment is not involved in either of the two recent agitations—the Maybrick case and the Arran tragedy; and it will be regrettable if attention is diverted from the constitutional and legal issues. Although, according to precedent, petitions are so worded as to request " mercy," reprieve or free pardon was and is asked for on grounds of justice, equity, and constitutional law. Law and precedent alike dictate that no one shall be tried for a murder until it can be proven somebody has murdered; and no one shall be condemned or held guilty of that " murder " upon mere suspicion, but only upon incontestible evidence amounting to proof. It is not proved that Mr. Rose was murdered in Glen Sannox. It is not proven that John Laurie was with him when he died, nor even that he afterwards had in his possession a single article on Mr. Rose's person when he met his fate. Laurie stole Mr. Rose's bag. That is proven, and for that he should suffer according to law. Mr. James Maybrick is not proven to have died from poison. There is literally no ground for suspicion of Mrs. Maybrick's felonious intent towards

Appendix IV.

him except confession and proof of previous immorality. In the evidence led at the trial there is no proof of any single instance in which Mrs. Maybrick administered arsenic to her husband. Yet, in face of these facts, both parties are pronounced guilty by a jury. Juries sometimes make mistakes; so do judges. Errors are inseparable from any conceivable human system—errors in judgment and errors in law. It is the business of the public to remember this, and to watch jealously the administration of justice. The Crown's "prerogative of mercy" is reserved in "order that the public sense of justice and equity" in such cases may not be outraged, and all confidence in the administration of justice be destroyed.

In cases where proof is clear, the question of capital punishment is worthy of discussion—the question whether mankind are justified, in any circumstances, in taking a life which they cannot restore.—I am, &c., J. L. F.

The Conservative Club,
Glasgow, 22nd November, 1889.

Sir,—Would you kindly allow me the luxury of one parting shot? My temper is not ruffled, nor is my courage enfeebled, by the hissing of the concealed snake in the grass. The position that I take up in this case is supported by Dr. James Adams, Senior Fellow of the Faculty of Physicians and Surgeons, a gentleman of large experience and undoubted ability; Dr. William M'Ewen, the distinguished surgeon, and one of the foremost authorities on cerebral surgery; Dr. James Lawrie, one of the clearest-headed men I ever knew. I prefer to err with Adams, M'Ewen, and Lawrie than to be "right" with the *canaille*. Au revoir!—I am, &c., D. Campbell Black.

115 St Andrew's Road, 23rd November, 1889.

Sir,—How reserved and utterly insipid are the clergy in the serious and momentous affairs of the people. Notwithstanding much illustrative material in the Old and the direct statements and tenor of the New Testament giving ample warrant for a "Church" movement on behalf of Laurie, they are lifeless and dumb. Were he one of their own sons, no doubt they would then find logic, philosophy, and Jesus Christ on their side, in addition to grand, eloquent effusions in their favour, on the ground of "brotherhood" and "common humanity."

If the Greenock magistrates had met, and unanimously determined to have nothing to do with the handling of that young, simple, and insane lad, it would have been more to their credit than being afraid to append their names to the document for reprieve in their official capacity.

That very opportune and most considerate and able letter by Dr. Adams should arouse sense and instant action among clergymen and magistrates, for the time is short and a life is in the balance.

John Watson Laurie.

Had Laurie been a "habit and repute," or had he been a "terror" in the land, there would be just reason to support the law, but the entire aspect of that young man's career is one deserving pity and not brutal treatment. The death of Laurie cannot now benefit the friends of Rose (and we greatly sympathise with them), nor undo the deed by whomsoever committed, neither can it possibly benefit the public. Surely the spirit of the people will assume the "higher standard" it has gradually been rising to, and scout with indignation a deplorable transaction that shall, if allowed, inevitably disgrace more than the town of Greenock.— I am, &c., ALEX. BROWN.

Kilmacolm, 23rd November, 1889.

Sir,—I see from to-day's *Herald* that 138,140 signatures in favour of a reprieve for Laurie have been forwarded to Lord Lothian. It would be very interesting to know what percentage of that number are ratepayers and entitled to a vote at either municipal or Parliamentary elections, for I consider that people who are not eligible to vote at these elections have no right or business, and should not be allowed, to sign petitions trying to alter the laws of our country. I question very much if 90 per cent. of those who have signed are not apprentices, office and message boys, servant girls, and mill workers. If petitions are to be signed, they should be signed in a legal manner, and with a few policemen knocking about. I'll be bound the petitions in this case would not have come to much.—I am, &c., W.

Helensburgh, 23rd November, 1889.

Sir,—The case of Laurie is, I think, an unprecedented one. There is no direct proof that Rose died by violence, or, if he did, that Laurie was the criminal. On the other hand, there is powerful evidence given by skilled medical men that the appearances on Rose's body were the result of a fall. The jury were divided in opinion, the majority of eight holding that there was a murder, and that Laurie was the perpetrator, and the minority of seven finding that there was not sufficient proof either of a violent death or of Laurie being guilty of it.

I see that some of your correspondents are very anxious for Laurie's execution, because the jury have found him guilty, and why, they ask, should there be any hesitation in carrying the sentence into effect? These persons forget that Laurie's case was submitted to 15 jurors, that seven of these were opposed to his conviction, that the verdict was therefore practically that of only eight men, or, I may rather say of only one juror, because if one of the majority had voted with the minority the verdict would have been different, and Laurie, instead of being sentenced to death, would have been freed from the charge and dismissed from the Bar. In point of

fact, if the execution is carried out, Laurie will die by the vote of one man. If the case had been tried in England, where the jury must be unanimous, there could have been no conviction. In Scotland the rule is different, as a majority of a jury is sufficient to procure a conviction. Perhaps it might be well that in a matter of life and death the same rule should be adopted in Scotland. But, passing from this point, I think I may safely say that no capital punishment was ever inflicted in Scotland where there was a minority of seven jurors opposed to the verdict. It is a trite legal maxim that where there is doubt of guilt the benefit of it should be given to the accused, and surely if ever there was a case of doubt it must be in this case, where seven of the jurors, conscientiously and on oath, declared themselves unconvinced of the prisoner's guilt.

Some of your correspondents speak of the persons seeking a reprieve as mere sentimentalists, as if it were sentimentalism to have a conscientious dread of depriving a fellow-being of life except upon the clearest and most undoubted proof of his guilt. When I first heard of the supposed murder, and of Laurie being suspected, I said to myself that if guilty he must have been deranged at the time. We have frequent cases of men becoming suddenly deranged and depriving of life their wives or children—the very people, to defend whom from danger, they would, when sane, have sacrificed their own lives. The small benefit to be derived from Rose's property could not be a motive for such an act, and it appears to me to be absolutely impossible for any but an insane man causelessly to deprive of life a fellow-being who had done him no harm and with whom he had previously been on friendly terms. A sane man would at once have perceived that from their known acquaintanceship suspicion would immediately fall upon him and very likely lead to his conviction. My supposition was afterwards confirmed by notices in the newspapers of Laurie having been medically treated on account of his mental condition, and his whole conduct before, during, and after his trial points in the same direction.

The object of punishment is to secure the safety of society and to deter men from the commission of crime. I am strongly of opinion that Laurie's execution will not serve this purpose, but, seeing that the great mass of the people is urgent for a reprieve, would cause a widespread mistrust of the law's administration, and would lead men to look on it not as a righteous retribution or salutary example, but only as a melancholy exhibition of reckless revenge.—
I am, &c.,   A. D.

---

(10) THE RESPITE OF LAURIE.

Saturday Review, 30th November, 1889.

It was announced last Thursday evening that the Provost of Greenock had received an official communication that morning that Laurie, the man recently convicted of the murder of the English tourist, Mr. Rose, had been respited. The convict, it was further

John Watson Laurie.

stated, "was made very cheerful by the receipt of the news," although when the intelligence was communicated to him he manifested no particular emotion, but confined himself to merely saying " Thank you." Before the public, however, can either share his cheerfulness or re-echo his thanks, it will be necessary to know a little more than we do at present as to the causes of his reprieve. The first impression, in some minds, may possibly have been that the advisers of the Crown felt uncertain as to the correctness of the verdict on the facts of the case, and thought it just possible that the prisoner's account of the manner in which Mr. Rose met his death may have been true. Nor is it even now quite certain that this is not one of the assumptions on which the respite has been based. Seeing, however, that it was Laurie's own behaviour subsequently to Rose's death which threw discredit on his explanation of that event, it will probably have been concluded by most people, on a little reflection, that the acceptance of some theory of his mental unsoundness must have been a condition precedent to the step which Lord Lothian has taken. And that conclusion was confirmed by the promptly following report that the reprieve had been granted by the Secretary for Scotland on the strength of the report of medical experts that the prisoner was of unsound mind.

We presume, however, that the public wish to be let a little more into official confidence. It may be a purely speculative curiosity, but we should certainly like to know what is the exact view taken at the Scotch Office as to the death of Mr. Rose, and in what precise way Laurie's insanity, assuming him to be insane, has operated to bring about his reprieve. Has it, that is to say, been treated as exculpatory or merely as explanatory? Is it the official theory that he killed Mr. Rose, but that, being of unsound mind, he is not criminally responsible? Or does that theory start with the assumption that Mr. Rose's death was, as Laurie protested in his defence, accidental, and that the latter's insanity only comes in to explain his flight and concealment after the accident took place? Our curiosity on this point may, as we have said, be rebuked as purely speculative; but we are not disposed at present to submit without protest to that reproof. On the contrary, it seems to us to be very material to know which of these two alternative reasons for reprieving the prisoner has in fact been adopted. It is notable that the difficulty which the ordinary mind would experience in assenting to the former theory is more considerable than it would prove in the case of the latter. But, for our own part, we must admit that we have seen nothing in the case from first to last to raise any presumption of Laurie's insanity, and that we trust the public will be informed, not only of the grounds on which certain medical experts unnamed have discovered a defence for him which was not, as far as we remember, so much as suggested on his behalf at the trial, but of the complete theory of his connection with the death of Mr. Rose, as that theory has definitely taken shape in the mind of the Secretary for Scotland.

Appendix IV.

(11) Letters to the Editor of the *Greenock Telegraph*.

Greenock, 2nd December, 1889.

Sir,—To test the real value of reprieve petitions, Lord Lothian ought to be asked to send a few sheets of the Laurie petitions to the police authorities in each town from whence petitions were sent, with instructions to ascertain by personal inquiry the ages and *bona fides* of the petitioners, as it is high time that school and message boys should be deprived of the opportunity of signing public petitions in the freehand style indulged in recently here, and doubtless elsewhere, in connection with the Laurie agitation, and of having their "fun" treated as the genuine expression of adult public opinion.—I am, yours obdt.,

AN EYE-WITNESS OF JUVENILE SIGNATURES.

Greenock, 2nd December, 1889.

Sir,—Every day I see almost all the morning and evening papers published in Scotland, and I have carefully watched how those journals have dealt editorially with the Laurie case. Almost without exception they have shown a childish change of policy utterly unworthy the traditions of the Scottish press. On the morning after the verdict they warmly accepted both that and the sentence as strictly justified by the facts of the case, but on the intimation of Lord Lothian's decision they at once "climbed down" and gave that the support they formerly gave the death sentence. Hence I have rejoiced to note the consistent attitude of the *Greenock Telegraph* in this matter, setting a much-needed example of fidelity to public duty to its fickle contemporaries. Your article in to-day's issue goes to the core of things, and it is to be hoped the information for which you ask will be forthcoming. A more miserable bungling of justice has not, to my mind, happened for many years than in connection with this brutal murder. It seems to me that the only insanity from which Laurie is suffering is that of shallow-patedness and insufferable vanity. How it comes about that such a being should have been made the object of a reprieve agitation passes my comprehension.—Yours, &c., INDIGNANT.

---

(12) LAURIE REMOVED TO PERTH.

Glasgow Herald, Tuesday, 3rd December, 1889.

Provost Rodger, Greenock, yesterday morning received a communication from the Home Office confirming Saturday's telegram that Laurie's sentence had been commuted to penal servitude for life, and that he would forthwith be removed to Perth Penitentiary. Laurie's brother visited Greenock Prison yesterday morning, but did not wait long. Laurie was in the afternoon removed from Greenock Prison to Perth Penitentiary, accompanied by Mr. Napier,

275

John Watson Laurie.

governor, and two warders, the former seeing the prisoner off with the train. He was driven in a cab to Greenock West Caledonian Station for the one o'clock train to Glasgow. Few persons were aware of the movements of the convict, and his departure was witnessed by about a hundred people only. He was dressed in the ordinary prison clothes—tight-fitting body dress, knickerbockers, thick stockings to the knee, and white skull-cap. A large rug was wrapped round his body, and he walked along the platform with great firmness, but his face was much flushed. There was a wait of a minute or so for the train, and in the interval, although the convict was taken to the furthermost end of the platform, the crowd pressed forward to get a good view. Laurie stood between the warders, his back turned to the people, and he kept biting his under lip as if under the influence of great agitation. Since his conviction he has had no shave, and he has consequently now a thin growth of hair all round his face. On the arrival of the train from Gourock he stepped to the front with alacrity, and leapt into an empty third compartment which had been reserved for the occasion. Scarcely a murmur was heard amongst the crowd. The train reached Cathcart Street Station in a couple of minutes. No one there evidently knew of Laurie's departure, but his presence was soon announced, and the compartment was in a moment surrounded by some scores of people. Laurie tried to hide his face behind the warders. He appeared to be much amused at the people, for he was seen to smile at their curiosity. The train left at once, many straining their necks to get the last look of Laurie at Greenock.

The train by which the convict travelled from Greenock arrived at the Central Station, Glasgow, at twelve minutes before two o'clock. There was only a meagre crowd at No. 2 platform, at which the train was drawn up. It was only indeed a couple of minutes or so before the train was due that the word was passed round that Laurie was one of the passengers. Even the railway officials were in ignorance, so well was the secret kept. Superintendent Orr, of the Central Division of police, was, however, upon the platform, and with him he had brought Inspector Carmichael, both ready to render whatever service might be required. Scarcely had the train come to a standstill than a prison warder stepped out of the carriage next the engine, his hand upon Laurie, who came immediately behind. A second warder came in the rear, he also having a grip of the convict. The few persons awaiting the arrival of the train at once made a rush forward to get a good look of the notorious criminal. Laurie was dressed in convict garb, a brightly coloured rug being thrown loosely over his shoulders to protect him from the cold. As he was rushed swiftly across the narrow footway for the nearest cab, Laurie looked up furtively at the onlookers who pressed closely in upon him. In a moment the convict was inside a cab, the two warders and Inspector Carmichael

276

Appendix IV.

beside him, and a brief space more and the cab was rattling out of the station on its way to the Perth train. There was a dead silence among the onlookers, who subsequently took to discussing the convict and the notorious case.

The Perth train left Buchanan Street Station at two o'clock. There were few persons about the station till near the hour, but when the cab arrived (about five minutes to two o'clock) the crowd greatly increased. Laurie stepped quickly out of the cab, and was taken along the platform to an engaged carriage attached to the Perth train. He looked pale and haggard, and from all appearance could not weigh more than 8 stones. Immediately on entering the carriage Laurie pulled his travelling rug over his shoulders, and, by cowering close behind one of the warders, a stout, tall man, he succeeded in screening himself from the gaze of the crowd, which had now swelled to considerable dimensions, and remained about the compartment anxiously trying to get a view of the prisoner till the departure of the train punctually at two o'clock.

Laurie arrived at the Perth General Station, under the charge of two warders, by the first train leaving Buchanan Street Station at two o'clock, and arriving at Perth at four o'clock in the afternoon. There is usually a large number of persons in the Perth Station, but as the news of Laurie's probable arrival in Perth during the afternoon had been published by the local papers, the usual crowd was considerably augmented, and when the train arrived there must have been between 200 and 300 persons on the platforms. A rush was made for the compartment where Laurie was seated, and the people crowded round to catch a glimpse of the convict as he emerged from the carriage along with his attendants. He wore the usual convict dress, but a travelling rug was thrown over his shoulders. He looked very cold, and was extremely pale. On stepping on to the platform he gave a hasty glance around, and then kept his eyes fixed on the ground as he made his way to the cab stance, about 100 yards off. He was followed by the crowd, but did not again look up. The party then got into a cab and drove off to the Perth Penitentiary.

---

(13) LAURIE IN GREENOCK PRISON.

Glasgow Herald, Tuesday, 3rd December, 1889.

Now that all doubt is over with regard to the fate of Laurie, a final word on the impression created by his conduct in prison will not be amiss. In the first place, to those who have been inclined to think as favourably as possible of the convict, and to hope that, notwithstanding appearances and circumstantial evidence, he may be at least a comparatively innocent man, it ought to be stated that, in the opinion of the persons who have been coming into closest contact with him since his incarceration, his hand and no other

277

John Watson Laurie.

committed the foul deed, and that had the respite been delayed for another day the world would have been apprised of all the circumstances relating to the crime. Laurie's first statement was that he and Rose parted on the summit of Goatfell; that he did not see him afterwards; and that consequently he had no share in his death. After his conviction, and when he had the imminent danger of execution pressing upon his mind, he wrote a letter to Lord Lothian which contained the admission that he had witnessed the fall of Rose from a high cliff; that he had gone to his assistance; that he had taken his bruised and bloody head between his hands; and that when he found Rose dead he robbed him of his valuables and buried the body. But as the day of execution drew nearer, the convict is said to have evinced a considerable degree of disquietude, and we believe it is a fact that just prior to the arrival of the first telegram announcing a respite he had made inquiries as to the proper person to whom to make a confession. The respite, of course, soon put all such thoughts out of his head.

From first to last the convict has maintained a consistent and absolute silence with respect to the crime. The utmost efforts to induce him to converse on the subject were unavailing. He was willing and almost eager to narrate the story of his wanderings while justice was on the search for him, but as soon as the deed itself was approached he drew back in a moment and closed his mouth. His general conduct in prison did not, in the opinion of those who were in a position to judge, look like that of an innocent man. He gave himself no chance to brood over the past. He was a voracious reader; he wrote much, sang, whistled, or talked; but he rarely sat down to think. We have said that he avoided speaking of the murder. The strong and convincing impression of his guilt produced upon the minds of those who were frequently about him was, therefore, not the result of explicit statements by the prisoner. It was the result of a multitude of little incidents and circumstances and conversations all leading to the one conclusion. His references to Rose were not marked by any exhibition of sympathy for that unfortunate gentleman. On the contrary, he spoke of him as a vain, proud man, always boastful of his money, and desirous of making his hearers believe that he was wealthy. The significance of Laurie's comment upon this point is striking. With a singular callousness, he added that Rose had not very much after all.

The apparent absence of motive for murder on the part of Laurie has been urged strongly in favour of his innocence. It is important for the public to know that apart from the belief that Rose had a large sum about his person—which might of itself have aroused Laurie's cupidity—it may be stated that he had at that very time a great and pressing need of money for the attainment of an object which was dearest to his heart; and that, had the sum possessed by Rose been anything like what was expected, Laurie would not have hung about the district so long, but would have endeavoured to get

278

Appendix IV.

clear of the country. What that dear object of his was need not be specially stated. So far as his mind and feelings could be understood, death had no terrors for him. At all events, his fear for the future never appeared to lie in that direction. He rather sorrowed that death would cut him off from all possibility of attaining that one desire of his life, a desire which had, and has, the strongest hold upon him of all things.

---

(14) WHY WAS LAURIE REPRIEVED?

Glasgow Herald, Tuesday, 3rd December, 1889.

It is strongly to be hoped that the Secretary for Scotland will reconsider his decision to say nothing more than he has said about the Laurie case. The public have surely some claim to know a little more than they know at present concerning the grounds on which Lord Lothian recommended to the Queen a commutation of the death sentence. We are unfeignedly glad that the wretched murderer is not to be hanged, for it is an awful thing to hurry a man into eternity with such a foul crime on his soul. But that is not the point now. The convict has escaped the gallows; and the public in general would be glad if they were put into possession of some satisfactory reason. There seems to be no doubt in the mind of the Secretary for Scotland, or of the Home Secretary, or of the learned judge who tried the case, that poor Mr. Rose was murdered and that Laurie is his murderer. These three men were in consultation, and the element of doubt on this point does not appear in the reason given for reprieve. The sole reason given is that Laurie is not of sound mind. If the man is insane now, that is, of course, quite sufficient reason why the sentence of death should be set aside in his favour. But what most people wish to know is whether in the opinion of the Commission that examined him he has been insane all along. Did Mr. Rose come to his sad end by the hand of a madman or by the hand of one of the most cowardly and callous of brutes? It will be noticed that Mr. J. B. Balfour, who is not often accused of losing a point, threw out no suggestion of his client being insane. Nor was any hint to this effect given by the witnesses. That Laurie is a man of strong personal vanity, and not strong brain power, seems to have been generally recognised among his friends; but it is to be hoped for the sake of the majority of mankind, at least according to Carlyle's verdict, that there is a wide gulf between such a person and a madman. For the sake of Mr. Rose's sorrowing family, who seem to have been too much forgotten in the matter, as well as for the sake of the public at large, it is not asking too much when we express a hope that Lord Lothian will give a somewhat fuller explanation than he has yet vouchsafed.

279

John Watson Laurie.

While dealing with this sad subject, it will not be amiss to call attention to the grotesque farce of allowing children of tender years to sign petitions for a reprieve on a matter of life and death. Some little children in Greenock have signed these hawked-about petitions over and over again. Surely those in charge of petition sheets might prevent this.

---

(15) THE CONVICT LAURIE.

Scotsman, Monday, 17th February, 1890.

Mr. PICKERSGILL asked the Lord Advocate whether he would communicate to the House the substance of the report of the three medical experts appointed by the Secretary for Scotland to examine the mental condition of J. W. Laurie, who was convicted of the murder of an English tourist in Arran; and whether these experts unanimously reported that, in their judgment, Laurie was " not irresponsible " ; and if so, upon what grounds the Secretary for Scotland advised Her Majesty to commute the capital sentence?

The LORD ADVOCATE—It would be quite contrary to practice for me to communicate to the House the substance of the report received by the Secretary for Scotland. I may, however, inform the hon. member that the words quoted in the question were not used by the medical experts.

APPENDIX V.

ATTEMPTED ESCAPE OF THE ARRAN MURDERER.

From the *Scotsman*, 25th July, 1893.

Considerable excitement was caused in Peterhead yesterday morning by a rumour that Laurie, the Arran murderer, had made an attempt to escape from the convict prison. The officialism surrounding everything connected with convict life within the establishment at Salthousehead makes it very difficult to obtain information regarding any incident that occurs to vary the monotony which characterises the everyday life of a convict. Although attempts at escape are so rare, this is the second within the last six months—both, however, ending in ignominious failure. On the previous occasion an Aberdeen burglar got away about half a mile, and ran into the arms of a policeman who was coming along the road. On this occasion Laurie, fleet of foot as he is, was overtaken before he got out of sight of the prison. It appears that Laurie, by his good behaviour, had advanced himself to be a prisoner of the first class, and as

Appendix V.

such had an amount of freedom which is denied to those in the lower grades. He is said to be surly in disposition, and to have at times annoyed the authorities by groundless complaints, but he is a good workman, and was entrusted with responsible work. He was employed in the carpenters' shop, and was one of a gang who were erecting scaffolding in front of an addition to a block of warders' houses, forming one of the lines of such blocks parallel to the Aberdeen turnpike road. The latest addition to this block is the sixth of a series of three-storeyed buildings, and is at the north end of the row. A high stone wall is built along the side of the road, upon the top of which is a sentry-box, one civil guard promenading from the centre of the wall to the respective ends, and overlooking the squads of convicts working in the space between this wall and the building. At the gable of the new house there is a close paling about 12 feet high running along the breadth of the house, and at the end of this paling there is another sentry-box. At one part of this wooden erection there is a section not so high as the rest— probably a door to the outside, and it is believed that it was over this part that Laurie leaped in making his exit. Part of the squad were picking the front wall of the house previous to pointing it, and Laurie was carrying a plank to be made part of the scaffolding at the time. About a quarter before eight in the morning there was a very thick sea fog hanging over the land—so dense, indeed, that it is said objects at a hundred yards distance were barely discernible. There is no doubt that Laurie had his plans made, and that a fog favoured him in his attempt to carry them out. In the near distance to the west there is what, in its present luxuriance of green, would look from the prison as a small forest, but which in reality is a series of plantations, with very limited tree-covered enclosures surrounding the house of Dales of Invernettie, and Laurie, doubtless, had the idea that if he could reach that apparent place of security he would be able to elude his pursuers. Between the prison and Dales there is a small clump of trees at the rear of Bellevue Cottage, and the fugitive had only reached that place when he was captured.

After clearing the wooden fence before referred to, Laurie had to pass up to the road, cross it, leap over a dyke about 4 feet high into a clover field, in which there are still some coles of hay standing, and on through a cornfield, his course leading him over three moderately high stone dykes. As soon as he emerged upon the public road he was discovered by Graham, the civil guard, who at once loaded his carbine, and, as he alleged, tried to fire, but the cartridge did not go off. Before he got it extracted and a fresh one substituted, the fugitive was hidden by the fog. This, it is understood, is Graham's version of the incident, and doubtless an investigation will follow. The alarm was at once given, and the whole army of warders and reserve civil guard on duty was ordered out for the pursuit. Only one warder could be spared from the

John Watson Laurie.

gang in which Laurie was working, and he at once started on his track. Unfortunately for the success of Laurie's daring exploit, the sun got out and dispelled the fog, and his line of flight was made visible. One warder got his bicycle and, seeing that Laurie must needs cross the Blackhills Road, sped along it to intercept him. Those who witnessed the pursuit describe it as very exciting while it lasted. Laurie had a good start, but he is a small man, and had no chance with the average 6-foot warder, nimble of foot though he proved himself to be. The people who live at Bellevue Cottage, hearing the whistling of the warders, looked out, but seeing a man in convict's dress approaching, they shut and bolted the door. Laurie, however, did not seek the shelter of a house, but made for the clump of trees behind, and there he was overtaken and held. He struggled violently, but the timely arrival of other warders made resistance futile, and he was securely handcuffed with his hands behind, and marched back along the road to the prison. On the way back to prison Laurie characterised his captors in language wholly inconsistent with the ecclesiastical office which he fills—that of precentor in the convict prison chapel. In less than half an hour after he threw down the plank and took to flight, the big gate again closed behind him, and another epoch of his eventful life was brought to an abrupt termination. It is understood that the punishment for an attempt to escape is that the prisoner has a belt of iron riveted around his waist, similar bands being put round his ankles, and these are bound together by heavy chains. He has to wear these ornaments night and day. His escapade will likely also reduce his standing from the first class, and in other ways restrict his liberties, besides probably adding to his term of servitude.

In regard to Graham, the civil guard, it is stated that his rifle was taken and tested with the cartridge which he alleged would not go off, and that it discharged without any hitch. It is further stated that he has been suspended from his duties, pending inquiry.

APPENDIX VI.

The Arran Murderer at Perth.

An Old Crime Recalled.

From the *Daily Record and Mail*, Thursday, 27th April, 1910.

The murder of the English excursionist, Edwin Robert Rose, on the slopes of Goatfell, Arran, over twenty years ago, was recalled yesterday by the removal of Laurie, who was convicted of the crime, from Peterhead penal establishment to the Perth Criminal Asylum.

282

Appendix VI.

It does not necessarily follow that because Laurie has been removed to the Perth Criminal Asylum that his mental condition has prompted the transfer. On this point the officials approached refused to speak.

Perth Prison is an old penitentiary dating back to the days of the French wars at the beginning of the last century, and before the prisons were under central control it was known as the Penitentiary, and was used for the detention of prisoners dealt with at the High Courts. The local prisons in those days had to accommodate the Police Court cases.

For years back male convicts have been sent to Peterhead, mainly to work on the breakwater there, and the greater part of Perth Prison has remained empty. A portion has been used as the Criminal Lunatic Department for Scotland; another part is used as the local prison; and another has been structurally altered to form a State inebriate reformatory.

Lately there has been talk of yet another part being converted into a place of detention under the Prevention of Crimes Act. Such a scheme would, of course, involve a lot of work by tradesmen of one kind and another, and it may be that Laurie, who is a patternmaker by trade, has been moved to Perth to assist in this work, though it may be recalled that during his incarceration at Peterhead he has on more than one occasion attempted to escape; and it seems improbable that the prison authorities would in these circumstances remove him from the convict establishment for labour reasons.

But, whatever his mental condition, he has been removed from Peterhead, where he has spent the greater part of twenty years in confinement.

He was removed yesterday in company with five other convicts. The tragic party left Peterhead in charge of three warders at half-past nine in the morning, and travelled in a specially reserved compartment, Aberdeen Joint Station being reached at 11.35. On arrival the convicts, all heavily manacled, were marched hurriedly to one of the waiting rooms, where they remained for an hour and a half awaiting the 1.10 Caledonian train for Perth. The coach employed for the conveyance of convicts was attached to this train (having left Glasgow in the morning with half-a-dozen men for Peterhead). This was coupled to the south-going train, and when all was ready Laurie and his fellow-convicts were put in.

Laurie was easily distinguished. The Arran murderer, however, has aged considerably. His hair, cropped close in accordance with prison rules, is quite grey, and his face is wan and haggard. He walks with a stoop, and his whole appearance points to his being in the latest stages of senile decay.

Perth was reached at about four o'clock, and a few minutes later Laurie and his convict companions were once more within the grim walls of a prison. At Aberdeen the *Daily Record and Mail*

John Watson Laurie.

photographer was able to secure a striking snapshot of the convicts as they were leaving the Aberdeen train, and the picture is reproduced on page 3.

The crime for which Laurie is incarcerated will for all time be known as the Arran murder. Its circumstances resemble more the imagination of the dramatist or novelist than an episode in actual life. The trial of John Watson Laurie before Lord Kingsburgh on the charge of murdering the young Englishman, Edwin Robert Rose, on the slopes of Goatfell, on the 15th of July, 1889, was heard in the High Court of Justiciary, Edinburgh, on the 8th and 9th of November of that year.

In summing up the case the judge described it as one of the most remarkable that had ever come before a Court of Justice. The evidence was purely circumstantial. After an absence of forty minutes the jury returned a verdict finding the prisoner, by a majority, guilty of murder, and he was sentenced to be executed in Greenock Prison on the 30th November. It was understood at the time that the verdict was arrived at by a majority of eight to seven.

Before the day fixed for the execution, however, Laurie was reprieved as being of unsound mind, and on the 28th of November his sentence was commuted to penal servitude for life.

Briefly stated, the facts of the crime were that Rose, an Englishman, was clerk to a builder in London. In the first week of July, at the suggestion of a brother of his employer, a clergyman, Rose left London for a holiday in Rothesay, and put up at the Glenburn Hydropathic establishment. Laurie, who was a joiner and patternmaker, employed at the Springburn Works, Glasgow, and who had a weakness for dandy dress, went on a holiday to Bute on the 6th of July and took lodgings under the name of Annandale at Port Bannatyne. Rose, on the 12th of July, accompanied a party of friends from the hydropathic on a day's excursion to Arran.

It so happened that Laurie, calling himself Annandale, was also on board the steamer and that he struck up an acquaintanceship with Rose. On the return to Rothesay the latter took "Annandale" to the hydro., and introduced him there as a friend. On the following day, the 13th of July, a Saturday, the pair travelled together to Arran and took lodgings in Brodick, occupying the same room. They started on the afternoon of Monday, the 15th, to climb Goatfell. The summit was reached, and shortly after six o'clock the two were seen standing on a boulder. From that moment Rose was never again seen alive. Laurie was observed leaving Glen Sannox about half-past nine in the evening; later he entered a hotel at Corrie and had a drink at the bar, and the next morning he was seen going on board a steamer and carrying two bags and wearing a hat which was afterwards proved to have belonged to Rose.

He went to Glasgow, returned once more to Rothesay, where he spent the rest of his holiday. He returned to work at Springburn

284

Appendix VI.

on the 22nd of July, but, when the hue and cry went forth, left on the 31st and began a most exciting career of wanderings which took him to Liverpool, Aberdeen, and other places, until his capture in a wood between Hamilton and Lesmahagow put a period to his exploits.

The search for the murdered man began on the 28th of July and was not brought to a successful issue till the following Sunday. The search party numbered about 200 men—150 from Brodick and 50 from Corrie—who scoured the whole of Goatfell. Eventually the body was found at a place called Corr-na-fuarin at the head of Glen Sannox, hidden beneath a great boulder and with the head and face smashed beyond recognition.

APPENDIX VII.

Death of Laurie.

The Goatfell Murder : Laurie's Death at Perth Penitentiary.

From the *Glasgow Herald*, 6th October, 1930.

One of the most remarkable dramas of crime and retribution in the judicial annals of Scotland is recalled by the death at Perth Penitentiary during the week-end [4th October] of John Watson Laurie, who was convicted in November, 1889, of the murder of Edwin Robert Rose in Glen Sannox, Arran.

The crime, which was generally referred to as the Goatfell [?Arran] murder, whetted public curiosity and interest from the date of Rose's disappearance in July, 1889, until the jury's verdict four months later. Laurie's disappearance, and a letter written to the editor of the *Glasgow Herald*, contributed largely to the sensation of the case.